BETWEEN WORLDS

Between Worlds

Access to Second Language Acquisition

THIRD EDITION

David E. Freeman & Yvonne S. Freeman

HEINEMANN ❧ PORTSMOUTH, NH

HEINEMANN
361 Hanover Street
Portsmouth, NH 03801–3912
www.heinemann.com

Offices and agents throughout the world

The authors and publisher wish to thank those who have generously given permission to reprint borrowed material:

Lines from the poem "Why Am I Dumb?" from *My Name Is Jorge on Both Sides of the River* by Jane Medina. Copyright © 1999 by Jane Medina. Published by Wordsong, an imprint of Boyds Mills Press. Reprinted by permission of the publisher.

Library of Congress Cataloging-in-Publication Data
Freeman, David E.
    Between worlds : access to second language acquisition / David E. Freeman and Yvonne S. Freeman. — 3rd ed.
        p. cm.
    Includes bibliographical references and index.
    ISBN-13: 978-0-325-03088-3
    ISBN-10: 0-325-03088-X
    1. Second language acquisition.   I. Freeman, Yvonne S.   II. Title.

P118.2.F74 2011
418.0071—dc22   2011009953

EDITOR: *Kate Montgomery*
PRODUCTION: *Vicki Kasabian*
TEXT AND COVER DESIGNS: *Jenny Jensen Greenleaf*
TYPESETTER: *House of Equations, Inc.*
MANUFACTURING: *Steve Bernier*

Printed in the United States of America on acid-free paper
15 14   VP   4 5

*We dedicate this book to our daughters, Mary and Ann,
our sons-in-law, Francisco and Christopher,
and to our grandchildren, Maya, Christiana, and Romero,
who continue to provide us with very personal lessons
about acquiring a second language and learning to live
between worlds.*

Contents

Acknowledgments

This third edition of *Between Worlds: Access to Second Language Acquisition* is a result of our reading current theory and research, our interactions with colleagues, and, especially, our experiences with teachers who are committed to improving the lives of their students. Our goal when we write is to translate theory and research into practice, but we couldn't do it without the real classroom examples that talented educators have provided us.

We wish to acknowledge the teachers with whom we have worked, and especially the following outstanding educators whose work we share in this book: Kristhel Allen, Gayleen Aoki, Loretta Aragón, Katie Bausch-Ude, Claudia Beymer, Christa Bryan, Janie Chapman, Leny de Ruijter, Rusty DeRuiter, Cándida Dillon, Ann Ebe, Kim Fuzco, Shelly Hernández, Mike Lebsock, Sandra Mercuri, Marjorie Miller, Helen Milliorn, Belinda Naso, Denise Rea, Susanne Roberts, Monica Rojas, Kathy Smith, Francisco Soto, Mary Soto, Lea Tafolla, Rhoda Toews, Kristene Vaux, Evelyn Patricia Yañez, Gustavo Yañez, Juan Carlos Yañez, and Marta Yoshimura.

In addition, we would like to thank our editor, Kate Montgomery. We also want to thank our friends in production, Vicki Kasabian and Abby Heim, who pay great attention to detail and find beautiful layout designs for our books. As always the Heinemann staff is a pleasure to work with. We appreciate their efforts to promote our work.

Introduction

Cavelier Elementary School is located in the downtown part of a border city in Texas. Its name belies its present student population of 530 Hispanic children, almost all of Mexican origin. Cavelier was the name of an early French settler who came to this part of south Texas in the late 1600s. His family members became important contributors to the community. In 1889 the first Grammar School in the city was built at the site. In 1947, fifty-eight years later and after several renovations, it was named after a descendant of the Cavelier family, a well-loved schoolteacher who later became principal. Cavelier Elementary School maintains much of its colonial Spanish-style structure, and welcomes newcomers from across the border.

There is a park across from the school that, at one time, was the town plaza. Now, this pleasant, grassy park has a fountain in the middle and paths around it. Families and neighbors from this part of town come often to walk around the park, much like people walk around the plazas in small villages in Mexico. Before and after school one can see mothers, grandmothers, aunts, older sisters, and even some fathers and older brothers dropping off or picking up their children. Almost all come and go on foot, as few have cars. This is a neighborhood school, with only one bus bringing in children from farther away.

After school, parent volunteers sell *palomitas* (popcorn), *raspas* (snow cones of different flavors), *leche* (sweet milk), and fruit with *chamoy* (spicy red sauce made from pickled fruit) or *limón* (lemon), to make money for the school. Spanish is heard everywhere. This school becomes a place where parents and relatives greet one another and share news and gossip.

The surrounding neighborhoods have small homes, and almost all the families living in the neighborhood struggle economically. Some sections have become dangerous, and gang members plague those who try to get ahead legally. Often children suffer because a parent is in jail or one parent has abandoned them. Relatives often take over the responsibility of raising nephews, nieces, and grandchildren. Adults struggle to feed and clothe their families, but know that education is the only way their children can hope to succeed.

The school and the park are a haven for the people living in this part of the city. The teachers are all extremely dedicated. They are all bilingual, many were once immigrants themselves, and all feel the responsibility of not only helping all the 530 children who attend the school to succeed academically but also of providing them a safe place to learn. The student body is 100 percent free breakfast and lunch, and over 80 percent of the children are second language learners of English. Still, the teachers must prepare them to pass high-stakes tests in English. For newcomers this is especially difficult, because there is only one year allowed before they must take the tests.

The challenges at Cavelier School are great, but they are not unique. While this school is on the border where one expects high numbers of immigrant children, there are similar schools with student bodies filled with immigrant children across our nation. Teachers, resource specialists, paraprofessionals, administrators, teacher educators, parents, and the general public need to understand who these students are and what the best ways are to help them succeed in this society. This book is an attempt to meet this need.

Why a Third Edition?

As the numbers of English language learners grow, the concerns about how to help them succeed in school increases. California has the largest number of students designated as needing English instruction, with about 1.5 million. One in four ELLs in the United States attends school in California. When the California State Superintendent of Public Instruction states that the achievement gap for linguistic minority students is "the most persistent and pressing nationwide challenge facing public schools" (Aguila 2010, 1), it is clear that everyone should pay attention to the schooling of English language learners (ELLs).

We have updated this text because we want to provide teachers with the latest thinking about language acquisition and to bring in recent important research studies. Educators should be able to apply current learning theory as well as articulate research and theory on language acquisition, bilingualism, literacy, and academic language. Of course, for teachers to help their students, they must know their students and understand the contexts of their lives. Our opening description of a border school is one attempt to do this. Our students come from rich and diverse backgrounds, and it is only when we teachers comprehend and appreciate our students that we can reach them.

Our schools reflect an increasingly linguistic and ethnic diversity, and this brings with it a challenge for teachers, because many more students at all grade levels have limited English proficiency. In 1994 when we wrote the first edition of this book, there were about three million second language learners in our schools. The number had grown to almost five and a half million in 2009. During this period, the second language population grew by 58 percent, while the total K–12 school population grew by only 4 percent. While states including California, Florida, Illinois, New York, and Texas have always had large populations of English language learners (ELLs), other states have seen an influx of second language students. States where second language learners make up at least 10 percent of the overall student population include Arizona, Nevada, New Mexico, Alaska, Oregon, and Colorado, along with California and Texas (Batalova and McHugh 2010b). However, it is important to understand that it is not only the states in the West that are seeing high numbers of English language learners. States with more than 200 percent growth in the last ten years include, in ranked order of growth: South Carolina, Indiana, Nevada, Arkansas, North Carolina, Delaware, Georgia, Alabama, Kentucky, and Tennessee (Batalova and McHugh 2010a).

As we have worked with educators in different states, we have seen many more teachers preparing themselves to work more effectively with ESL students. We have given workshops for teachers in small communities as well as in major cities in most of the states across the country on the topic of effective approaches to teaching their multilingual/multicultural students.

While teachers are becoming better informed, misconceptions among the general public about new immigrants and their needs have also grown. Immigrants have been blamed for economic and social ills, and there have been strong movements to limit immigration to the United States. In California, Arizona, and Massachusetts movements against bilingual education have led to outlawing the use of students' first languages for instruction. Throughout the country anti-immigrant movements have been a concern for all those teaching second language students. We believe that it is perhaps more important now than ever before for educators to be aware of the many issues affecting the academic performance of immigrant students in our schools so that they can be advocates for all their students.

Certainly, no magic formula will ensure the academic success of any group of learners, and while this book offers examples of practices that have proved effective with a variety of students, we are aware that each learning situation is different. What works in one classroom may not apply down the hall, much less in another part of the country. We hope, however, that by identifying and discussing the linguistic, social, and psychological factors that impact students who are learning academic content in their second or third or fourth languages, we can help professionals examine their programs and their classroom practices to ensure that they are providing what is best for all their students.

The approach we develop here recognizes that any student's second language development and academic-content learning are the result of many interacting forces. No one factor determines success or failure for a particular student or group of students. Yet, in the past, some educators relied on single-cause explanations to account for students' progress. For example, some have focused on English proficiency. However, learning English is not the only key to academic achievement. English proficiency, by itself, does not determine success or failure. Cummins (1989) expresses this clearly:

> Understanding why and how minority students are failing academically requires that educators dig a little deeper than superficial linguistic mismatches between home and school or insufficient exposure to English. Underachievement is not caused by lack of fluency in English. (33–34)

Even when lack of English is not seen as the cause of failure, the students themselves or their backgrounds are sometimes blamed. Such single-cause explanations are often based on social or cultural stereotypes. For example, some teachers might say that Hispanic students lack motivation, so they do not do well in school, but that Asians get good grades because they are influenced by high parental expectations. Recent research has disproven these stereotypical beliefs as well as others. In this book, we hope to help readers understand the issues related to the schooling of linguistic minority students at a deeper level so that we can all become advocates for our students and help them succeed in our schools and the greater society.

Our Title

The title for this book, *Between Worlds*, reflects our conviction that providing the best education for second language students requires that we understand that our students must negotiate between the world of their families and their native countries and their new world. In a sense, school is a place that is between two worlds for all students. Students entering school are leaving the smaller world of their home and entering the larger world of the school. For English language learners, these two worlds are often very different. In school, language minority students are often taught by teachers whose experiences have been limited to the mainstream culture and whose attitudes and values have been shaped by mainstream views. Teachers benefit from examining their attitudes and values and also by considering the values and attitudes that their second language learners bring to school. By doing this they can help all their students fully experience the best of both worlds.

Some students are unable to move successfully between worlds because they never fully enter the mainstream school community. They are marginalized by the instruction they receive and the attitudes they encounter. Eventually, many of them drop out or are pushed out of school. Unfortunately, these students also often lack a sense of belonging in their home community. They may be in a state of cultural ambivalence, not completely accepted either at school or at home. When this happens, increasing numbers of students turn to alternate communities, such as gangs. Rather than experiencing the best of both worlds, they cannot participate fully in either one.

Other students succeed in school, but in the process they become alienated from their home community. These are students who enter school as monolingual Spanish, Arabic, or Korean speakers and leave school as monolingual English speakers. They are unable to communicate fully with family and friends in the home community. These students may reject their heritage language and culture in order to become part of the mainstream. Rather than experiencing the best of both worlds, they simply trade one world for another.

We have chosen *Access to Second Language Acquisition* as the subtitle for this book because we believe that a number of linguistic, psychological, and social factors interact to permit or deny students access to the acquisition of a new language. However, the subtitle also has another purpose. We hope that this book gives those involved with English language learners access to recent research, language learning theories, and effective classroom practice. We hope to bring the research and theories alive for the readers of this book by providing numerous examples of classroom practice. Educators who understand research, theory, and the implications for teaching can provide English learners with access to their new language.

Who Is This Book For?

The idea for writing the first edition of this book came to us as we taught a course called *Language Acquisition and Cross-Cultural Communication*. The teachers in our graduate program needed a text that described different theories of language acquisition and also provided examples for putting theory into practice. In addition, as we worked with teachers in schools, we were reminded daily that teaching multilingual/multicultural learners involves much more than an understanding of theory, methods, and materials. We realized that this text needed to address linguistic, social, political, and cultural factors that influence students' learning. Our goals for this third edition are not different. We bring to readers what we now understand even more deeply as the result of our own work, the work of teachers around us, and the work of recent researchers and theorists.

Many of the examples in this text appeared in the first and second editions. Teachers found them useful and often told us how much they related to them. Some of the stories are new ones, vignettes we wanted to share because they helped us to better understand teaching and learning and the ever-changing immigrant populations who come to our schools. We have spent eight years now along the Texas/Mexico border working with large numbers of Latino teachers and administrators. They have taught us much and have provided us with new insights.

All of the examples come from our own experiences and from the experiences of teachers we have worked with. It is our hope that teacher educators continue to find this book useful in courses dealing with learning theory, first and second language acquisition, and linguistic, social, political, and cultural factors that influence learning. These courses might be part of a preservice program for prospective teachers, part of a program for teachers wishing to continue their professional development, or part of a graduate program of study.

However, we do not intend that the audience for this book be restricted to people taking formal coursework or to designated ESL or bilingual teachers. We hope that mainstream teachers will also find this book useful. In fact, we wrote this book with several possible audiences in mind, including teachers, counselors, paraprofessionals, and others who work with second language students and who wish to continue their own professional development through independent reading. As student populations change and increasing numbers of English learners enter our schools, it is important for all the professionals working with these students to be knowledgeable about current theories of language acquisition and to be aware of the linguistic, social, and cultural factors that influence students' academic performance. We have presented explanations of theory and examples of successful classroom practice that should clarify many of these issues. We encourage educators who are not taking formal courses to meet with colleagues in pairs or small groups to reflect on the ideas presented here.

We have also written this book for school administrators. Administrators provide leadership in curriculum, and they support the efforts of classroom teachers. School demographics have changed radically. In many schools, language minority students have become the numerical majority. For administrators to carry out their role, they need to be aware of the linguistic, psychological, and social factors that influence the academic performance of second language students as well as their curriculum needs.

Finally, we have written this book for parents and for community members interested in school improvement. Parents and other community members play a key role in the academic success of language minority students. We discuss in some detail ways in which the social context of schooling influences the educational context. We also describe successful programs that involve parents and other community members. Second language students can succeed when home and school work together to provide them access to the best possible education. We hope that parents and other members of the general public will find the examples and explanations here helpful as they increase their own involvement in programs to improve schooling.

At the end of each chapter we have included a section called *Applications*. These are not intended as end-of-chapter tests or exercises that must be completed for a grade. Instead, they are invitations to explore in more detail the concepts raised in the chapter. We hope that they will help readers apply the ideas to their own experiences. We believe that people learn by doing, and the applications ask readers to do something with what they have read or to read related material. We have asked our own students to try these activities, and they have reported that the applications enabled them to relate the concepts being studied more directly to their own teaching. Since we also believe that learning takes place in social interaction, we have often suggested that the activities be completed in pairs or small groups. With our students, this sharing has led not only to the expansion of ideas but also to the building of a supportive community.

Terms to Describe Students

We wish to comment on the terminology we use to refer to the students we write about in this book. It is always difficult to choose a descriptive term for any group because the words used may, in fact, label or limit the people in that group (Wink 1993). For example, the frequently used label for non-English speakers, LEP, focuses attention on what students cannot do. All of us have limited (or no) proficiency in a number of languages.

In the past, we have referred to students in our schools who do not speak English as their first language as *second language learners*, or *bilingual learners*. We use these terms to make the point that these students already have another language, and English is an additional language. However, we are aware that many English language learners are, in fact, adding a third, fourth, and even fifth language to their repertoire. Therefore, the terms *bilingual learners* and *second language learners* might also be seen as limiting.

Another term often used is *language minority students*. As the numbers of these students grow in different areas, this term is a misnomer. For example, in South Texas where we live, many of our schools are 98–99 percent Hispanic, and often more than 50 percent of the students come to school speaking a language other than English. These students are in the majority although their languages do not carry the social power of English.

The term most often used is *English language learners* (ELLs) or simply *English learners* (ELs). Even native speakers of English are English language learners in a sense, but students for whom English is not the native language face the task of learning English. This term focuses on what these students are trying to do, what they have in common, so it is the term that we will use at times.

A more recent term that has been suggested is *emergent bilinguals*. García (García 2009, 2010; García, Kleifgen, and Flachi 2008) has proposed that this term validates the language students bring to school as well as the fact that, as they learn English or another second language, they are becoming bilingual. They are not simply learning English, as the term *English language learner* implies; they are emergent bilinguals. We will move back and forth among the different terms as we write this book, being always aware that it is important to be cautious about the use of any label.

The Chapters in This Book

The nine chapters in this book focus on the students who are in our classrooms and the factors that affect their school success, the teachers who teach those students, and the research and theories that provide the basis for effective practice for teachers of ELLs.

Chapter 1 poses the question, "Who are our English language learners?" and explores factors that influence their academic performance. In this chapter, we present a series of case studies of English learners to show the complex factors that influence their academic development. We look at English language learners with a variety of language and cultural backgrounds who are living in different contexts, and we analyze each. Chapter 2 asks, "What factors affect the school success of English language learners?" Here we describe different types of English learners, including those with adequate schooling, limited formal schooling, long-term English learners, and potential long-term English learners. We review Ogbu's distinction between immigrant and involuntary minorities and the characteristics of each of these groups. We end the chapter by reviewing perspectives on failure for ELLs and laying out a model that helps us identify factors that lead to student success or failure.

Chapter 3 raises the question, "What influences how teachers teach?" In this chapter we consider the many different influences on teachers working with language minority students. We then trace the experiences of one teacher over many years of teaching and analyze what influenced her teaching. In Chapter 4 we turn to learning theory and the role of the teacher because, ultimately, teachers teach based on how they believe students learn. We discuss social learning theories and connect them to teaching emergent bilinguals. We then connect learning theory to language learning and describe the different functions of language that students must acquire. Different language learning strategies are described. Throughout the chapter we provide examples of students learning a second language.

Chapter 5 answers questions related to first and second language acquisition: "How do people acquire a first language?" "Can people acquire a second language in the same way they acquire a first language?" "Are the processes involved in acquiring a language the same as in learning other things, such as how to solve a math problem?" and "What are the principal theories of second language acquisition?" We review theories and give examples of how the theories apply to real students and real schools. We also discuss a key question in language teaching, "What is the role of the teaching of grammar?"

In this book we dedicate Chapter 6 to a topic we did not fully cover in our first two editions: bilingualism. In our global society, it is critical that we promote bilingualism for all. We know that rather than eliminating our students' first languages, we should develop them. Language use in the twenty-first century includes moving back and forth between and among languages, and educators need to understand the value and power of using different languages at different times and in different contexts. In this chapter we review the principal theories of bilingualism and the different models of bilingual education.

In Chapter 7 we further discuss students' first languages and whether we should view their language as a problem, a right, or a resource. We explore orientations toward teaching ELLs as being either assimilationist or intercultural. As we develop these topics, we talk about the role of the parents of second language learners and how to encourage parents to participate in schooling. We provide examples of transformative pedagogy, and discuss how educators can take an advocacy role in assessment.

Chapter 8 develops another new topic for this third edition, one that has received a great deal of attention because of its importance for the school success of ELLs: literacy. In this chapter we describe the concerns we have that many second language students have become "word callers" but cannot comprehend the textbooks they need to read. We suggest the gradual release of responsibility model for the teaching of reading and provide readers with ways to choose and use culturally relevant books that support literacy development for bilingual students. In particular, we discuss culturally relevant bilingual books and review three false assumptions about teaching bilinguals that have made some teachers hesitant to use bilingual books.

In the last chapter of the book, Chapter 9, we address two topics that have been widely written about and discussed in the past few years: academic language and assessment. Academic language is the particular kind of language that our students need for academic success. Many ELLs develop conversational language fairly easily, but without academic language, they cannot hope to read, discuss, and write about the subjects they study in school. In this chapter we contrast conversational language with academic language and explain the importance of developing academic language for emergent bilinguals. We discuss academic language at the word, sentence, paragraph, and text levels.

The last section of the final chapter includes the important topic of assessment. We explain how teachers need to develop both content and language objectives in the different content areas, and we describe different approaches to the assessment of ELLs.

We also review the research on standardized tests and second language learners and discuss modifications designed to help these students succeed. We end the chapter with an explanation of the standards and performance indicators that the international organization TESOL (Teachers of English to Speakers of Other Languages) has developed to help educators assess students' academic language proficiency.

We hope that the information in this book will be useful to teachers, counselors, paraprofessionals, administrators, parents, and others involved in the education of language minority students. We are aware that there are no easy solutions to closing the achievement gap for our emergent bilingual students, but we are convinced that all students benefit when educators working with them are aware of current research, theory, and effective classroom practice.

We began this introduction with a description of a school with many emergent bilinguals, dedicated teachers, and families who look to the school for children's success, for hope of a better future. This school is not that different from many schools across the country. By studying language acquisition and bilingual theories, the sociocultural influences on bilingual learners, and the effective practices of teachers working with diverse populations, educators can better provide the best instruction for all those students who are living and learning between worlds.

Who Are Our English Language Learners?

"I was amazed. I had no idea!"—these were the words John kept repeating as he told fellow teachers in his second language acquisition (SLA) class about an experience he had while trying to choose one of his students for a case study, a major class assignment. John teaches choral music, and he began by polling his small class of eleven students:

> First I asked, "Do any of you speak English as a second language?" All raised their hands. To be sure they understood, I asked, "Does anyone speak Spanish?" Again, all raised their hands. I was amazed. I had no idea.

John is a new teacher, trying to prepare himself to work effectively with his students. He recently earned his teaching credential, and now he is returning to graduate school to take the courses for his English as a Second Language (ESL) endorsement. He knew that the student population had changed in recent years, but he "had no idea" that so many of his students speak English as a second language. John's teacher-education classes gave him a good foundation for his teaching assignment, but he now knows that he needs additional information about second language learning if he is to reach all his students.

In his graduate class, John is beginning to learn that the academic success of English learners depends on many factors and that he needs to understand learning theory and second language acquisition theory. Students learning in a new language and in a new culture have unique needs. In a school like John's, the students and the teachers are worlds apart—almost literally. It is critical that educators understand that many elements interact to influence the school performance of students who are acquiring English as another language.

We begin this book with case studies of several English language learners. Teachers who wish to understand the complex interaction of factors that affect the performance of their students can benefit from reading these stories and from conducting case studies of their own. These studies help show the different factors that influence the academic performance of second language students. Case studies provide a good starting point for understanding the research, theory, and practice described in this book, and this knowledge can help educators respond in an informed way as they work with their English language learners.

Each case study is based on a real student in a real school setting. Since we have lived in several multilingual communities, some of the case studies reflect our personal experiences with English language learners. Others are based on our observations of schools and our conversations with teachers, students, and parents as we work with teachers across the country. The remaining case studies were conducted by teachers studying second language acquisition in the graduate education programs at universities where we have taught.

To help our graduate students discover the strengths of their second language students, we have them read about and discuss second language acquisition (SLA) theory and the importance of students' first languages and cultures. They also study the ways the community context affects schools. Then the teachers choose one second language learner to work with closely. We wrote of John's experience in making his choice in the beginning of this chapter. The teachers read, write, and talk with their student. They share with each other what they are learning from their experiences as they write up their case studies. Through their research on one student and their interactions with their peers, many of these teachers begin to change the way they view the language minority students in their classes and the way they teach.

The teachers in our classes agree that it is one thing to read about English language learners and discuss SLA theories in the setting of a university classroom; it is another to work with the students directly and apply what they have read. However, when our teachers take the time to study one student carefully, they gain a new perspective on all their English learners. Desiree, an elementary teacher in one of our classes, wrote:

> I am now a strong advocate for case studies. It is too bad that a case study is not mandatory for all teachers. A case study forces you to really get to know the children. I know that what I have learned will help to make me a much better teacher.

Another teacher, Katie, whose case study we describe below, explained even more specifically how her experience would influence her in the future:

► I will expend more effort in getting to know my students personally.

► I will provide individual time for each student as often as possible.

► I will never again assume that "what I hear" is "what they know."

► I will arrange my classroom/curriculum around whole, real, purposeful, meaning-filled experiences.

► I will find, value, and exploit each student's contributions and talents.

While we realize that no two students are alike and that no two students have the same needs, there are commonalities among learners that help us approach our teaching in a more informed way. We include here the case studies of eleven students at different grade levels and with different educational, cultural, and linguistic backgrounds. After each, we list several of the factors that may have influenced that student's success or failure. It is important to be aware of the different forces involved and consider them as we work to provide our students who are between worlds access to second language acquisition and content-area knowledge. Our students need both for academic success.

We ask readers to compare the students in the case studies below to English learners with whom they have worked and to think about the differences and similarities in the factors that may have influenced them.

Eugenia

Five-year-old Eugenia attends a bilingual kindergarten in a small rural community in the Central Valley of California. She was born in the United States in the apartment of a family friend, because her mother, an undocumented immigrant, was afraid to go to a hospital. Shortly after Eugenia's birth, her parents became legal residents under the amnesty laws for migrant laborers who had worked in the United States over a period of years. For several years her parents were seasonal field laborers, moving often and leaving the children with relatives in Mexico at times, but after both parents got jobs in a canning factory, the family settled down.

Though neither of Eugenia's parents speaks English, and neither has had much formal education, both parents believe that her education is very important. They see school as the hope for their children's future. At first they were concerned about the fact that Eugenia's teacher used Spanish for some instruction. One of their high school sons had had negative experiences with bilingual education and had recently dropped out of school. However, Cándida, Eugenia's energetic Puerto Rican teacher, was able to explain to the parents why she teaches in Spanish and how building a strong first language base would help Eugenia in English in the future. Cándida convinced Eugenia's parents to sign the waiver form to allow her to receive primary-language instruction. Because Cándida speaks Spanish and has shown an interest in them and their child, Eugenia's parents now come to the school frequently to ask for advice or offer to help.

Eugenia has thrived in Cándida's classroom. Cándida provides many opportunities for her kindergarten students to begin to read and write. For example, the classroom playhouse doubles as a "restaurant," and includes paper, pencils, and lots of cans and boxes so that the children can "take orders" and "prepare meals." The class spends time every day reading predictable books, singing, and reciting poetry in both Spanish and English. Because the class creates language experience charts and class books and does lots of brainstorming, Eugenia is comfortable with writing and experiments with writing in both Spanish and English for different purposes.

Eugenia has had a very positive year in kindergarten. Cándida believes that Eugenia will succeed in school. "She is lucky enough to have a supportive and caring home environment," Cándida explains, "which will help her weather academic difficulties or disappointments and tolerate and defeat racism and expectations of failure. She has strong self-esteem."

Perhaps Cándida is optimistic because she is seeing these Hispanic children at the very start of their school experience, and she has such a strong belief in them. In her own words, Cándida describes why she feels she can work well with her students:

> I believe that being a Latina from the South Bronx helps me understand my kids not only linguistically, but also philosophically. I know the challenges that face these children, but I also know that if someone cares, their chances for success are great.

Analysis

At this point Eugenia is doing well. Cándida is giving her a positive start, and she has supportive parents who are eager for her to succeed and are willing to help her in any way they can. Her teacher, a Hispanic herself, is sensitive to the needs of both Eugenia and her parents. In addition, her teacher is giving Eugenia the kind of curriculum she needs, including first language support, a print-rich classroom environment, opportunities for social interaction, and experiences with meaningful literacy activities.

However, other influences may affect Eugenia in the future. Eugenia's parents have low levels of education and do not speak English. They will not be able to help her with her academic studies as she moves into the upper grades. Though they are now in the United States legally, the uncertainty and transience of the past and their socio-economic status may keep them from being as confident as they need to be in dealing with schools. An older brother has already encountered problems and dropped out of school while the parents watched helplessly.

As Cándida herself points out, many Hispanic children face challenges of racism. Eugenia's teacher is optimistic, but her background as a New York City Puerto Rican is different from that of her students, whose families come from rural Mexico. We have hope for Eugenia, but we must look at both the positive and negative influences that might affect her in the coming years.

Mony

Unlike Eugenia, who lived most of her early years in the United States before attending school, Mony arrived here from a refugee camp in Thailand just as she was entering kindergarten. The school she attended was a large, inner-city elementary school of over one thousand students from many different linguistic and cultural backgrounds. Since most of the students were Spanish speakers from Mexico or Hmong speakers from Laos, Mony had only a few other Khmer speakers from Cambodia she could communicate with. Her parents, also overwhelmed by their new surroundings, were of little help, as they spoke no English and were concerned about finding work and maintaining a household for Mony and her siblings in a new country.

Mony's kindergarten teacher recommended that she be placed the next year in Katie's prefirst class, a transition year for students who were not ready for first grade. Katie's classroom had twenty-eight students, and many were English language learners from Mexico, Laos, Vietnam, Cambodia, and Korea. Katie was intrigued by Mony, who "seemed 'deeper,' more serious than students who, though 'silent' in English, converse freely with their L1 [first language] peers." Mony followed directions and participated silently in most activities. Her artwork was so impressive that Katie, a veteran teacher of ten years, commented that Mony was "the most advanced six-year-old artist I'd ever seen." Mony avoided eye contact with most people and preferred the company of the one other Cambodian child in the room. In fact, if her peers paid too much attention to her, Mony would stick her tongue out at them, trying to make sure Katie didn't see her do it.

Though Katie could coax Mony to come close to her for cuddling during quiet times and comforted her when she had crying periods, she could not convince Mony to converse with peers in Khmer or discuss her fears and concerns in her first language. Just as Katie felt she might be beginning to connect with her, Mony was transferred to another school. Katie wrote a note to administrators at the transfer school. "I worried that [Mony's] darting tongue and serious look might get her into unfair trouble, that her lack of oral language would be confused with lack of intelligence, and I wanted someone to know of her treasured artistic ability," she explains. She received one brief follow-up call.

Since Katie teaches at a year-round school and went on vacation shortly after Mony left, she chose to do her case study on Mony in her new school setting. She decided to visit Mony in her new classroom, talk and read with her, and continue an interactive journal she had begun with Mony when she was in Katie's class. Katie visited Mony ten times and kept anecdotal records of their time reading, writing, and talking. In this smaller classroom environment, Mony seemed almost like a different student. Katie's reflections reveal how much her visits taught her.

> I was amazed at Mony's proficiency in English and shocked at what I'd wrongly perceived it to be when she was in my class. It sounds so simple, but if we as teachers put more effort into *who* we're teaching, more of the *what* would take care of itself. When we concentrate on programs, or strict timelines, we lose sight of the important human element.

Looking closely at one student helped Katie see that human element anew.

Analysis

Mony is a refugee child who arrived in the United States with no preparation for the dramatic changes she encountered. Busy teachers who have many other things to be concerned about often do not realize just how traumatic the changes are for refugee children who leave behind war-torn countries or homelands ravaged by natural disasters.

Mony found little support at the large school she attended. Her response was to watch silently and try to absorb what was going on around her. As we will see later, many English learners have a silent period as they acquire the language, and Mony was no exception. Her silence and seeming defiance were wrongly perceived by her kindergarten teacher as lack of ability, and even Katie, who recognized her skill in art, underestimated her proficiency in English. She was surprised at Mony's rapid progress when she visited her new school.

Many immigrant children get lost in our school system. Yet, if we can find ways to get to know them as individuals, show an interest in them, and meet their specific needs, we give them greater chances for future school success. Although Katie did not see the effects she was having on Mony while Mony was in her class, Katie's teaching and her attention to Mony paid off in the new school. Katie was fortunate to see the change. Often, teachers are not aware of the effects they have on students because those effects do not appear until after they leave the classroom and move on to another class.

Salvador

Salvador entered Ann's multiage second- and third-grade bilingual classroom as a third grader. His previous teachers had warned Ann how difficult he was and had pretty much written him off as unreachable. He had been in a bilingual kindergarten and first grade and then had been transitioned to an English-only second grade because he was not learning to read and write in Spanish, and his teacher thought he might do better in English. When he failed in English, he was put into Ann's Spanish/English bilingual class, which was designed for struggling students.

Salvador was disruptive in Ann's class and refused to try to read or write in Spanish or English. He would often cry and throw tantrums and start arguments with classmates both in class and on the playground. Ann spoke with Salvador's mother, who was also at a loss about what to do with him. His behavior at home was similar to his behavior at school. His mother's response was to give him what he wanted, to placate him. She had a high school education in Mexico, was attending English classes, and hoped to get a job soon. She could help Salvador at home, but he would not often let her. Ann learned that his father was frequently absent from the home, since he worked in other parts of the state or returned to Mexico. She also came to discover that Salvador's worst outbursts occurred when his father returned home, even though Salvador was always very excited about his father's homecomings.

Ann's classroom offered many opportunities for students to do shared and pair reading in Spanish and English. She organized her curriculum around inquiry units and encouraged her students to write in journals, create books, and summarize content readings by making charts and graphs. She suspected that much of Salvador's behavior stemmed from his lack of confidence in his own reading and writing.

She gave Salvador responsibilities, such as having him take roll or track for the class when they read a poem or big book. Ann celebrated any and all of Salvador's positive responses, but was frustrated by his frequent disruptive behavior. By the end of the year, Salvador had improved somewhat in his ability to take part in the classroom routines, but Ann and his mother decided that he was not ready to go to fourth grade, where the academic content was demanding and the curriculum was entirely in English. Salvador was still struggling to read and write in Spanish.

The next year, Salvador's teacher was Francisco, who also found Salvador to be difficult. Francisco helped Salvador to see that anger was a response that was hurtful not only to his classmates but to Salvador himself. His teacher's gentle insistence on positive behavior and cooperation was calming for Salvador. Francisco also played soccer with the students during recess, and Salvador loved soccer.

Since Francisco had a similar routine to the one Ann had used, Salvador was more ready to read and write and participate in group projects. By midyear, Francisco began to see real progress. Salvador actually wrote a book on his own, following the pattern of a class book about farm animals and the sounds they make. This seemed to be a breakthrough for Salvador. He wrote and read more confidently in Spanish and began to read and write in English.

Salvador's year with Francisco was important. He continued to get literacy support in his first language, with routines similar to the year before. In addition, Francisco was a Latino male who insisted on good behavior and maintained high expectations. By the end of the year, Salvador was beginning to show significant academic gains.

Both Ann and Francisco have watched Salvador's progress in fourth and fifth grade. While he is not the strongest student, he is progressing well and his former behavior problems have all but disappeared. When Francisco visited the school two years after he was in his class, Salvador greeted him and told him how well he was behaving and how much better he was doing in school.

Analysis

Salvador is an example of a student who had many complicated forces influencing him. Though his mother wanted to help, she seemed at a loss, and her husband was seldom home. The school had no specific proof, but there was a suspicion of violence in the home when the father was in residence. This seemed to affect Salvador's behavior.

Salvador was first placed in a bilingual class. Teachers soon labeled him as a troublemaker and did not appear to know much about him. He was later placed in an all-English classroom when he was not yet literate in his first language. Before coming to Ann's class, his teachers didn't perceive him as a capable student and largely ignored him.

Ann gave him responsibilities and held high expectations for him. Her classroom provided a consistent routine of reading and writing in Spanish and English, and

Salvador was expected to participate in all activities with the class. Although he still misbehaved frequently, Ann laid a foundation for his eventual success. Francisco built on that foundation, and Salvador is doing much better now.

Even though Salvador has made great progress, his home situation is unstable. He will soon enter his teen years, always a difficult time. He will also have to make the transition to middle school. These outside forces will make success more difficult, but he has developed better self-discipline and his academic skills are steadily improving, so if he continues to get good teachers, he has some chance for success.

Sharma

Rhoda, a fifth-grade teacher in an elementary school in a rural farming community, describes her first impression of her Punjabi student, Sharma, and Sharma's mother.

> She walked into my classroom and smiled at me with warm, giving brown eyes. Her dark brown hair was neatly braided, and she politely introduced me to her mother and her baby sister. The woman's traditional Indian silk was embroidered in rich primary colors setting off her beautiful olive skin. In accented English she asked for a few moments of my time. She asked that I arrange for the school's Punjabi aide to spend time with her daughter so that she would not fall behind the rest of the class. I was intrigued by this caring mother and wanted to know more about her soft-spoken daughter.

As Rhoda gathered information for her case study, she learned a great deal about her. Sharma and her family had moved back and forth between India and the United States several times since her birth in California. The family's middle-class life in India was comfortable, but Sharma's parents were concerned that the primitive rural school near their home would not provide their daughter with the future they wanted for her. They tried twice to succeed economically in the United States and once even left their children with relatives in India while they looked for work in the States. Finally, both parents found jobs in the community where Rhoda taught. The father worked for local farmers and the mother was employed at a packing plant.

Sharma's parents speak English, but they use Punjabi with Sharma and her two younger sisters, who were also born in California. Sharma and her sisters dress in Western clothing for school and make an effort to fit into the activities in which the other students participate. The parents have allowed their children to give up some of their traditions, because they think that adopting Western ways is necessary for school success. They believe in hard work and have high academic expectations for their children. On weekends the girls go to a Sikh temple in a nearby city to develop their first language abilities and to learn about their religion. They also participate in Punjabi holidays and traditions.

Sharma has attended the same rural school from kindergarten through fifth grade. Though the school has a bilingual program for Spanish speakers, only limited primary-language support is available for Punjabi students. Sharma is an active member of her fifth-grade classroom community. She especially seeks out friends among the native English speakers in her class. Her social English is animated and full of the same idioms used by her peers. She tends to avoid contact with other newer and less proficient Punjabi students, although she is willing to be helpful with information about India or to support the newcomers when asked.

Sharma is categorized as proficient in English by the test the school administers to its second language students. However, Rhoda has noticed that the language of some content-area texts is a challenge for Sharma, and Sharma, on her own, looks for resource books, pictures, and charts to help make sense of some of the more academic content.

Rhoda hopes that Sharma will continue to study her native language so that she will develop that resource as she progresses in English. Rhoda summarizes her concerns about Sharma's future as follows:

> Although Sharma has had some advantages other language minority students have not had, she still has a problem with not being able to work to her potential because of lagging academic language development. As she continues to be exposed to comprehensible input, and continues to develop academic language, concepts will become less cognitively demanding. Because Sharma does not have a strong background in reading and writing Punjabi, it would appear that her primary language needs continued support. Teachers should continue to appreciate new Punjabi students for who they are and model this acceptance to their classroom communities. They should allow them to speak out of their personal experience so that students like Sharma can understand that "traditional" Punjabis have as much value as their Americanized counterparts.

Analysis

Many factors have influenced and will continue to influence Sharma's progress in school. Her parents are both educated and speak English well when compared with other immigrants. On the other hand, their socioeconomic status is not high. The family has experienced financial stress in the past and for this reason has had to move often. They presently live in a small farming community where there are many Spanish-speaking immigrants but only a few Punjabis. Teachers at the school have little understanding of the Punjabi way of life and customs.

The family maintains their home language and culture; yet her parents want Sharma and her siblings to succeed academically in a society that is very different from their own. Their expectations for their children are very high, almost demanding. Sharma must do well in a competitive school system but also maintain, to some extent, traditional Punjabi customs. This creates a struggle for Sharma, who even avoids social contact with Punjabi students who have recently arrived.

Sharma seems to be thriving despite these difficulties. Though no teachers speak her first language, a Punjabi-speaking aide works with those students who need first language support. Sharma's parents are quick to seek assistance from the school when they think their daughter needs it. Sharma herself interacts freely with her Anglo peers and seems well adjusted socially. Presently, she is able to function well in both the Punjabi social context and the school context. It remains to be seen if she will continue to be able to do this successfully.

Farrah

Farrah came from Iraq to Dallas, Texas, at age nine with her parents and her younger brother, Abrahem. Both of Farrah's parents speak English quite well, but like many Iraqi refugees, they have had trouble finding work. A recent economic downturn has made jobs scarce. Farrah's mother, Lelya, was a doctor in Iraq but works as a part-time case-worker here. Her father, Hussein, was educated as an engineer. When the war started, he took a job as a translator for English-speaking military personnel because the salary was so high. However, when it became too dangerous to stay in Iraq because of constant death threats, the family came to the United States with special immigrant visas under the Defense Authorization Act.

Hussein now is an interpreter in a meat-packing plant near the housing complex where they live on the edge of the city. The family is having trouble making ends meet, and their jobs certainly do not match their skills. They talk often of moving to Chicago because it has the largest Iraqi population in the country, and they have friends there.

Because she attended a good school in an upper-class neighborhood in Iraq, Farrah was close to grade level in academic content areas when she arrived despite some interruption of schooling from the war. She had studied some English at school in Iraq, and her parents paid for some private lessons as well, but Farrah still struggles understanding the English of her teacher, her peers in class, and her textbooks.

Her fourth-grade teacher is nice, but not certain how to help her. She has several students in her class who do not speak English as their first language, and she is not certain what to do with any of them. She is taking a series of inservices about working with English learners offered by the district, but she still feels overwhelmed most days. She admits she is relieved when the ESL teacher comes to take her second language students out for special help. While there are three other Arabic speakers in her ESL class, most of the other ELLs are Spanish speakers. Farrah sometimes believes she is learning more Spanish than English in her ESL class, though at recess and lunch she uses Arabic with the other Muslim girls, who also wear the traditional *hijab* or head scarf.

Farrah studies a great deal at night, but she realizes that she is missing much of what her native English-speaking classmates are learning. She is very aware of her accent and of the many words she still does not understand. Farrah is old enough to recognize her parents' stress and her responsibilities. She takes that and her other worries with her to school.

She studies very hard at home, but she hesitates to bother her parents too much. They seem to lose patience with her quickly. She manages to do all right with most assignments, but is terrified of the tests that are coming in the spring. Last year she did not have to take the tests because she was still a newcomer, but this year she will have to. Farrah envies her kindergarten age brother, who seems to be picking up English quickly and is making lots of friends at school and in the neighborhood. Abrahem fits in well with the other refugee children in their apartment complex, but Farrah feels like an outsider.

Farrah has nightmares. Sometimes the nightmares come from the violence she witnessed in Iraq, sometimes they come from worries about money that she hears her parents talking about, sometimes they are from her fears of not speaking enough English to do well in school, and sometimes they come from the taunts she hears that express anti-Arab and anti-Muslim sentiments.

Analysis

Farrah is an interesting student because she comes to school in this country with both advantages and disadvantages. Farrah arrived in fourth grade at grade level academically. She attended a quality private school in Iraq and understands what school is about and what is expected. However, she also is old enough to realize that she has a huge academic challenge because she does not speak English, and she knows she is not understanding critical instruction that students who speak English do. She knows she needs to study hard in order to compete with her classmates.

However, Farrah's challenges go beyond academic ones. Socially, she understands the racism that exists around her and only seems to feel really comfortable with girls who share her cultural and linguistic background, while her younger brother interacts happily with his peers, oblivious to what Farrah is old enough to understand. She also realizes that her family is struggling financially and seems to take that burden too upon her shoulders. Farrah's parents are so concerned with their own struggles that they don't realize the problems she faces. With another possible family move on the horizon, Farrah's academic future is difficult to predict.

Osman

Like Farrah, Osman is a Muslim refugee who has experienced the violence of war in his home country and racism in the United States, but his situation is very different than hers. When he entered middle school at age twelve, it was the first formal schooling experience Osman had ever had. He and his mother left Somalia with his uncle and aunt and four cousins when he was five. His father was killed during one of the many clan conflicts within the country.

Osman and his family lived in a refugee camp in Kenya where schooling was extremely limited. At times, children attended classes during the morning, sitting on the ground and repeating lessons after the teacher. However, most of the time in the camps was spent trying to obtain the basic necessities to stay alive. Osman and his cousins stood in line for food and water for many hours.

Osman is one of over a million Somalis who have been displaced since the late 1980s. In 2004 officials estimated that between one and three million Somalis were living abroad. Many had emigrated to Europe, Canada, and the United States. In December of 2009, the estimated number of Somalis in the United States was almost 84,000 (Corcoran 2009). Osman's family immigrated to the Minneapolis–St. Paul area, home to the largest number of Somali refugees in the United States.

For Osman and many of the other refugee children, life in the big city is overwhelming. Moving from a refugee camp where thousands of people slept on the ground with no modern conveniences to a large U.S. city with tall buildings, public transportation, and modern technology has been a shock. For the first time in his life, Osman held a pen and kept his own books in a locker.

The challenges for Osman are daunting. He has to learn English and learn the subject area content at the same time. Although he brought many experiences with him, those are not the experiences that help him understand the school system and the expectations the system has of him. His family cannot help him too much because they also have so many adjustments to make coming to a new country, looking for jobs, and finding a new home. In addition, they had very limited formal education in Somalia and are trying to learn enough English to survive in the United States.

In addition to struggles in school, Osman finds that the climate and the customs are very different in the new place. The cold is hard for Osman and his family to get used to, and they have to learn how to adapt to dressing, eating, and cooking differently. The religious holidays and customs in his new country are very different from the Muslim traditions Osman was raised with. Stories of communities across the country who do not welcome Somalis and mistrust Muslims concern the Somalis in Minneapolis–St. Paul despite the fact that there is an effort in local schools and the community to understand their refugee populations.

Although Osman worked hard and learned quite a bit of English in his first year in school, he realizes that he is significantly behind his native-English-speaking peers. Because he did not attend school during his time in the refugee camp, he is behind in all subject areas. Now, in this new country, he often doesn't understand what is being taught. Even though his teachers mean well, they do know how to help these older students who arrive with little to no formal schooling experiences.

Analysis

Osman's academic challenges seem overwhelming. He had no previous schooling and cannot read or write in his first language. He is living in a new country, trying to learn a new language, and also trying to learn school subjects at the middle school level. His parents cannot help him with his academics. He is starting school at age twelve. He does not have very much time to develop the academic content and academic English he will need to graduate from high school in five years. His teachers will need to give him specific kinds of support so that he can learn English and the content he needs, but even with the best instruction, the chances of his succeeding academically are slim.

Other challenges are also daunting. Osman lived in a warm, dry climate; now he is living in a state known for its 10,000 lakes, forests, and snowy winters. While Minneapolis–St. Paul has refugees from many parts of the world, it is a traditional midwestern U.S. city. Osman has always lived in a Muslim world, and now he needs to adjust to different holidays and customs. He is determined to do well in school, but there are many factors that will make academic success difficult for him.

Tou

Kathy, a junior high school English teacher, chose Tou, a Hmong student, for a case study because he is typical of other junior high school students she has. The population at Kathy's school is approximately 75 percent Hispanic, 10 percent Asian, 8 percent

African American, and 7 percent Caucasian. Tou, like many of Kathy's students, speaks English well, but he tested substantially below the fiftieth percentile on reading and struggles academically. Kathy described why she chose Tou for her case study:

> Tou is not generally well liked. His small stature and immaturity certainly contribute to this unpopularity. I have witnessed several instances of racial slurs aimed at Tou and the isolation that has ensued. The normal adolescent self-doubt and low self-esteem combined with the hostility he encounters daily seem a certain formula for failure.

Tou, now fourteen, is the youngest of seven children in a refugee Hmong family. He was born in a refugee camp in Thailand but spent only a few months there. After his birth, his family moved to the midsized city in California where he now lives with his father and two of his older brothers, who are married with children. His mother is living with a daughter and her family in another city several hours away. Separation of parents is difficult for any child, but because the Hmong place great value on family unity, Tou is deeply affected as his family stands out as an exception.

The family came to the United States with the hope of finding a better life. Economic and emotional problems, however, have kept them from achieving their goals. Tou's father, who was a farmer in Laos, does not speak English, is not literate in Hmong, and does not have any job skills appropriate to his inner-city neighborhood.

Tou has attended seventh and eighth grades in Kathy's inner-city school. Most of the students at the school are from low-income families living in run-down apartment complexes. Many of the parents are unemployed laborers or refugees on welfare.

Tou is generally an extremely reluctant participant in most class activities. Kathy describes his frequent pattern of absences:

> He often would come to school toward the middle of the week and then start his weekend early—kind of a two-day school week, five-day weekend model! When he was there, his antisocial behavior was more obvious, and students began to ask me not to seat them close to Tou.

This behavior eventually led to an emotional conference in which Tou's father, with the help of a Hmong-speaking aide, told of his hopes and dreams, of what America meant to him, and of his aspirations for his children. He told how one older brother had dropped out of high school because of involvement in gang activity and how worried he was that Tou was following the same failed path.

After that conference, Kathy saw that there was a change in Tou's behavior, though not a transformation. "Truthfully, it was old-fashioned parental hovering, teacher monitoring, and weekly progress reports sent home requiring Dad's signature that kept

Tou in school the last two months of school." His teachers and father did manage to get him through seventh grade, and he was promoted to eighth, an event Kathy explained as "not lifelong success, exactly, but an achievement nonetheless." However, in eighth grade it became obvious that Tou had become part of a gang. He attended school, but was in trouble outside of school. He was eventually transferred to a continuation school.

Kathy summarized her concerns for Tou and students like him at the end of her case study:

> This experience made me sadly aware that my students are all individuals with diverse and complicated needs and that I can never hope to solve them all. Just my one-on-one interviews with Tou and my special efforts to talk at least briefly with him every day pointed up that all my students need that attention. I feel stretched to the limit.

Analysis

As Kathy points out, Tou's situation is a complex one. Many negative factors are at work, and they appear to be outweighing the efforts his father and his teachers have made to help him. Tou is the youngest in a large family that is caught in a struggle to survive in a new and challenging culture, a culture that has little in common with their own. The home situation for Tou is stressful. His parents are separated, a situation that is unusual in traditional Hmong culture (Bliatout et al. 1988) and is a source of embarrassment. He lives with his father, who does not speak English and cannot find work. Tou has little support at home and few personal examples of school success. Older siblings either did not get schooling or had trouble in school themselves. One brother has a history of gang membership.

In his large inner-city junior high school, Tou is like many students with social and economic problems who become involved in gangs. He is not well liked even among Hmong students. In the classroom, he is a loner and does not work well with others. He frequently cuts classes.

The teachers in Tou's school have made an effort to meet their students' needs by forming teams so that they can share students and get to know the students better. However, for Tou, these efforts appear to have come too late. Tou has now entered a continuation school that provides a last chance. One fears that this change will not be enough for him. In fact, Kathy told us that the caring teacher there works very hard with students, but spends more time at his students' funerals than any other type of event. Students have often lost hope and many commit suicide or are killed during family violence or in gang warfare. The outlook for Tou is discouraging.

José Luis, Guillermo, and Patricia

We first met these three teenagers in 1984, less than a week after they arrived in Tucson, Arizona, from El Salvador. A few days before they flew to Tucson, they had watched as their father, an important military official, was assassinated in front of their home in San Salvador. The three had narrowly escaped being arrested and perhaps even murdered themselves. In fact, sixteen-year-old Guillermo had two bullet wounds in his leg when he arrived in the United States.

Their stepmother in El Salvador distanced herself from the three teens for her own safety and that of a two-year-old daughter, who was their stepsister. José Luis, Guillermo, and Patricia, alone in a country that had suddenly become hostile, sought asylum with their aunt, a fellow doctoral student and friend of ours at the university. Through that connection, we often had the opportunity to spend time with these remarkable teens over the next six years. We have maintained contact up to the present over twenty-five years later.

Although they had studied English at private bilingual schools in San Salvador, their comprehension of English and their ability to communicate in English was extremely limited when they first arrived. Their aunt, a dedicated academic, was anxious to get them into school and working toward school success. All three were enrolled in a local high school almost immediately and admonished by their aunt that they must do well in all their subjects. She warned them that there was no time to be wasted, and that she would not tolerate irresponsibility.

The aunt, who had an older, ailing husband, found them an apartment near her and supported the three financially the best she could. They also received some sporadic financial help from aging grandparents in El Salvador. The teenagers were soon almost entirely on their own, trying to cope with a new culture and language. Each handled the situation in a different way.

The oldest at seventeen, José Luis felt responsible for the other two. He also felt somehow at fault for not having saved his father, and wrestled with that guilt. He studied day and night, smiling little, and taking almost no time for relaxation. English was a struggle for him, and he spent hours with a dictionary, translating his textbooks and studying for tests. He ignored jokes his classmates made about the fact that he studied all the time. Classes in algebra, calculus, and physics were less linguistically demanding, so he soon concentrated on them as a possible specialization. He graduated from high school with a President's Award for excellent academic scholarship just two years after arriving.

Guillermo responded in a totally different way to his new surroundings. He was the most outgoing of the three. He worked hard to make friends and joined high school clubs almost immediately. He talked to anyone who made an effort to understand him, even when they made fun of his accent, and he soon became involved in school government. His grades were not high, but he studied enough to earn a B-minus average and qualify to attend the university.

Patricia depended more on our family for emotional and personal support at first. At thirteen, she was the youngest of the three and the only female. Her aunt wanted her to be responsible for the cooking and cleaning of the apartment the three siblings shared, but those responsibilities and the adjustment to the new language and culture were often too much for her. Her brothers seemed to understand. They helped with household chores. She studied and made friends, but in some ways was the most affected by the move and the loss of her father. English probably came faster to Patricia than to her brothers. She spent more time with our family, and our two daughters helped introduce her to customs and fads in the United States.

The three teens and their aunt became involved in our church shortly after their escape from El Salvador. The church family was especially important when they applied for asylum in the United States. At that time, refugees from El Salvador had to prove their lives were endangered to be granted asylum. Even though they had newspaper articles about the assassination of their father, it was difficult to establish that the three children were in danger. When the hearing for their asylum was held, church members took time off from work to attend. That show of support impressed the judge and probably was instrumental in his filing a positive report with the federal government.

All three eventually attended The University of Arizona and graduated. José Luis completed a master's degree in engineering and is presently working for the City of Los Angeles. Guillermo studied engineering and international economics as an undergraduate and completed a master's degree in architecture at the University of Southern California. Patricia finished a degree in chemistry and is now living in the San Francisco area where she works in a supervisory position for a large pharmaceutical firm. They are now all financially secure professionals. The three enjoy traveling in the United States and Europe and have returned to El Salvador several times to visit family and friends. They consider the United States home and probably will not return to El Salvador to live, despite intentions to do so when they first arrived.

Analysis

Certainly the three teenagers faced overwhelming obstacles when they came to the United States. Their only relative here was an aunt who had never had children and who had her own personal responsibilities, including the care of a sick husband, graduate studies, and teaching. The three young people had to learn to live on their own almost from the beginning. Money was tight and had to be budgeted, something they had never had to do before.

The trauma of their father's assassination was difficult to cope with, and the three rehashed the scene many times and speculated about what might have been. They were immediately enrolled in a public school where they had to deal with the academic work in English, and establish their own identities apart from the other Hispanics at the school. They were not Mexicans, and their background was very different from almost all the other students.

That background was probably what helped them the most. They were from a prominent family in El Salvador. Their relatives, including their aunt, knew high government officials, including former presidents. They had pride in their past and a strong sense of their worth. They had attended good private schools in San Salvador and had traveled to the United States and Europe. Although they did not speak and understand English well, they had studied English grammar and had a strong background in Spanish language and literature as well as in academic-content areas such as math and science.

Once José Luis, Guillermo, and Patricia arrived in Tucson, they found different kinds of support. Their aunt provided the money for the basics of living, and they received some funds from family in El Salvador. Eventually, with the encouragement of their aunt and others, they earned academic scholarships. They also had emotional and social support from people in the community.

Our family often did things with them on weekends, delighting in introducing them to American culture and advising them about schooling and finances. The church provided another important support. They had weekly and sometimes biweekly contact with Americans with whom they had the chance to use English for real purposes. Their past experiences in El Salvador, their aunt's academic expectations, their social interactions with an American family, and the support of a church community placed José Luis, Guillermo, and Patricia in contexts that influenced them positively.

Conclusion

English language learners are a very diverse group of students, as the case studies we report on here show. Despite their differences, they all face the same academic challenge. As Short and Fitzsimmons (2007) point out, ELLs face double the work of native English speakers. They must learn English, and they must learn academic content through English. In addition, they often live in neighborhoods where the schools are underfunded and are staffed by inexperienced teachers.

Second language students face challenges outside of school as well as in school. New immigrants must adapt to a new culture and a new language. Many immigrant families are poor. Some immigrants face hostility because of their race or religion. Even for ELLs born in the United States, the culture of the school is usually very different from the culture of the home.

Despite these challenges, some ELLs succeed in schools. They succeed because they have caring and knowledgeable teachers like the graduate students whose case studies we have reported here. They succeed because of their strong motivation and persistence. And they succeed because their parents support them, even when their parents are not highly educated and don't understand the U.S. school system. However, many other ELLs fail their classes and drop out of school. In the following chapters, we examine the factors that affect the success and failure of ELLs, and we provide information and ideas teachers can use to better serve the increasing number of second language students in our schools.

Key Points

- English language learners are a very diverse group of students.
- Factors both outside and inside school affect their academic performance.
- Case studies can help teachers understand English language learners.
- Teachers should understand second language acquisition theory and the social and cultural factors that affect their ELLs.

APPLICATIONS

1. Of the students discussed in the case studies, choose one that reminds you of a second language learner you know. Compare and contrast the factors that affect the schooling of both. Discuss your comparison in pairs or in a small group.

2. In small groups choose a case study described here, or the story of a second language learner you know. On a SMART Board, butcher paper, or an overhead, list the factors that seem to predict school success and those that seem to limit success in each case. Share your results with the large group, and make a composite list of positive and negative factors.

3. Choose a second language learner who seems to be especially successful in school or one that seems to be struggling. Interview that student and/or family members to try to determine what factors might be influencing school performance. Before the interview, compile a list of possible questions with others and discuss culturally appropriate ways of approaching the interview.

2

What Factors Affect the School Success of English Language Learners?

Types of Students

All the case study students we described are English language learners. They all have had to learn in a new language, and many have had to adjust to schooling and to life in a country with different customs. However, there are some important differences in their backgrounds that influence their chances for academic success in this country. These differences are related to their previous educational experiences and to their life experiences both before they arrived and after they began their schooling here. It is important that educators understand the factors that affect the academic performance of ELLs so that they can best meet their students' needs and help them succeed in school.

Researchers (Olsen 2010; Freeman and Freeman 2002, 2009; Menken and Kleyn 2009) have categorized English language learners into three major groups: recent arrivals with adequate schooling, recent arrivals with limited formal or interrupted schooling, and students who are long-term English learners. In addition, some students are potential long-term ELLs. In planning for instruction, it is helpful for teachers to be aware of the differences among these groups. Figure 2–1 lists the characteristics of the four types of students. In the following sections we describe the characteristics of each group. We also give examples of students who fit into each group.

Recent Arrivals with Adequate Schooling

Students who fall under the category of recent arrivals with adequate schooling have come to the United States within the last five years. When they arrive, these students bring with them the schooling experiences of their native country. They are literate in

Newly arrived with adequate schooling	• recent arrivals (less than 5 years in U.S.) • typically in grades 2–12 • adequate schooling in native country • soon catch up academically • may still score low on standardized tests given in English • social and economic factors can influence positively or negatively
Newly arrived with limited formal schooling	• recent arrivals (less than 5 years in U.S.) • typically in grades 2–12 • interrupted or limited schooling in native country • limited native language literacy • below grade level in math • poor academic achievement • social and economic factors can influence positively or negatively
Long-term English learner	• 7 or more years in the U.S. • typically in grades 6–12 • limited literacy in both native language and English • some may get adequate grades but score low on tests • struggle with content classes • often have been retained and are at risk of dropping out • are *vaivén* students or students with inconsistent/ subtractive schooling • have had ESL or bilingual instruction, but no consistent program
Potential long-term English learner	• recent arrivals in grades K–1 • students in grades K–5 who have lived in the U.S. most of their lives and begin their schooling speaking a language other than English • parents with low levels of education • parents struggling financially and/or socially

FIGURE 2–1. *Types of English learners (adapted from Olsen and Jaramillo 1999; Freeman and Freeman 2002; Menken and Kleyn 2009)*

their first language, and their content knowledge is at grade level. While these students may catch up academically fairly quickly, they still struggle with standardized tests and exit exams because they have not fully developed English, and there may be gaps in their understanding and knowledge because tests are written with the assumption that all students have the background of native English speakers.

Recent arrivals with adequate schooling may or may not adjust well socially. The school and community factors that influence them are extremely important. The economic situation their families find themselves in also makes a difference in whether or not they succeed academically. Looking at two of the case study examples helps us understand these students and assess their chances for achieving academic success.

José Luis, Guillermo, and Patricia

These three teenagers fit the description of recent arrivals with adequate schooling. All three arrived in this country at grade level academically. In fact, due to their private schooling, they were probably more advanced in some subject areas than their English-speaking classmates. In addition, their international travel had given these students life experiences that helped them adjust to a new country and new school. They had even studied and practiced a little bit of English. While their English ability was not equal to school tasks, they could communicate minimally socially.

Certainly, the three young people suffered trauma as they watched their father's assassination and had to flee as refugees. However, they had academic, community, and social support. Their aunt was a graduate student and understood what was necessary for her niece and nephews to succeed academically. She encouraged them to study hard. Our family was also connected to the university and provided academic support. In fact, David was José Luis' composition teacher when he reached the university. We also provided important social support. Our two daughters, though younger than the three teens, introduced them to U.S. culture and traditions. Because our daughters were younger, their indirect lessons were perhaps less threatening than having to learn from peers. Their church community also was important. These young people never felt alone in a new country.

Farrah

Farrah was also a recent arrival with adequate schooling. Like José Luis, Guillermo, and Patricia, she attended a private school and arrived with grade-level literacy and academic content knowledge. Her parents spoke good English, and she had some private English lessons before coming to this country. This background may help her eventually.

Although her academic background was similar to that of the teens from El Salvador, Farrah lacks the kinds of supports they had. Farrah's home situation in this country is much more traumatic, mainly because her family had no relatives or friends waiting for them when they arrived. While there are government agencies to help Iraqi refugees, her parents had to accept jobs for which they were overqualified. These jobs provided some money, but the family still struggles financially. Agencies do not provide the same kind of support that relatives, family friends, and a church community can provide.

Farrah's friends are other refugee children. She faces racism from some Americans both in and outside of school. Her parents, though academically prepared, are not emotionally ready to help her in school because they are busy establishing themselves economically in the United States. In sum, Farrah's academic background may ultimately enable her to succeed, but she lacks family and community support that would help her.

Limited or Interrupted Formal Schooling Students

A second type of ELL is the recent arrival with limited or interrupted formal schooling. Students in this group are also referred to as Students with Interrupted Formal Education (SIFEs) because of their inconsistent schooling. These students face all the problems of any new immigrants, but they are much less prepared academically than students like the Salvadorans or Farrah. When they arrive, they have either had little or no schooling or schooling that was so often interrupted that they are significantly behind their peers in literacy development and academic content knowledge.

Limited formal schooling students have limited or no native language literacy to draw upon as they learn to read and write in English. Sometimes teachers can tell if a newcomer is a limited formal schooling student either by the student's poorly developed handwriting or by the student's inability to do even basic math computation, such as addition or subtraction. Because of their limited experiences in school, they lack basic concepts in the different subject areas and are often at least two to three years below grade level in the content areas.

Limited formal schooling students are faced with the complex task of developing conversational English, becoming literate in English, and gaining the academic knowledge and skills they need to compete with native English speakers. Because they do not have the academic background to draw upon in their native languages, they often struggle with coursework in English and receive low scores on standardized tests. Many also lack an understanding of how schools are organized and how students are expected to act in schools. Further, in most cases, they live in families that struggle economically as they try to adjust to living in a new culture.

OSMAN

Osman is an example of a limited formal schooling student. He escaped the terrorism of his country at age five and spent the next seven years of his life in refugee camps in Kenya. In Minneapolis–St. Paul his family is struggling to adjust to living in a new country. He had limited schooling in the refugee camps and does not understand the routines of school. Osman has no first language literacy or content knowledge to draw upon as he studies different subjects in English. Although he is working hard, he has double the work of his peers because he has to learn both English and academic subject matter. It is not surprising that students like Osman often have poor academic achievement even when they try very hard to do well in school.

Long–Term English Learners

Long-Term English Learners (LTELLs) are increasingly attracting attention among educators across the country. The 2000 census reveals that over half of the LEP secondary school children were U.S. born (Fix and Capps 2005). This is disturbing because LTELLs are students who have been attending school in this country for more than seven years and yet are still struggling academically. These students are generally misunderstood or overlooked. Recent reports have highlighted these students because of the growing concern about them. In a report on large urban school districts across the country, Horwitz and her colleagues (2009) state:

> Leaders and staff in each district were quick to point out the specialized needs of adolescent, newcomer students, yet they acknowledge that a majority of the students falling through the cracks are long-term ELLs who have been in the system for years. (29)

Olsen (2010) has authored a report about long-term English learners in California. This report has been referred to as "a wake-up call to California educators and policymakers." Olsen expresses the concern that so many secondary students, despite many years in California schools and "despite being close to the age in which they should be able to graduate, are still not English proficient and have indeed incurred major academic deficits" (iii). Researchers have published reports about long-term English learners in other states, including Texas, Colorado, and New York (McNeil, Coppola, and Radigan 2008; Olsen 2010; Menken, Kleyn, and Chae under review; Menken, Kleyn, and Chae 2007).

Menken and Kleyn (2009) have studied long-term English learners with colleagues in New York City and identified common characteristics of this student population. LTELLs are typically found in grades 6 to 12, speak different languages, and come from different countries. They are often orally bilingual and speak English like a native speaker, but they have limited literacy skills in English and in their native languages. LTELLs perform below grade level in reading and writing and, as a result, struggle with their content-area classes. Usually, these students have low grades, often they have been retained at some point, and they are at high risk of dropping out. The needs of these students are different from those of secondary newcomer ELLs, "yet the language programming at the secondary level is typically for new arrivals [because] most educators are unfamiliar with the specialized needs of this population" (Menken and Kleyn 2009, 2).

Since there are so many of these long-term English learners, researchers have divided them into subcategories. Menken, Kleyn, and colleagues (2007, 2009, 2010) have listed two main types: *vaivén* students and students with inconsistent and/or subtractive U.S. schooling. We will discuss each briefly.

VAIVÉN STUDENTS

The first group is referred to as the *vaivén* transnational students because, as the label indicates when translated from Spanish, they "go and come." *Vaivén* students, though primarily U.S. educated, move back and forth between the United States and their country of origin. Many of these students also fit the Students with Interrupted Formal Education (SIFE) designation since their schooling is interrupted as they move back and forth between countries.

Carlos is a good example of this type of student. He lives near the Mexico/Texas border. He grew up in Mexico. His mother is a single parent. Carlos began school in Matamoros, Mexico. When he was eight, his mother met a Mexican-origin man who had legal residency in the United States and lived across the border in Brownsville, Texas. When she got pregnant with his baby, he wanted to get married and have the baby born and educated in the United States. Carlos, his mother, and the baby moved to Brownsville, and Carlos started second grade in Texas.

Since then Carlos has moved back to Matamoros twice to live with relatives. Once he attended school, but the other time he did not. He says he hates schools in the United States and doesn't like his stepfather. Although he tries to impress Mexican friends and relatives with his fluent oral English, he struggles academically in English. At sixteen Carlos is back in Mexico for the third time. He isn't attending school there, and his relatives can't support him in hard economic times. He will probably return to Brownsville soon, but one wonders if he will attend school there or not.

INCONSISTENT/SUBTRACTIVE SCHOOLING LTELLS

A second type of LTELL is the English language learner with inconsistent and/or subtractive schooling. Students with inconsistent schooling receive various types of support. For example, some ELLs may be placed in bilingual programs when they first enter schools in the United States. However, as soon as they develop some conversational English, they are mainstreamed. Other ELLs are only given ESL classes. In states like California or Arizona, which have English-only laws, ELLs are put directly into English immersion programs with no primary language support. ESL and English immersion programs are considered subtractive because many ELLs in these programs lose their first language as they learn English.

Alicia is a good example of a student who received inconsistent, subtractive schooling. She started school in a rural district in Southeastern Texas when she was in kindergarten. Though born in Mexico, she came to the United States when she was three after her parents crossed over to find work in the fields. The school district where she first attended provided bilingual classes, so she started school with first language support. However, since her family needed to move to find work, Alicia became a migrant child, spending spring, summer, and fall in Michigan, and then returning to south Texas for the winter. When she was in Michigan, Alicia was in all-English classrooms often without any kind of instructional support.

In second grade in Texas, she was also placed in all-English classrooms since she spoke English well. However, when her family began living in South Texas year-round, Alicia's struggles with academic English became evident. Now in sixth grade, Alicia cannot read or write at grade level, and teachers are concerned that she might not be able to pass state-mandated exams and go on to junior high school. Alicia is a typical example of an LTELL who speaks English well, but struggles in academic reading and writing. As a result of her inconsistent, subtractive schooling, she has not developed age-appropriate oral ability in her first language. She is not literate in Spanish and has limited English literacy.

Potential Long–Term English Learners

A fourth group of English language learners are students who are either new arrivals in grades K–1 or students in grades K–5 who have lived most or all of their lives in the United States and started school speaking a language other than English. While these students can succeed if community, family, and school factors are positive, many of them are not successful. They are best seen as potential long-term English learners who need a great deal of support to achieve well academically.

New arrivals in kindergarten or first grade do not fit into the categories of recent arrivals with either adequate or limited schooling simply because they have had little or no previous schooling. For these students, the kind of support they receive in school is extremely important. For example, if they are placed in a bilingual program, they can build on their first language skills as they learn English. Support from their families is also crucial. If their parents are well educated and financially successful, their chances of adjusting quickly to school in the United States improve.

However, many new arrivals live in difficult family situations and receive little or no first language support. Mony, the Cambodian girl in Katie's kindergarten class, is a good example of a potential long-term English learner. She received no support in her first language. Mony had great difficulty adjusting to life in a new country. Her parents were overwhelmed and not stable financially, so they could offer little support. Fortunately, Katie is an excellent teacher who provided both academic and affective support. From Katie's observations, it appears that Mony is doing much better in school. However, without continued strong support at both school and home, Mony remains a potential long-term English learner.

A second group of students who are potential long-term English learners are those in grades K–5 who either came to the United States at a very young age or were born here and entered school speaking a language other than English. If their family situations are stable, and if the school provides a strong bilingual program, these students can succeed at a high rate. However, students who live with parents who struggle economically and who have had low levels of education themselves are less likely to succeed, especially if the school does not provide first language support.

Salvador, a student we described previously, is a good example. He was born in the United States and entered school speaking only Spanish. In kindergarten and first grade, he received bilingual education. However, due to his home situation, he was a discipline problem. Salvador was not learning to read and write in Spanish, and school officials decided he should be put in an all-English classroom for second grade. By the time he reached Ann's second-/third-grade classroom, he was labeled as a troublemaker and was not able to read or write in either Spanish or English.

It was a struggle for Ann to work with him at all. However, he did get consistent reading and writing support from Ann. Despite making some progress, Salvador repeated third grade. His new teacher, Francisco, also supported his reading and writing. Francisco seemed to turn Salvador around, but early schooling made his learning a struggle. Fortunately for Salvador, Ann and Francisco could begin to help him catch up academically, and he has continued to improve both in his behavior and his academic abilities.

Salvador has made great improvements in school. However, his home situation has not changed, and so he remains a potential long-term English learner. With continued strong support in school, he should succeed. Nevertheless, he can still be classified as a potential LTELL because factors from the family and community may counter the efforts of school personnel.

It is important that teachers find out about their students' backgrounds. Teachers we have worked with do this in a variety of ways. Sometimes teachers give students questionnaires asking them how they feel about reading and writing in English and what their strengths and challenges are. Other times they ask students to interview each other about their past schooling and report back. Other teachers examine writing samples and then conference with students. The more information teachers can gather, the better they are able to help students. Of course, the factors that influence the academic success of ELLs go beyond the instruction they receive. We now turn to other factors that researchers have identified as influential in the school success of second language learners.

Ogbu's Classification of Immigrant and Involuntary Minority Students

Ogbu (1991) and Ogbu and Matute-Bianchi (1986) have studied the schooling of immigrants. These researchers have found that certain types of immigrants succeed in school at higher rates than other types of immigrants based on factors other than language or previous schooling. These researchers distinguish between immigrant minorities and involuntary minorities. Figure 2–2 lists the characteristics of these two groups.

Immigrant Minorities	Involuntary Minorities
Groups immigrated recently	Groups may have lived in the U.S. for decades or generations
Not highly influenced by mainstream values and attitudes	Highly influenced by mainstream values and attitudes
Measure success by homeland standards	Measure success by mainstream standards
Believe they can go back home and use skills and degrees	Cannot go back home or do not believe they can
Can alternate behavior between home and school	Cannot alternate behavior
Characterized by primary cultural differences that existed before cultures came into contact (food, clothes, language, religious practices)	Characterized by secondary cultural differences that developed after cultures came into contact (ways of talking, walking, dressing)
Minority group members recognize the differences and are willing to work to overcome them to succeed in school.	Minority group members have created the differences to distinguish themselves from the mainstream. They do not attempt to cross self-imposed cultural boundaries.
Minority group members don't suffer emotionally as they work to overcome differences. They're motivated to learn the things that will help them to succeed. They can alternate behavior. They develop a folk theory for success that places a high value on education.	Minority group members may suffer emotionally and physically if they try to overcome differences. Group members exert negative peer pressure. It is not possible to alternate behavior. They develop a folk theory that puts a low value on education.

FIGURE 2–2. *Immigrant and involuntary minorities*

Immigrant Minorities

Ogbu classifies immigrant minorities as groups who are new arrivals in the United States and who exhibit certain characteristics. In the first place, immigrant minority groups are not highly influenced by the attitudes and values of the mainstream society because they measure their success by the standards of their homeland. New students from Somalia or rural Mexico, for example, might be from families living in poverty by U.S. standards, but their condition in the United States is probably much better than what it was in Africa or the Mexican countryside. Moreover, if they experience prejudicial treatment because of their country of origin, they may not be strongly affected by other people's attitudes toward them. Osman is a good example of an immigrant minority. While he struggled to adjust and had challenges, including suffering from racism, he worked hard even though his chances for academic success were minimal.

In addition, as Ogbu points out, the cultural differences between immigrant minorities and the mainstream are primary differences that existed before the cultures came into contact. These differences are specific and easy to identify. They include such things as language, food, customs, and clothing. So, for example, Osman celebrated Muslim holidays including daytime fasting during Ramadan, the monthlong religious holiday that celebrates the period when the prophet Muhammad received the first revelations of the Koran, the holy book of Islam.

In his research Ogbu found that immigrant minority students like Osman could alternate their behavior between home and school. They assume that they must do this to succeed at school. At the same time, they feel it is important to maintain cultural traditions and values at home. Many immigrant minorities believe that they can go back to their homeland someday and use the skills and academic degrees they earn in the United States.

José Luis, Guillermo, and Patricia also fit Ogbu's classification of immigrant minorities. They made a point of learning how things were done in the United States. They worked hard to learn English and do well in school although they spoke Spanish at home. They were not bothered when students made fun of their English or were rude to them. They knew what they needed to do to succeed in this country, and they were willing to work hard to get ahead. In fact, though they never returned to live in their own country, they talked often about getting an education to return and help rebuild their native El Salvador.

Ogbu found that immigrant minorities often succeed in schools at a higher rate than involuntary minorities. However, many older immigrant minority students have interrupted or limited formal schooling. In addition, both older and younger immigrant students live in families who are struggling to adjust to living in a new country. These factors may limit possibilities for success.

Older immigrants like Osman face a particularly great challenge. A recent, comparative long-term study of new adolescent immigrants by Suárez-Orozco, Suárez-Orozco, and Todorova (2008) makes it clear that not all students who fit Ogbu's immigrant minority category succeed. Suárez-Orozco and colleagues studied immigrant adolescents from China, Haiti, the Dominican Republic, Central America, and Mexico on both the East and West coasts of the United States in an attempt to understand the influences on their school success or failure. Their findings showed that multiple factors both inside and outside school affect the academic success of immigrant students. We examine a number of these factors in the following chapters. However, in general, immigrant minorities fare better in school than ELLs whom Ogbu would classify as involuntary minorities.

Involuntary Minorities

The second category of students Ogbu identified, involuntary minorities, includes groups like African Americans, Mexican Americans, and Native Americans. Many of them have lived in the United States for generations. These are minority groups who either were in the United States before it became a country, were brought here as slaves, or lived in regions such as the Southwest where wars resulted in border shifts. Members of these groups have typically not experienced academic success.

Refugees from Southeast Asia are another group that falls into the involuntary minority category. Many were placed in camps in Thailand or the Philippines for several years and then given asylum in the United States. They did not choose to leave their homeland and come to a new country. In fact, they cannot return to their homeland. For children of these refugees, whether born in the camps or in this country, the United States is often the only permanent home they know. By the second or third generation most have lost their native language and culture. These Southeast Asian refugees exhibit many of the characteristics of involuntary minorities.

Ogbu found that involuntary minorities are highly influenced by majority group attitudes and values and measure success by mainstream standards, and they do not believe they can export skills or academic degrees to a distant homeland. For most students who are involuntary minorities, the United States is the only home they have ever known.

According to Ogbu, involuntary minorities are characterized by secondary cultural differences. These are differences that developed after the cultures came into contact, and they are more a matter of style than content. They might include different ways of walking, talking, or dressing designed to signal identity in a particular social group. In some cases, involuntary minorities join gangs. In those cases, they may wear gang colors and dress using styles that other members of their gang do. Of course, not all involuntary minorities are gang members. Since these secondary differences are intended to indicate distinctions between the minority group and members of mainstream culture, involuntary minorities generally do not alternate behavior. They act the same way at school and outside school.

In many cases, involuntary minority members develop a folk theory for success that puts a low value on education. Successful members of involuntary minority groups generally move away from the area where they grew up, so they don't serve as positive role models for other group members. Involuntary minorities, then, do not see that education improves life conditions, and in fact, see few, if any, examples of success resulting from education. Not surprisingly, involuntary minorities have higher rates of school failure than immigrant minorities. Many long-term English learners and potential long-term English learners have the characteristics of involuntary minorities.

Tou, Kathy's Hmong student, is an example of an involuntary minority. He was born in a refugee camp in Thailand and came to the United States when he was very young. He seems to be losing touch with his Hmong culture and language. His family has not followed traditional Hmong values, with both divorce and gang membership in its history. He cannot alternate behavior between home and school because he really has no model of Hmong traditions to follow, or he considers them old-fashioned.

Tou sees almost no role models who have succeeded academically in his community. His gang membership is probably an attempt to find some place where he belongs. All his schooling was in the United States, in a large school system where he seems to have been overlooked. When his teacher, Kathy, tried to help him with his academic struggles in junior high school, it appears it was already too late. Tou had no primary-language support in school and fell behind. Family and community factors have both had negative effects on his school performance.

Mexican–Origin Categories for School Success

Hispanics make up the largest group of ELLs, almost 80 percent. Among Hispanics around 65 percent are of Mexican origin (U.S. Census Bureau 2006). For this reason, we believe it is important to discuss two research-based categorizations relevant to Mexican-origin student school success. Matute-Bianchi (1991) did in-depth interviews with immigrant and nonimmigrant Mexican-descent students in rural California. From this work she suggested five categories of students, which she then linked to academic achievement: (1) recent Mexican immigrants, (2) Mexican-oriented students, (3) Mexican American students, (4) Chicanos, and (5) Cholos.

According to Matute-Bianchi, the first group, the recent Mexican immigrants, consists of students who have been in the United States for only three to five years. They are essentially newcomers and fall under Ogbu's category of immigrant minorities. The second group, Mexican-oriented students, may have lived here longer than the three to five years, but they have maintained their *mexicano* identity and still speak Spanish even if they also speak English. The third group Matute-Bianchi identifies as Mexican Americans. These students were born here and have acculturated to U.S. culture. They may speak some Spanish, but many have lost most of their Spanish and do not really consider themselves more American than Mexican.

The fourth group is Chicanos. These are generally second-generation Mexican Americans. The term came from the Chicano Movement of the 1960s, which included political agendas such as restoration of land grants promised to Mexican peoples, farm workers' rights, enhanced education for Mexican-origin children, and voting and political rights. Chicanos generally want to know about their history and culture. The final group is the Cholos, who may be associated with Mexican gangs and may be identified by the ways they dress or act.

Matute-Bianchi argues that school success is not associated with more acculturation, which is often thought to be important by schools and society. She found that students with strong ethnic identity, including the new Mexican immigrants, the Mexican-oriented students, and the Mexican Americans, did better than the Chicano or Cholo groups. Matute-Bianchi found that these last two groups believed they were stigmatized and had limited opportunities. This is consistent with Ogbu's involuntary minority classification. Students in these groups displayed secondary cultural differences. Matute-Bianchi emphasizes the effect of ethnic identity and beliefs about minority status on school performance.

In her study of Mexican border families, Valdés (1996) came to some of the same conclusions as Matute-Bianchi. She found that Mexican immigrants often feel little identification with Mexican nationals. They self-identify as American, but see themselves as having low status in U.S. society. She found that Mexican Americans believed that because they were of Mexican origin, they would automatically experience discrimination and that their opportunities were limited. At the same time, they believed that education was the route to success.

Recent research by Gándara and Contreras (2009) suggests that the earlier research Matute-Bianchi and Valdés carried out with Mexican Americans applies to Latinos in general. In fact, the authors title their recent book *The Latino Education Crisis* because their research shows that Latinos, an increasingly large percentage of the U.S. school-age population, are failing in schools and in society at alarming rates. Like Ogbu and Matute-Bianchi, Gándara and Contreras found it is not the new immigrants who are failing; it is the native-born Latinos who have lived in the United States and gone to school here and who have become long-term English learners who struggle most in school. As Gándara and Contreras state:

> . . . Latino students typically experience a host of impediments to success in school. Any one of these barriers is daunting, but to be challenged simultaneously by multiple obstacles and a lack of social, psychological, and educational support at school and in the community does limit the potential of many Latino students. (120)

Ogbu's distinction between immigrant and involuntary minorities helps explain the academic performance of many second language students. Of course, within each group there are exceptions. Many ELLs from both groups struggle in school and experience low rates of graduation from high school and even lower levels of college success. Nevertheless, as our own research has shown, some students also succeed. One key to the success of ELLs is effective and caring teachers who understand the multiple factors that affect their students' school performance. Figure 2–3 combines the categories of ELLs we discussed as types of learners with Ogbu's classification of immigrant and involuntary minorities.

Type of Student	Grade	Ogbu Classification
Recent arrivals with adequate schooling	2–12	Immigrant (José Luis, Guillermo, and Patricia; Farrah)
Recent arrivals with limited schooling	2–12	Immigrant (Osman)
Long-term ELLs	6–12	Involuntary (Tou)
Potential long-term ELLs	K–5 K–1	Involuntary (Salvador) Immigrant (Mony)

FIGURE 2–3. *Types of learners and Ogbu classification*

Factors Leading to Student Success or Failure

Our focus in this book is primarily on the world of the school. Teachers do not have control of all the forces in or out of school that affect student learning. Nevertheless, it is important for teachers to be aware of these factors. By studying the particular factors that affect their students, teachers begin to take on new attitudes and try new teaching strategies to support their students and to build on the strengths they see in their students.

We recognize that whether a particular student succeeds or fails may have little to do with curriculum itself. Success or failure may be more related to what goes on outside the classroom than what goes on in school. As Sue and Padilla (1986) comment:

> There is no question that English proficiency is essential to educational success, occupational achievement, and socio-economic mobility, but these occur in a sociocultural context. Understanding this context can help to explain educational attainments of ethnic minority students and to provide alternatives that can lead to improved educational outcomes for these students. (35)

An understanding of the various elements that influence student school performance can help teachers in several ways. First, it can keep teachers from blaming themselves, the curriculum, or student ability if students are not doing well. Second, when teachers understand the role of external factors, they can begin to work for changes that would benefit their students in areas beyond the classroom. Finally, teachers can resist the acceptance of negative stereotypes about minorities, and they can help their students develop positive attitudes toward school and toward themselves. They can do this by discussing with students the various factors that contribute to their academic success or failure, including the negative attitudes others may hold toward them because they are members of minority groups. They can become advocates and enlist the support of students, parents, politicians, and community members as they work towards creating positive environments for learning.

Perspectives on Failure

Sue and Padilla (1986) and Díaz, Moll, and Mehan (1986) point out that there are many explanations for minority-group failure that simplify complex issues. These explanations tend to be context free. That is, the explanation is applied to all immigrant students who fail, without considering any specifics about the individual students, including their background and experiences in and out of school. Context-free explanations, then, are applied to a group of students and assumed to fit all situations and all students. These explanations are also usually single-cause explanations. In other words, they put forward one sole reason for behavior or results and do not consider alternatives.

Cortés (1986) notes that we often attribute success or failure to single causes because we confuse cause and correlation. Just because two things occur together, we cannot conclude that one causes the other. For example, students who speak English as another language may do poorly in school, but speaking a second language does not cause school failure. Cortés notes the "tendency to decontextualize explanations"(16). Often, factors such as race, language, or socioeconomic status may contribute to school success or failure, but looking at any one of these factors, or even some combination, out of context may lead to false conclusions. According to Cortés, the question we need to ask is, "under what conditions do students with similar socio-cultural characteristics succeed educationally and under what conditions do they perform poorly in school? In other words, within what contexts—educational and societal—do students of similar backgrounds succeed and within what contexts do they do less well?"(17).

Next we discuss the three most common single-cause, context-free explanations of school failure for immigrant students: genetic inferiority, cultural deficit, and cultural mismatch. Even though these perspectives have been discredited, some people assume they are the causes for the school performance of second language students. These perspectives are summarized in Figure 2–4.

Single cause, Context free		
Genetic inferiority	**Cultural deficit**	**Cultural mismatch**
Certain groups fail to do well because they are genetically inferior (single cause) not because of any factors in the environment (context free).	Certain cultural groups fail to do well because their culture is seen as deficient (single cause) not because of any factors in the environment (context free).	Certain cultures fail to achieve because their culture is different from mainstream culture (single cause) not because of any factors in the environment (context free).
Multiple cause, Context specific		
Contextual interaction		
Certain groups fail to achieve because of the complex interaction of many factors including background experiences, social factors, and school setting (multiple cause and context specific).		

FIGURE 2–4. *Perspectives on failure*

Genetic Inferiority

A context-free interpretation that was once widely accepted is genetic inferiority. The argument has been that certain minority groups do better than others because of genetic factors. Oftentimes the groups labeled as inferior have been the newest immigrants to arrive; so, for example, at one time the Irish received this label, at another time the Polish immigrants, and more recently the Hispanics. Unfortunately, this view has not entirely disappeared. A Hmong leader who publishes a Hmong/English newspaper described the kinds of calls the paper sometimes receives:

> Some of the people who called me at my office were terrifying, telling me that American people don't need the Hmong; Hmong people came to America to collect American tax dollars; Hmong people are lazy, just like the Hispanic and African-American people. Hmong people just want to produce babies after babies and they don't want to work. (Yang 1992)

The calls this publisher received reflect a genetic inferiority perspective, which blames the minority group for any failure to succeed. It precludes any possibility for change, since hereditary factors are permanent. No consideration is given to Hmong individuals, such as the newspaper publisher, who is obviously succeeding, nor to the factors that challenge the Hmong in society.

Cultural Deficit

Cultural deficit explanations differ from explanations based on genetic inferiority because here the focus is on cultural factors rather than hereditary factors. Comments such as "What did you expect? José is from mañana land" or "You can't trust those people—in their culture, it's okay to cheat" are examples of cultural deficit attitudes. The cultural deficit view is another single-cause explanation of failure. Student failure is understood to result from a deficient culture, and no other factors are seen as relevant. This view also assumes that the mainstream culture has no deficiencies, but that any deviation from mainstream practices represents a deficit that schools should some-how fix.

Not long ago, we learned that a university supervisor wrote an evaluation of a student teacher in which he commended her for working "hard to challenge and reward her pupils, especially those with learning or cultural handicaps." The supervisor's comments revealed that he held a cultural deficit view of the students, many of whom were English language learners. This is a stance that labels certain cultures as flawed and students who come from those cultures as handicapped. The comment on the evaluation sent a negative message to the student teacher about those students and what her expectations for them should be. It also might have kept the student teacher from examining other factors that were affecting her students' school performance.

A possible response to a cultural deficit interpretation of minority-group school performance would be to attempt to change what are regarded as deficient cultural conditions or practices. Parent or family intervention programs are an example. However, there are caveats that should be considered. Valdés (1996) studied ten Mexican migrant families in depth. She discusses the culture of the families and the concerns she has for intervention programs that are based on a cultural deficit view. Valdés comments:

> It is true that the families were not producing successful schoolchildren. It is true that there were many things they did not know about American schools and American teachers. It is also true that they were poor and they were struggling to survive. What is not true is that the parents in the study were bad parents, or that they did not know how to parent well, or that they did it poorly. (200)

In her study, Valdés identified many important values that the families passed on to their children, values that should not be lost. She is worried about programs that attempt to "cure" the "problems" that "deprived" students have in order to make them more like the mainstream population. A context-free interpretation would assume that "fixing" the parents so that they reflect the mainstream culture is the solution. Valdés would call for a more context-specific approach in which the schools and parents would work together to draw on the strengths within the culture and validate the values and abilities children bring to school in order to lead them toward academic success.

Cultural Mismatch

More recently, rather than speaking of a cultural deficit, researchers have presented the idea of a cultural mismatch. The word *mismatch* may refer to differences between the language of the home and the school or differences in how cultures typically interact. While the term *cultural mismatch* is more positive than *cultural deficit*, the underlying assumptions are usually the same. According to the cultural mismatch view, something must be done to change the culture so that it can be more like the mainstream, which is perceived as clearly superior. As with the previous two perspectives, this viewpoint may be used as a single-cause explanation to account for failure and is often applied in a context-free manner. In other words, other factors in the situation need not be considered to solve the "problem." Since students from many different cultural backgrounds have succeeded in schools, the mismatch between their culture and that of the school cannot be considered the only reason that some students fail.

If teachers or other school personnel take the view that a cultural mismatch is the cause of a student's poor academic performance, they may send the message that something is wrong with the student's culture and stress the importance of the student's adopting school norms at the expense of his or her native language and culture. Loretta, a Hispanic high school teacher, has struggled with how she had to give up so much of her culture to get where she is now. In response to reading about how the denial of the first language at school confuses students about their identity, she wrote:

> In the book, we read about the idea of "language mismatch," where the language at home is different from the language of the school. I understood this concept as what we, my family, called Spanglish. I feel that I fall under this category. My spoken and written English is not as good as I would like it to be, and my Spanish is even poorer. As a Mexican American, I used to feel alienated from both groups of kids. I really did not fit in with the Anglo Americans because we did things differently at our home (for example, we ate with a tortilla instead of using a fork). Also, I did not fit in with the Mexican American students who spoke Spanish and were more traditional in their customs than my family. As a student, I was not proud of my culture because I felt I did not belong to any group. As an adult, I feel I was deprived of my language and of being proud of my culture. Presently, my goal is to become proficient in Spanish.

The most obvious kind of mismatch occurs when students enter school speaking a language other than English. Teachers generally recognize that English learners need to develop a new language to function in school. What is frequently overlooked is that these students may also need to learn new ways to use language. As Heath (1986) says, "Not only is there the general expectation that all children will learn to speak English but also the assumption that they have internalized *before* they start school the norms of language used in academic life" (148).

Schools require children to use language in certain ways. If children's patterns of language use at home are different in significant ways from the uses at school, children may experience difficulties. Heath (1983) has written extensively about differences between uses of language, or ways with words, between homes and schools. She points out that "for all children, academic success depends less on the specific language they know than on the ways of using language they know" (144). For example, in school students are expected to answer questions that a teacher asks, even when it is obvious to them that the teacher already knows the answer. Outside of school, people seldom ask questions to which they already know the answer.

When children don't know the ways of using language that the school expects, they may fail. However, this does not necessarily imply that home language use must change. Heath also argues that "the school can promote academic and vocational success for all children, regardless of their first language background, by providing the greatest possible range of oral and written language uses" (144).

None of the three single-cause explanations of school failure—genetic inferiority, cultural deficiency, and cultural mismatch—should be used to explain the school performance of language minority groups. All three views have been discredited by research. A better approach is to recognize that school performance depends on the interaction of a number of factors both inside and outside the school.

The Contextual Interaction Model

As we look at the many factors that influence emergent bilinguals in schools, we must consider societal influences at different levels, including the national, state, community, and family levels as well as school influences. We base our consideration of the factors that affect student success on Gándara and Contreras' (2009) schooling and social context models for Latinos; Suárez-Orozco, Suárez-Orozco, and Todorova's (2008) findings from their research on different groups of immigrant students in American society; and Cortés' Contextual Interaction Model (1986). Figure 2–5 combines many of the factors that these researchers discuss.

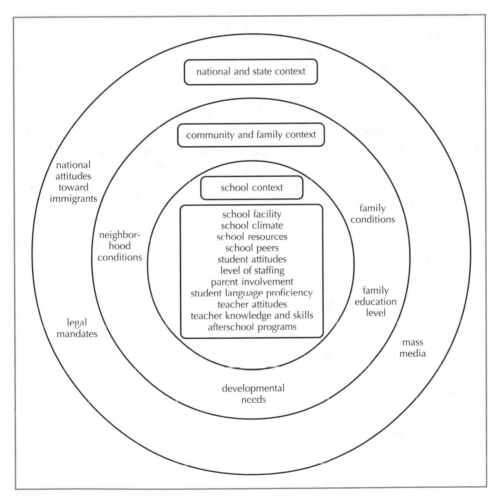

FIGURE 2–5. *Contextual Interaction Model*

National and State Contexts

The outer circle of the Contextual Interaction Model includes factors from the national and state levels. These include attitudes toward immigrants, the mass media's coverage of immigrant issues, and legal mandates that regulate education, including the requirement that English language learners pass high-stakes tests after only a short time in the United States. Second language students are very much aware of attitudes toward immigrants. Many ELLs are involuntary minorities, not recent immigrants. Nevertheless, the general public may treat them as similar to new arrivals. In many communities attitudes toward recent arrivals is negative. These attitudes are shaped by the mass media, including TV shows, newspaper articles, and radio talk shows. A negative attitude toward immigrants is not new in this country. Little more than a century ago, Irish, Italian, and Jewish immigrants were often ostracized and were only gradually assimilated into the mainstream.

Legal mandates reflect national attitudes. A good example of how legal mandates affect schooling for ELLs is the No Child Left Behind Act. This Act requires that schools test ELLs after only a short time in the United States. While the Act has had the positive effect of drawing attention to the needs of ELLs, the overall impact has been extremely negative. The testing requirements are not aligned with the research on the time it takes ELLs to attain academic proficiency in English. As a result, many ELLs fail mandated tests. This reflects poorly on the schools and also causes many ELLs to become discouraged and, eventually, to drop out.

Legal mandates at the state level have also impacted schooling for ELLs. Three states, California, Arizona, and Massachusetts, have passed laws restricting the use of students' native languages for instruction despite research showing the benefits of first language instruction for academic success (August and Shanahan 2006). In addition, Arizona has recently passed controversial laws including one that requires immigrants in Arizona to carry their registration documents at all times and allows police to question individuals' immigration status in the process of enforcing any other law or ordinance.

A second Arizona law bans ethnic studies programs that advocate for solidarity among ethnic groups that might threaten American values and solidarity (CNN 2010). The law seems to be targeting Latino studies programs in particular (Strauss 2010b). Further, the State Department of Education has ordered school districts to remove from classrooms teachers who speak English with a very heavy accent or whose speech is ungrammatical (Strauss 2010a).

In 2010, the Texas State Board of Education approved changes to the requirements for state-approved social studies textbooks. These changes are consistent with the conservative Christian views of the board's majority. Since social studies textbooks are the de facto curriculum in most secondary classes, the changes directly impact students.

The new textbooks play down the role of Thomas Jefferson among the founding fathers, question the separation of church and state, and minimize their coverage of movements for equity.

In an action that led one dissenting board member to walk out of the meeting, the board decided to reduce the role of Latinos in American history. Commentator Michael Preston explained, "This kind of rewriting reeks of a certain sort of cultural superiority" (Preston 2010). Historians are concerned that some of these changes may not be historically accurate. Certainly, laws and decisions like these do and will continue to influence the schooling of English language learners and the communities they live in.

Community and Family Contexts

Gándara and Contreras have examined the effect of the community and family context on the schooling of Latinos. The neighborhood conditions include the availability of preschools, social services, and recreational facilities as well as segregation in housing, and the prevalence of poverty. The family is often crucial, and within the social context for the child, Gándara and Contreras look at parent education, family income, family structure, whether there is mobility or stability, and whether the family has social and/or cultural capital in society. They also consider children's developmental needs, including physical care, mental health care, nutrition, language, and identity.

Suárez-Orozco and colleagues (2008) investigated factors related to the family. They discuss the difficulties of the process of migration for new immigrants and the profound effect that both family separations and then later reunifications have on newcomers. Immigrant children often not only have to adjust to a new language, a new school, and a new country, but to a new family.

For example, our son-in-law, Francisco, from El Salvador, was separated from his mother for seven years, from the time he was seven until he was fourteen. While she established a home in the United States, Francisco's grandmother took care of him and his older brother with only two short visits from his mother. When the time came to move to the United States, Francisco felt he was going to live with a stranger. To this day, some twenty-five years later, he still feels his grandmother is more like his mother. Francisco's experience is not unusual among immigrant children in our schools.

The School Context

These factors from contexts outside the school have a significant effect on school success for ELLs. At the same time, factors in the school context also play a crucial role. Cortés (1986) points out the importance of teacher knowledge and skills as well as teacher attitudes as impacting the school context. In addition, he lists factors such as level of staffing and parent involvement. ELLs have a greater chance for success in a school with adequate numbers of highly qualified teachers with background in second language acquisition, second language teaching, linguistics, and cross-cultural communication. The presence of counselors with training in working with second language students is also essential. However, many schools have only limited numbers of counselors. In addition, ELLs succeed at higher rates in schools with strong parent involvement programs that include the parents of ELLs.

Both Cortés and Gándara and Contreras list resources as an important factor in the school context. When assessing school resources, Gándara and Contreras ask questions such as, What kind of facilities do the schools have? What kind of curriculum is available and how skilled are the teachers and administrators? Is the technology up to date and available, and what kinds of special programs are offered? Is the general school climate positive and safe?

Both Gándara and Contreras and Suárez-Orozco and colleagues are concerned about the segregation that new immigrants and other English learners experience at school. Gándara and Contreras point out that

> [a]pproximately half of all Latino students in Texas and California attend intensely segregated (90 to 100 percent minority) schools, and more than three-quarters of these schools are also high-poverty schools. (2009, 113)

This segregation does not only apply to Latinos, however. It affects all immigrant and language minority groups. As Suárez-Orozco and colleagues (2008) point out, "The new segregation tends not just to be about color, but about poverty and linguistic isolation—so-called triple segregation" (89). Within the segregated schools immigrant students tend to spend time with other immigrant students, rarely interacting with native-born students, even those of their same ethnic groups.

The school climate in these segregated schools is also a concern. Safety, in particular, was an issue cited by both sets of authors. Gándara and Contreras found that 10 percent of Latino students do not feel safe at school or on their way to school. In describing the schools they studied, Suárez-Orozco and colleagues state that "[r]ather than providing 'fields of opportunity,' all too many were 'fields of endangerment'" (89).

For example, they describe in detail a large, poorly cared-for school in a run-down neighborhood with buildings covered with graffiti announcing the presence of five different gangs. The school has students who are Latinos, African Americans, Asians, Filipinos, Pacific Islanders, Native Americans, and a few White students, but the racial groups stay separated. As the authors point out, "When the groups come together, it is usually to fight" (98). A murder suspect was arrested on campus, and on one section of the school grounds an Asian boy was beaten up by a Mexican boy who saw the Asian talking to his girlfriend. In another incident, a girl was gang raped there. No school guards ever watched that part of campus. It is clear that this campus was not a safe place for learning.

Evidence suggests that children who participate in high-quality afterschool programs tend to spend more time on educational activities and perform better academically (Lauer et al. 2006; Miller 2003). Extracurricular activities, however, are often difficult for English learners to participate in because of the cost, lack of transportation, afterschool jobs, family responsibilities, or simply because English learners do not feel welcome.

Conclusion

The Contextual Interaction Model is dynamic. Societal and educational contexts constantly change as new families enter the community and the school. For example, when we visited the Midwest, educators were talking about the impact large numbers of refugees from Somalia was having on their classrooms. These educators had adjusted for their immigrants from Mexico, but immigrants from another part of the world brought new challenges. Teachers in the Southeast had questions about the growing numbers of Hispanics and Hmong students in their schools. There had been some Mexican students in the past, but now their Hispanic population was changing, and the Southeast Asians brought new cultural and educational considerations to be considered.

The model is a two-way model. The school context is influenced by the larger social context at different levels from national to family. It is also important to understand that the social context is impacted by attitudes, knowledge, and skills of the students who graduate and achieve some economic success. Some do return to their neighborhoods where they serve as role models for students still in schools, but many move away. These immigrants change the mainstream community, but their departure from the neighborhoods where they attended school negatively impacts the immigrant communities. Parents and grandparents often feel abandoned. On the other hand, if educated immigrants return to their communities, they often present a challenge to traditional values.

The children of educated immigrants may feel conflicted because they are not sure of their own values or identities. Suárez-Orozco and colleagues (2008) describe poignantly the feelings of the immigrant Chinese and Haitian parents whose children are succeeding academically, but losing some of their Chinese and Haitian roots.

Students' success or failure results from complex interactions of dynamic contexts. Our case study stories above certainly show this. No single factor can explain success or failure, but change in any one area may alter the dynamics of the whole system in such a way that success is more likely.

In the following chapters as we consider factors that affect the schooling of emergent bilinguals, we want readers to keep the stories of real-life second language learners, like the students we described in the case studies, foremost in their minds. We will refer to these examples, as well as others, as we discuss the different factors that have influenced and continue to influence the academic success of students who are living between worlds.

KEY POINTS

➡ English language learners can be classified based on their previous schooling.

➡ Four types of English language learners are recent arrivals with adequate schooling, recent arrivals with limited formal schooling, long-term English learners, and potential long-term English learners.

➡ Long-term English learners include *vaivén* students and students with inconsistent, subtractive schooling.

➡ Ogbu classified minorities based on sociocultural factors as involuntary or immigrant minorities.

➡ Matute-Bianchi and Valdés both provided further classification of Mexican immigrants into several different groups based on their orientation to Mexico and the United States.

➡ Gándara and Contreras argue that a number of factors in and out of schools contribute to the current Latino education crisis.

➡ Three discredited single-cause perspectives on the academic failure of minority groups are genetic inferiority, cultural deficit, and cultural mismatch.

➡ The Contextual Interaction Model illustrates that a number of factors in both the school context and the societal context help account for the school performance of English language learners.

APPLICATIONS

1. Choose two of the case study students described in Chapter 1. Compare and contrast the factors that have influenced, are influencing, and may influence school success for each. Refer to the Contextual Interaction Model. Discuss your comparisons in pairs or a small group.

2. Interview a second language student to find out his or her background. Then categorize the student using the types of students described in this chapter as well as Ogbu's classification of immigrant and involuntary minorities. How does the student you interviewed fit?

3. Interview five people of different ages in and out of education. Ask them what they think has caused the achievement gap between minority-group students and native-speaking mainstream students. Categorize their answers using the different perspectives on failure discussed in this chapter.

3

What Influences How Teachers Teach?

When we visit classes, we see teachers using a variety of techniques and methods to help their students learn English and academic content. This variation is not surprising. In fact, even within the same school and at the same grade level with a similar student population, teachers differ considerably in how they teach. Why is this?

In this chapter we turn from looking at second language students to considering their teachers. The basic question we wish to explore in this chapter is "What influences how teachers teach?" A number of factors seem to be at work, and these help to account for the variation in classroom practices we have observed. For one thing, teachers have been students themselves, and often the way they teach reflects the way that they were taught. In addition, teachers have studied teaching methods, and what they learned in their education classes affects how they teach.

Teachers, especially new teachers, are influenced by the other teachers at their school and by their administrators. Sometimes teachers use new techniques in their classrooms because they have heard about them in the teachers' lounge or during a professional development session. In some school settings, administrators require teachers to use certain methods. If teachers change schools or grade levels, new colleagues with new ideas may influence their practice. Another factor that plays a role in how teachers teach is the materials that are available (or required) for them to use. Teachers also adjust their teaching in response to the needs of their students. With the increase in the English language learner population, many teachers have adopted new methods to meet these students' needs.

Legislative Requirements

In addition to these factors, legal mandates have always influenced how teachers teach. For example, several initiatives—Proposition 207 in California, Proposition 202 in Arizona, and Question 2 in Massachusetts—have severely limited the use of primary-language instruction in educating English language learners. Despite considerable research support for bilingual programs that make extended use of students' first languages (Rolstad, Mahoney, and Glass 2005; Slavin and Cheung 2003; Greene 1998; August and Shanahan 2006), schools in these states are generally limited to providing only English language development or structured immersion programs for ELLs. The legislation has limited how teachers teach ELLs in these states.

The passage of the Elementary and Secondary Education No Child Left Behind Act (NCLB), which replaced the Bilingual Education Act in 2002, has exerted an even broader influence on how teachers teach ELLs. Baker (2006) lists some of the requirements of NCLB:

> In essence, NCLB makes states, districts, and schools accountable for the performance of LEP [Limited English Proficient] students. The requirement is to (1) identify languages other than English in the student population; (2) develop academic assessments; (3) use English language (oral, reading, writing) proficiency assessment with LEP students on an annual basis; (4) include LEP Grade 3 to Grade 8 students in the assessment of reading and mathematics with appropriate accommodations; (5) administer reading assessment in English to students who have been in US schools for at least three years. (198–99)

As a result of NCLB, there has been an increased emphasis on accountability for all students. High-stakes tests hold students accountable for demonstrating the knowledge and skills identified in the state content standards. In addition, all states have now developed English language proficiency standards, and ELLs are required to show progress toward meeting these standards as well as progress in academic content areas in English. The increased attention to standards and accountability is intended to ensure that all students are given access to the basic knowledge and skills of the different academic content areas.

Although most educators would agree in principle with basing curriculum on standards and holding students accountable for demonstrating learning, the requirements for student progress, in many cases, are not realistic or based on research. For example, although extensive research has shown that it takes from five to seven years for ELLs to reach native-like proficiency in academic English (Collier 1989; Cummins 2000), ELLs are given much less time than that to meet state standards on grade-level tests given in English. The emphasis on having students pass the tests has had a strong influence on how teachers teach.

NCLB has had a profound impact on schools as well as on teachers. As Fix and Capps (2005) report, NCLB:

▶ Compels schools to report scores on statewide standardized tests separately for LEP students as well as those of low-income, minority, and disabled students;

▶ Allows students in schools that do not meet state standards in terms of student test performance for more than two years to transfer or receive additional instructional services;

▶ Forces schools to close or restructure after several years of poor performance;

▶ Requires that every classroom—including those with LEP students—have a "highly qualified" (i.e., fully certified and properly educated) teacher; and

▶ Requires schools to notify parents—in the languages they speak—of their children's academic performance, their schools' progress toward meeting NCLB goals, and, in the case of LEP students, the type of language instruction they are receiving.

As Fix and Capps explain, these requirements put a burden on schools, especially those with high concentrations of ELLs in areas that have had recent immigration. Such schools do not have the experience or the personnel to meet these requirements in many cases. Teachers, of course, are strongly influenced in how they teach when they work in schools that are under pressure to provide these required services and to raise student test scores.

A good example of the effects of NCLB on a school district comes from research conducted by McNeil, Coppola, and Radigan (2008). They looked at high-poverty high schools with a large minority student population in a large urban district in Texas. A careful examination of assessment data of nearly 271,000 students coupled with extensive ethnographic study of these schools revealed, among other things, that many minority students were retained in ninth grade. This was done so that school test scores on the tenth-grade high-stakes test would be high. However, the consequence of retaining students for up to three years in ninth grade was an extremely high dropout rate. African American and Latino youth dropped out at nearly a 60 percent rate. As McNeil and his colleagues write:

> The study carries great significance for national education policy because its findings show that disaggregation of student scores by race [a requirement of

NCLB] does not lead to greater equity, but in fact puts our most vulnerable youth, the poor, the English language learners, and African American and Latino children, at risk of being pushed out of their schools so the school ratings can show "measurable improvement." High-stakes, test-based accountability leads not to equitable educational possibilities for youth, but to avoidable losses of these students from our schools. (2)

High-stakes tests affect teachers as well as schools. McNeil and colleagues found that teachers in the schools they studied were under tremendous pressure to raise student test scores. In theory, high-stakes tests were supposed to improve teaching. Instead, as interviews with teachers and administrators showed, "the obsession with gaining high test scores forced teachers to abandon their regular curriculum to teach to the test and to seek other ways of boosting scores" (20).

Schools face severe penalties if students fail to meet state standards, and teachers are put under great pressure to teach to the test, often using prescribed curriculum materials. The result of the emphasis on standards and accountability, in many cases, such as the schools McNeil and colleagues studied, has been that teachers have not been able to tailor instruction to the needs of individual students. Instead, they have been required to use a one-size-fits-all curriculum designed to raise test scores. The No Child Left Behind legislation, then, has perhaps had a greater influence on how teachers, especially new teachers, teach than any other factor. Figure 3–1 summarizes the factors that influence how teachers teach.

Influences	Results
Past academic experiences	Teach as we were taught
Educational training	Teach as we were taught to teach
Colleagues/administrators	Teach as others teach or as we are required to teach
Changes in teaching situation	Adjust teaching to new school or level or new students
Materials	Teach using available or required materials
Students	Teach in response (or reaction) to the students
Legislation	Teach to ensure that students meet the requirements of state and federal legislation

FIGURE 3–1. *Influences on how teachers teach*

Teacher Attitudes

All the factors listed in Figure 3–1 may influence how a teacher teaches. In addition, teachers are also influenced by specific experiences they have. Loretta, the Mexican American teaching high school whom we discussed previously, reflected on her student teaching experience:

> During my student teaching experience, I had the opportunity to work with ESL classes in math, history, and English. In one of these classes the teacher was trying to give me some of her educational insight. She told me that the Asian students (Lao, Hmong, etc.) were much better students than the Mexican students. She went on to say that these children wanted to learn and were not a behavioral problem like the others. I do not think she knew that I was Mexican. Needless to say, I was extremely bothered by her remarks, and I immediately went home and shared this experience with my parents. They were both angered by her false statements. They felt that this new wave of immigrants is being treated much better than they were when they were in school.

The teacher Loretta worked with during her student teaching reflected an attitude that teachers working in schools with large numbers of immigrant students sometimes develop. As we mentioned earlier, teachers' opinions about students have an important influence on how they teach. We believe that some teachers may need to develop new attitudes for the new students in their schools (Freeman and Freeman 1990).

Almost every state now has a significant number of ELLs in schools at every grade level. Working with ELLs is both challenging and rewarding. Teachers have responded to changes in the school population in different ways. We have seen five common responses from teachers in schools with high populations of English language learners. In describing these responses we will use hypothetical situations that represent what we have observed. In each scenario, teacher attitudes and perceptions, developed in response to the influences listed in Figure 3–1, play an important role in how teachers teach. In these scenarios, we focus especially on the effect of a changing school population on teachers. We briefly analyze each scenario and then offer some possible positive responses.

"Teaching Isn't Like It Used to Be"

Mrs. Brown has taught kindergarten at Baker School in the south end of town for fifteen years. When she first began teaching there, the neighborhood was made up mostly of middle-class whites, but over the years large numbers of African Americans, Hispanics, and Southeast Asians have moved into the area, causing a "white flight" to the north. The majority of her present students arrive with little or no English.

Mrs. Brown complains that these new students cannot do what her students in the past could. She remembers the past fondly. On the first day of school, children arrived eager to learn, holding the hands of parents who offered support. Now, she complains, the students, especially the Southeast Asian children, enter the classroom reluctantly. They are either alone or with parents who don't speak English and seem anxious to escape as quickly as possible. Though she has an English-only rule for the classroom, she constantly has to remind students not to speak their native languages. Her biggest complaints are that the children don't seem motivated and the parents don't care.

ANALYSIS

There are several reasons that Mrs. Brown may be responding as she is. In the earlier days, most of her students spoke English and came from a background similar to their teacher's. She now finds herself trying to teach students who not only do not speak the same language literally, but also do not understand her customs and values any more than she does theirs. Previously, Mrs. Brown had strong parent support, but now she is not sure how to communicate with the parents. Mrs. Brown does not know how to change her teaching to help students, and she responds by blaming them and their families.

POSITIVE RESPONSES

Many teachers who suddenly find themselves with large numbers of English language learners make it a point to inform themselves about their new students. They read and discuss books and articles about other teachers working with non-English speakers. They talk with their fellow teachers and share materials and ideas that have been successful. They attend workshops offered by school districts and local universities. They join professional organizations for teachers of bilingual and second language learners.

Once they learn more about English language learners, they become advocates for them. They seek people and materials that can provide first language support, and they promote school events that highlight different cultural traditions. In addition, they make an effort to include the parents of their new students, not only at special events but in the regular classroom day. Even if parents do not speak English, they are invited to class to read a book in their first language, cook, or do crafts. Though all of these things require extra effort, they make these teachers' classrooms exciting places where all their students learn.

"Language Minority Kids Make Me Look Like a Failure"

Ms. Franklin is a second-year second-grade teacher. Like most nontenured teachers in the district, she has been assigned to a classroom of diverse students, mostly Hispanic but also including African Americans, a Somali refugee, two students from Iraq, and one student from China. Many of her students are classified as LEP. Ms. Franklin's teacher-education program included some coursework in second language acquisition, ESL methodology, and diversity. As soon as she began to work with her English learners last year, she fell in love with them. She read with the children, encouraged them to write often, and, in general, created activities that drew on their interests and background knowledge. The children responded well to this type of curriculum, and she could see tremendous growth in their English.

Despite this success, Ms. Franklin has encountered problems. She teaches in a school that has not met the state goals for annual yearly progress. The test scores for her students have remained low, and the principal has talked about this with Ms. Franklin. Even though he did not threaten her directly, Ms. Franklin now feels her job is on the line. From the coursework she has taken and her own experiences, she realizes that standardized tests do not chart the progress of her bilingual students fairly. Still, she is tempted to try this year to "teach to the test," despite the fact that she does not feel that worksheets and drills are meaningful to her students, especially to her second language learners. She is beginning to view her students as having deficits— deficits that could have direct consequences for her career. She is also beginning to wish that she could transfer to a school in another part of town with fewer English learners.

ANALYSIS

Ms. Franklin began her teaching with enthusiasm and caring. Her college coursework prepared her to work effectively with English learners. However, Ms. Franklin is a new teacher and not really experienced enough to defend her curriculum. The emphasis on test scores has begun to erode her confidence in doing what is best for her students. She is beginning to view the students she once was trying to help as the source of her problems. Her solution is to try to get away from her present teaching situation.

POSITIVE RESPONSES

Many of the teachers who take our graduate courses are like Ms. Franklin. They are new teachers who want to help their students and are studying second language acquisition. However, they are concerned because they feel pressure from standardized testing and do not want to be judged by the poor performance of non-English speakers. After taking further graduate coursework, these teachers begin to understand how long it takes to speak, read, and write a second language with near-native proficiency and how critical first language support is for content learning. They begin to view their teaching and the testing of their students differently. Despite their knowledge, though, most new teachers are not able to successfully implement effective practices unless they receive mentoring and support from other teachers and their administrators. With the right support, new teachers can implement effective practices and also ensure that their students are prepared for state tests.

"It's Not Fair to the Rest of My Class to Give Those Students Special Attention"

Mr. Martin teaches in a farming community where he has lived since he was a child. At the beginning of the year, his sixth-grade classroom consisted of a nice group of Anglo and Hispanic children who were all fairly proficient in English and all reasonably successful learners. At the end of the first month of school, the principal called Mr. Martin in to explain that five sixth-grade migrant children had just arrived from Mexico and that they would be placed in Mr. Martin's class.

Mr. Martin wasn't sure what to do with these new students, whose English was extremely limited. The district paid him to take training to learn new techniques, but he resented the idea that he had to attend extra classes and learn new ways to teach, especially when he had been successful for a number of years. Why should he be the one to change? If these students couldn't meet the expectations for his class, maybe they weren't ready for it.

Nevertheless, the students were in his class, and the principal was not about to transfer them out. Since he was a good teacher, Mr. Martin knew he should be doing something for them, and he felt guilty that they just sat quietly in the back of his classroom. On the other hand, it seemed to him that giving those students special attention wasn't fair to the rest of the students, who were doing just fine with his traditional instruction. At the same time, the extra training he was receiving also made him feel guilty because it stressed that students should not simply be given busywork, but that they should be engaged in meaningful activities with other students in the classroom. However, Mr. Martin's teaching style did not include much student interaction. He became doubly frustrated, as he felt that he was not only being asked to deal with new students, but also to change his way of teaching.

ANALYSIS

Mr. Martin, like Mrs. Brown, is a conscientious teacher in a school system that is changing. He has succeeded in the past and resents the fact that he has been designated to deal with the new students. It is probable that the principal chose Mr. Martin because he was an experienced teacher, and she believed he could handle the new challenge. However, Mr. Martin feels picked on and resentful of the extra time and training necessary to work with second language students. In addition, he believes that giving them special instruction is actually going to be detrimental to his other students. At this point, Mr. Martin does not understand that what is good instruction for second language students might also benefit his other students.

POSITIVE RESPONSES

Teachers we have worked with have come to realize that it is impossible to use a traditional teacher-centered model of teaching to reach a very diverse student body. In addition, as they try interactive activities in which heterogeneous groups of students work on projects together, they see that all their students, including their native English-speaking students, learn more. Several teachers who entered our graduate classes determined never to change their teaching styles later gave enthusiastic testimonials of how exciting teaching can be when it is organized around units of inquiry and includes literature studies, creative writing, and projects involving art, science, music, and drama.

"Who Wants to Be the Bilingual Teacher?"

Mr. González went into bilingual education because he himself had come to the United States as a non-English-speaking child, and he knew how difficult it was to succeed in school as a second language learner. His education classes had taught him that instruction in the first language helps children academically and actually speeds their success in English. During his first two years of teaching, he enthusiastically worked with his fourth graders, supporting their first language and helping them succeed in their second language.

By the end of the third year when he was tenured, his enthusiasm began to wane. Mr. González was troubled by the subtle way his fellow teachers treated him. The bilingual program was considered remedial, and constant remarks in the teachers' lounge showed him that fellow teachers did not really believe bilingual kids were capable of the kind of success other students could achieve.

On top of that, Mr. González soon discovered that Hispanic children who were discipline problems were transferred into his class throughout the year even though they were not English language learners. When he objected, the principal always explained that since he was Hispanic, he could understand those children better. Mr. González's attempts to explain that his program was geared to work with Spanish speakers to help them succeed academically, not with discipline problems, fell on deaf ears. He began to feel that his expertise was not respected and that his classroom was becoming a dumping ground. He put in a request to be taken out of the bilingual program.

ANALYSIS

Mr. González's situation is one that has repeated itself many times in different school districts. When there is little understanding of what bilingual education really is and why it is important, bilingual teachers feel isolated and misunderstood. Often, uninformed teachers make commonsense assumptions about bilingual learners and do not hesitate to express their opinions about the limited potential of that group of students. Administrators who have heard about the importance of ethnic and cultural role models but do not really know the theory behind bilingual education try to find quick and easy solutions to problems of minority students. In this case all Hispanics are lumped together, and Mr. González is asked to solve all the "problems" of the Hispanics at the school. Bilingual teachers such as Mr. González find themselves, like their bilingual students, suffering from prejudice and a lack of understanding. It is no wonder that many bilingual educators request to teach nonbilingual classes.

POSITIVE RESPONSES

Bilingual teachers we have worked with have not found an easy answer to this situation. Attacks on bilingual education and negative public opinion have undermined the efforts of schools and teachers trying to implement good bilingual programs. Because the general public often has a negative view of immigrants, bilingual teachers like Mr. González have the challenge of not only defending what they are doing but also keeping others from undermining the programs they have. A bright spot in the area of bilingual education is the continued increase in the number of dual-language bilingual programs. These programs have had positive results for native English speakers and those learning English, as both groups become bilingual and biliterate (Dolson and Mayer 1992; Collier and Thomas 2004, 2009; Freeman, Freeman, and Mercuri 2005). If Mr. González could teach in one of these programs, he would probably have more support.

"Don't Expect Too Much of These Students"

Mrs. Williams is a pullout ESL instructor who works with children grades K–8. Most of her students are either Hispanics whose parents are migrant workers or new immigrants from Africa. Mrs. Williams likes teaching small groups of children and, in fact, volunteered to become a district pullout teacher because the idea of working with small groups of polite, respectful children appealed to her.

Mrs. Williams has had no special training in ESL teaching, but because she has seen lots of English language learners over the years, she feels she understands their problems. She firmly believes that many non-English speakers enter school with no real language ability since they don't speak English and they don't speak their first language correctly. "After all," she explains, "their parents don't speak English, nor do they read or write in their first language. What these children need is lots of oral-language development in English."

In her pullout classes, the students get practice in pronouncing words, and they often do worksheets that focus on phonics. Since the students don't have control of the oral language, Mrs. Williams does not have them do much reading or writing. "They simply aren't ready," she concludes. Mrs. Williams and her students appear to have reached a sort of truce. She won't push too hard or expect too much, and they will be orderly and complete the assignments she gives them. The regular teachers from whose classrooms the students are pulled out don't complain. They are happy to be relieved of the responsibility of teaching these students for a part of each day, so this arrangement seems satisfactory to all concerned.

The parents of Mrs. Williams' students don't pressure the school to do more either. They seem reluctant to talk to her and do not show up for the conferences she schedules, thus reinforcing Mrs. Williams' belief that the parents do not care about their children's school success. Since the students, their parents, and the other teachers are satisfied with her program, Mrs. Williams sees no need to change and resents the suggestions from a new district ESL specialist that she needs to incorporate her students' first languages and cultures, challenge her students with more reading and writing, and work with the mainstream teachers to support content instruction for her students.

ANALYSIS

Mrs. Williams is a classic case of a teacher who loves her students and perceives herself as doing the best she can for these *pobrecitos* (poor little ones). However, it is important to realize that a limited view of students' potential leads to a limiting curriculum (Valdés 2001). Often, people believe that simply knowing English qualifies a person to teach English as a second language. Mrs. Williams does not see the need for any further education about English language learners or the teaching of a second language. If she had done some further study, she might have learned that ELLs need lots of reading and writing as well as speaking and listening (August and Shanahan 2006; Freeman and Freeman 2000), and that worksheets and drills do not help with the natural acquisition of language (Krashen 1992). Mrs. Williams believes that the students' first language and culture are not really important for learning English. Stereotypes about the parents' lack of interest in the students' school success keep her from attempting to form links between the home and school. Perhaps most disturbing of all is the fact that the rest of the school is actually relieved that Mrs. Williams will take care of the "problem" of the second language children.

POSITIVE RESPONSES

Mrs. Williams needs coursework in the areas of second language teaching and cross-cultural studies to make her more aware of the need to change her teaching style. She should be encouraged to involve her students in challenging reading and writing activities as well as oral language development. Mrs. Williams could also collaborate with the mainstream teachers and align her curriculum with what is being taught in the students' math, science, social studies, and language arts classes.

Although it still happens, it is less likely that teachers like Mrs. Williams would be assigned to teach English language learners without professional preparation. In almost every state there are programs at universities that help prepare teachers working with multilingual students. States have developed English language proficiency standards, and most states require special certification for teaching English language learners. This is part of the requirement under No Child Left Behind that schools employ highly qualified teachers. Additional training is an important first step toward preparing teachers to work effectively with their ELLs.

Coping with Change

Despite the positive changes that are taking place in some schools, there is still much to be done to improve the education of English language learners. Each time we read and discuss these five scenarios with the teachers in our graduate programs, we are saddened to learn how many of them tell us these situations are entirely representative of what is still going on in many schools. Rusty, a sixth-grade teacher, reflected on what he has seen in his school by writing a poignant poem (see Figure 3–2).

Although many teachers are learning about English language learners and are doing wonderful things in their schools, other teachers and schools still have a long way to go before they begin to meet their students' needs. Suárez-Orozco, Suárez-Orozco, and Todorova (2008) in their extensive study of immigrant youth in high schools found that only 10 percent of the students named a teacher as someone they would go to for help, 21 percent named a teacher as someone who respected them, and only 3 percent named a teacher as someone who was proud of them.

When the researchers talked to the teachers and administrators about the students, they responded that they were happy to have new immigrants who "have a desire to learn, are more disciplined, and value education" (134), but for long-term English learners there was less enthusiasm. In a teachers' lounge in a largely Dominican and Puerto Rican high school, the researchers heard a teacher ask her colleagues who nodded as she spoke: "What do you expect me to do with these kids? Within the next few years, most of the girls will be pregnant and the boys are going to be in jail" (137). In an interview with a superintendent of a highly diverse district with a large number of immigrants, the researchers asked, "What is the hardest thing about your job?" He responded, "To get the teachers to believe these children can learn" (137). With the growing number of second language students, the importance of developing the skills,

School Days, School Days

You cannot see it,
So well it does hide,
Yet subtly it whittles,
Away all self-pride.

Through teeth straight and shiny,
You see the bright smile.
Yet no love is shown there,
Not even for a while.

The pros they can fake it,
They act like they care,
"No, Honey, not here,
You sit over there."

"You don't speak our language,
I'm sure that will change."
She pokes little Susie,
"Her home's on the range."

"Your mom calls you Carlos,
Now Charles is your name.
I'm sure that you realize
It all means the same."

"Oh, look at your free lunch,
Why, isn't that rice?
It's just like your home, dear,
Oh, isn't that nice?"

Yes, each day it happens
In room after room.
And kids really do wish
They'd stayed in the womb.

The talk, it is subtle,
Its impact so cruel,
Like slow-burning fire
when you've added some fuel.

It strikes at the heart
And pulls at the brain.
Like a strong locomotive,
That pulls the whole train.

We know what the law states,
and that is a start.
But can you really legislate,
Affairs of the heart?

We've had great examples,
In religions and creeds,
You'd think that would do it,
That's all we would need.

Yet man's basic nature,
His seeking of wealth,
Has caused him to stumble
All over himself.

And so often the children
They stand in the way.
And push comes to shove,
And the children, they pay.

Oh, teacher you must see,
You're the last hope
In helping that small child
With life just to cope.

His face may be dirty,
His clothes might have holes,
His stomach is growling,
He's had only stale rolls.

So reach out a hand please,
Bring a smile to his face.
Give each child a hug
Regardless of race.

No matter his language,
His color, his creeds,
As God is your witness
You must meet his needs.

And if you can't do it,
then please leave our ranks.
Go work in a factory
Or in one of the banks.

We're looking for teachers
With hearts big as stores
Who love all the children
And do a lot more.

So if you are willing
To look to the heart
Come quickly new teachers
We'll give you a part.

To show kids some justice
Some fairness and love,
With an abundant supply
That comes from above.

Challenges? Why yes,
Of course, that is true.
But no greater work
Can you ever do.

—*Rusty DeRuiter 1992*

FIGURE 3–2. *Rusty's poem*

knowledge, and positive attitudes for teaching the changing school population effectively becomes more critical daily.

For all teachers, though, coping with change is not easy. In their report on how California teachers responded to the influx of immigrant students, researchers from the group California Tomorrow interviewed thirty-six teachers. Kate Duggan, a middle school teacher in a Los Angeles school with a high second language population, expressed the views of many teachers across the country:

> Change in itself is extremely stressful, and teaching now immerses you in change. Changes in the student population and cultures and races who enroll. New kids coming in and out all the time. And because traditional methods don't work, you always have to be experimenting with different approaches so there are changes in what you're doing as a teacher. All this change affects the entire tone of the school. (Olsen and Mullen 1990)

Change *is* stressful, but a number of teachers are not only coping with it, they are learning how to celebrate the growing diversity in their classrooms.

Yvonne's Story

A teacher's practice, then, changes over time in response to new experiences, new studies, new materials, new types of students, new legal mandates, and a new emphasis on standards and accountability. While teachers can learn from all their experiences, effective teachers develop a set of principles that guide their teaching. These principles are based on their understanding of research and theory in second language acquisition and second language teaching. These principles help teachers choose methods and techniques for working with their second language students. Yvonne's story provides a good example of a teacher who has developed principles that guide her teaching. As she has read theory and research and as she has experienced new teaching situations, she has continually refined her teaching to provide the best education she can for her students.

Yvonne has moved through different stages of understanding about how language is learned and how language and content might best be taught to English language learners. Her teaching has been influenced by several of the factors listed in Figure 3–1. We hope that Yvonne's story will help our readers reflect on their own beliefs and practices. Greater awareness of why we teach the way we do can help us refine our principles and make the changes necessary for providing the best education for all our students.

Yvonne studied several different languages in high school and college. Her four years of high school Latin were taught through a grammar translation method in which students memorized grammar rules and vocabulary and carefully translated excerpts from great works such as *The Odyssey* and *The Iliad* from Latin to English. The study of Latin was considered a good scholarly exercise that would provide a base for English vocabulary development, but there was never any consideration that knowledge of the Latin language might be useful outside the Latin class.

As a high school junior, Yvonne, who at the time had no intention of ever becoming a teacher, decided to study Spanish. Students in her Spanish class studied less grammar and vocabulary than in the Latin class. Instead, they memorized dialogues that they practiced and recited. The most memorable and enjoyable activities in the Spanish class were learning and performing the Mexican hat dance and singing songs in Spanish. Yvonne continued her study of Spanish at the junior college. The advanced class was tedious, with grammar tests and long hours spent repeating drills in the language laboratory.

It wasn't until she went to the university as a junior majoring in Spanish that it dawned on Yvonne that there was more to language learning than memorizing rules and taking tests. Her Spanish grammar class was going well, but she was put into a Spanish literature class with an instructor who lectured only in Spanish. For the first three weeks of class, she took limited and inadequate notes because the language seemed to fly by her unintelligibly. She knew something had to be done, so she made plans to go to Mexico that summer.

The Mexican summer experience was a turning point in her Spanish proficiency. Yvonne's train trip to Guadalajara gave her the opportunity to put the language she had learned to real use. She was amazed when her carefully formed sentences were understood, and somewhat shaken when rapid answers came shooting back. She and three fellow students stayed with a family while she studied in Guadalajara, and because she had the strongest Spanish language background of the three, she soon found herself in the role of language negotiator. Her success communicating with the family, a brief romantic interlude, and exciting weekend travel excursions convinced Yvonne that she had found her niche. Her interest in the Spanish language and the Latino culture led naturally to her decision to become a Spanish teacher.

Back in the United States, Yvonne enrolled in a cutting-edge teacher education program. In just one year, students in this program got both a teaching credential and a master's degree in education. Teacher training included videotaped micro-teaching sessions that allowed student teachers to view their performance and critique their lessons. Methodology classes presented the latest techniques of leading different kinds of audio-lingual drills. These techniques were based on a behaviorist view of learning. In fact, one of her education-methods professors was considered an international language teaching expert. Yvonne accepted the idea that learning, and especially language learning, consisted of forming habits. All her own language instruction had assumed that kind of a model. In her classes, students had memorized dialogues, and teachers had corrected errors quickly. Yvonne and her classmates had repeated their lines as their cheerleading teachers led them rapidly through carefully selected language-pattern exercises. Yvonne's teacher-education classes prepared her to teach as she had been taught.

She received her credential and landed a job in an inner-city high school. Despite all her preparation, her first teaching position was a real eye-opener. She was teaching five classes a day of Spanish 1. Her audio-lingual method (ALM) Spanish 1 book included lesson after lesson of dialogues and drills. Her students hated what they called the "boring repetition" and "stupid dialogues." Yvonne was devastated. She wanted her students to love speaking Spanish as much as she did. She remembered her positive experiences in Mexico but had forgotten how bored she had been when forced through similar drills.

Faced with 150 resisting and restless high school students each day, Yvonne began to look closely at the lines from the dialogues that the students were repeating. Instinctively, without really knowing what she was doing, she began to change the dialogues to make them more relevant. *A mi no me gustan las albóndigas* (I don't like meatballs) became *A mi no me gustan las hamburguesas con cebolla* (I don't like hamburgers with onion), and the students were encouraged to expand the talk to include other things they did not like. She even gave them choice in the dialogues they practiced. Yvonne wanted her students to realize that Spanish is a language that real people use for real purposes. She invited some friends visiting from Mexico to her class. The students prepared and asked questions they wanted to know about teenagers in Mexico. That class period was one of the best of the year.

The classroom context for learning was improving. However, contexts interact, and what goes on outside the classroom has a great impact on curriculum. Yvonne soon found herself in trouble on two very different fronts. In the first place, the department chair discovered that Yvonne was giving students vocabulary lists with words that were not part of the department curriculum and was encouraging students to create their own dialogues. The problem, of course, was that the students were not always saying things correctly and were undoubtedly learning some incorrect Spanish. The department chair, a strong advocate of ALM, did not want students to develop bad language habits. In the second place, as she attempted to use more authentic Spanish with her students, Yvonne realized that she had not learned enough "real" Spanish to truly help her students say everything they wanted to say.

Yvonne decided to find an opportunity to improve her Spanish proficiency. She and her adventurous husband, a high school English teacher, decided that they should live abroad, so they both took positions at an American school in Colombia, South America. Yvonne found herself with absolutely no background for her teaching job.

Educated as a high school Spanish teacher, she was assigned to teach fifth grade in Colombia using curriculum from the United States. Some of her students spoke English as a foreign language and would never visit the United States. Others were native speakers of English whose parents expected them to attend college in the United States.

Like many teachers faced with a difficult assignment for which she was not prepared, Yvonne relied heavily at first on the textbooks the school provided. Basal readers from the United States as well as social studies and science textbooks were the center of her curriculum. Again, however, she found herself responding to her students. Many of the basal reading stories were boring or completely unrelated to the students' interests and needs. The social studies and science texts were almost impossible for the students to read and understand. Though other materials were not easy to find, Yvonne centered much of what she and the students did around projects, stories, and discussions. Since most of the teachers in the school were experiencing the same problems, they shared ideas about what was working in their classrooms.

The teaching couple returned to the United States after a year, more fluent in Spanish. Yvonne's husband found a job teaching high school in a small city, but there were no high school Spanish jobs. When a local welfare agency in their new town called to ask if she would volunteer to teach English to Spanish-speaking adults, Yvonne decided to try it. Her first class of students included two Mexican women with no previous schooling and a college-educated couple from Bolivia. With no materials, not even paper or pencils, and diverse students, Yvonne, in desperation, asked the students what English they wanted and needed to learn. Starting with any materials she could get, including maps, pamphlets, and resource guides, Yvonne soon found herself teaching a class that had grown to forty adults on a variety of topics including nutrition, shopping, community services, child care, and geography.

Yvonne's class became a part of the public school's adult education program, and Yvonne began teaming with another teacher who also loved teaching adult ESL. The two collaborated daily, making up skits, writing songs, organizing around themes, and creating a community with students who came from Mexico, Central America, South America, Northern and Eastern Europe, the Middle East, Japan, Korea, and Southeast Asia.

Though Yvonne had come a long way from having students memorize dialogues and do drills, she was still uncomfortable about what she should be doing to teach language. She and her team teacher, a former high school English teacher, often would pull out traditional grammar sheets and do a part of their daily lesson with some of those exercises "to be sure the students understood the structure of the language." When those lessons seemed to go nowhere, especially with adults who had little previous schooling, the grammar books were dropped in favor of books with stories and discussion questions. However, the readings were seldom related to student needs and experiences, so the two teachers kept returning to skits, songs, and projects created around relevant themes.

Yvonne and her partner had an additional experience that stretched them in new directions and strengthened their conviction that language learning was more than memorizing grammatical rules and repeating pattern drills. The two were asked to teach as adjunct instructors in an intensive English program at the local university. A large group of Japanese college students had arrived, and although these students had extensive background in English grammar and vocabulary, they understood and spoke little English. Initially, the Japanese students resisted classroom activities that were not carefully organized around grammar exercises, but Yvonne and her partner worked hard to get the students to take the risk to speak English in class and in the community. Several of the Japanese students came to appreciate the emphasis on using English for real purposes and began to attend the adult ESL classes as well as the university classes.

After she had taught the Japanese students for two years and the adults for nine, Yvonne and her husband decided that they would like to teach abroad again, taking their children along. They moved to Mexico City, where new learning and teaching experiences awaited them. They first taught professional adults English in a large language institute. The institute was moving away from using a textbook based on audio-lingual methodology to a new series using the notional-functional approach, so both Yvonne and her husband learned about teaching language communicatively around functions such as apologizing, giving directions, and making introductions, and around notions such as time or space.

Since their teaching schedule did not fit the school schedule for their young children, Yvonne left her job with adults and began teaching fifth grade at the bilingual school her daughters attended. The school was typical of most private schools in Mexico City. The student body for the kindergarten through sixth grade had about five thousand students. The playground was a huge expanse of cement with no trees or play equipment of any kind. Classrooms had one chalkboard in the front of the room, with a raised platform for the teacher's desk. There was one bulletin board, decorated monthly by the teacher and checked by the supervising administrator. Desks were bolted in rows filling up the entire room.

The school where Yvonne taught had classes of only forty students. This school was popular because of the small class size. Other schools had sixty or more in a class. Yvonne soon learned that most parents in Mexico City, if they could scrape together any money, sent their children to a private school such as this because public schools had larger classes and fewer materials.

At this bilingual school, half of the day was taught in Spanish and the other half in English. The English curriculum was centered around basal readers and textbooks from the United States, as it had been in Colombia, and the Spanish curriculum around

Mexican government texts. The school required teachers to follow the textbook-based curriculum carefully. All assignments involved copying and memorizing. Students' needs were viewed only in terms of passing the textbook or government tests that were administered by the school monthly. Discipline was strict. Students stood up to answer questions and were not to speak otherwise.

Fortunately, the administration of this school discovered that Yvonne had a master's degree in education, a very high degree among Mexican teachers at schools like this. Many elementary teachers in Mexico have little training beyond high school.

After teaching a month of the regimented fifth-grade curriculum, Yvonne found herself the administrator in charge of the English curriculum for twenty-three teachers. She began to reflect on how many times she had found herself in positions she was unprepared for and yet how similar her conclusions were each time. Again, she wondered how meaningful the curriculum was for the students. If the Mexican students were studying at a bilingual school so that they could learn to read, write, and speak English, were the U.S. textbooks appropriate? Should they be reading in basal readers about blond, blue-eyed Americans going to an American birthday party or going ice-skating in snowy weather? Would they really learn English when their teachers rarely allowed them to speak English, or any language, in class, and when the teachers rarely spoke to them in either English or Spanish?

Yvonne encouraged the teachers to center their curriculum around themes of interest to children of various ages. She collected stories and information related to celebrations, science topics, and biographies of famous people that seemed to lend themselves to language use and content learning. She encouraged teachers to involve students in drama and music using English songs and plays. She helped teachers write plays for their students and tried to encourage conversation activities. However, all of this was done on a limited basis, as the school requirements were stringent and any activities beyond preparing students for tests were considered frills.

After two years of teaching in Mexico City, Yvonne and her husband moved back to the United States, where her husband began graduate study and she took a position teaching senior composition and freshman English at a private high school. The composition class was organized around a packet of materials that students were to follow carefully, completing assignments at their own pace with no class discussion. The freshman English class curriculum included short stories, a library unit, the play *Romeo and Juliet*, and study of a grammar book written in England. Again, Yvonne looked at her students, this time all native speakers of English, and wondered about teaching to their interests and needs. In this situation, unlike the Mexico and the high school Spanish experiences, the English department chairperson was flexible and sympathetic to deviations from the set curriculum. Before the year was over, Yvonne had students in the composition class meeting in groups, having whole-class discussions, writing joint compositions, and sharing their writing. She largely ignored the grammar book for the freshmen, had them write and edit their own compositions, and encouraged discussion of their reading. Before teaching *Romeo and Juliet*, Yvonne planned with another freshman English teacher to have their students view the movie *West Side Story*, which provided them with valuable background for the Shakespeare play.

However, Yvonne did not feel that her previous experiences were best utilized by teaching English to high school students, so the following year, she went back to graduate school and worked as a graduate teaching assistant in the Spanish department. Her graduate work included both a second master's degree, this time in English as a Second Language, and doctoral work in education. In her ESL program she studied SLA theory and second language teaching methods. Many of the writers advocated a communicative approach to teaching language. She was especially impressed by the work of Krashen (1982), who differentiated between acquisition and learning, a distinction that made sense to Yvonne because of her own language learning and teaching experiences.

While her ESL classes were interesting, it was her doctoral studies that really challenged Yvonne to think seriously about learning and teaching and the relationship between the two. She majored in language and literacy and minored in bilingual education. This combination seemed to fit her interests and her experiences. She began studying about language learning with a focus on the development of second language literacy. As she read the work of Ferreiro and Teberosky, K. and Y. Goodman, Halliday, Graves, Kolers, Heath, Lindfors, Piaget, Smith, and Vygotsky, Yvonne began to make connections among her language learning and teaching experiences and the theories she was studying. She realized two things: First, what she was learning about made sense because of what she had experienced in her own language learning and her many teaching jobs. Second, much classroom practice was not consistent with current theory.

As she studied, Yvonne made her beginning college Spanish classes her laboratory. With her first-year Spanish classes, she talked about how children learn language, how language is acquired naturally in a risk-free environment, and how language must have meaning and purpose for learners. Students wrote in Spanish daily in their journals, and she responded in writing. Students read current articles of interest to them, working in groups to interpret the Spanish. Students learned Spanish in the course of investigating themes such as friendship, professions, and dating customs. One of the most successful projects was a pen pal exchange between students in different college classes. Yvonne realized that students would devote more energy to writing a nongraded assignment, a letter to a peer, than to writing a theme in Spanish for the instructor to grade.

After graduation, Yvonne and her husband found teacher education positions at a small, private university in California that was known for innovative literacy practices but needed to expand its program offerings for teachers to include teaching English language learners. Yvonne was hired to teach language acquisition and bilingual education courses for students working on a master's degree in ESL or bilingual education. A teacher always learns more than his or her students, and for Yvonne this seemed to be especially true. She did a great deal of reading to be sure that her students were reading the latest theory and research, and at the same time, she worked hard to be certain that her practices as a college professor reflected what she had learned about how people learn best. Her assignments for her students always combined theory and practice as students applied what they were learning to their own emergent bilingual students and then shared with other teachers what had been successful. An outgrowth of the reading she was doing, and of the projects and work with the practicing teachers at the university, was the co-authoring with her husband of teacher education books on the topics of ESL methodology, language acquisition, reading for English learners, and linguistics.

After ten years of teaching at this university, Yvonne and her husband were awarded Fulbright Scholarships to teach at the University of the Andes in Venezuela. Here again, Yvonne experienced lessons in second language acquisition. She had become more proficient in Spanish. However, since she had developed a high level of grammatical competence in Spanish, and could converse with her colleagues at the university fluently in Spanish, she worked to become more communicatively competent in this social setting. Was she saying the right thing to the right person at the right time? Yvonne now had to be careful not to be rude unintentionally. She could not apply her U.S. English communicative norms to her colleagues at the university. For example, she soon learned that trying to communicate with people efficiently and quickly was frowned upon. It was much better to stop by an office of someone several times and miss them than to leave a note. The note was perceived as an emergency that had to be taken care of immediately. While discussing the details of a surgery and displaying scars with a casual acquaintance was acceptable, blowing one's nose in public was not! All these types of lessons helped Yvonne understand language learning at new levels.

After returning to California, Yvonne had another important experience with language learning. She wrote and directed two Title VII bilingual dual language grants. They were to prepare preservice teachers to teach in Spanish or Hmong dual language classrooms. Through this experience with schools and preservice Mexican and Hmong bilingual teachers, Yvonne grew to understand more deeply the challenges involved in learning how to teach and learn bilingually.

The passing of Proposition 227, banning bilingual education in California, made it difficult to attract students into the graduate programs in bilingual education. Colleagues in Texas encouraged Yvonne and her husband to move to Texas, a bilingual-friendly state with a growing number of dual-language bilingual schools. They spent three years at one university. During this time she had the opportunity to work in several of the Texas border one-way dual language schools where Hispanic students learned in both Spanish and English and both languages and cultures were valued. This work, the experience with the dual language grants in California, and research in different kinds of dual language schools led her to write a book with her husband and a California colleague on dual language education.

Yvonne now works at a different Texas university that has a doctoral program in curriculum and instruction with a specialization in bilingual studies. She teaches teachers and administrators who work in schools with second language learners. Most of these teachers and administrators began school speaking a language other than English. They were ELLs at one time in their lives. Now, as master's or doctoral students, many of them find they still struggle with reading and writing academic English. Yvonne works with these students to help them develop the academic language they need to succeed as future professors themselves.

With every teaching experience she has had, Yvonne's beliefs have been confirmed that teaching must be geared to student needs and that learning occurs when students are engaged in the topic they are studying. Yvonne has learned many lessons through her experiences, but perhaps the most important of these is one she came to gradually throughout her teaching career: that theory and research inform practice, and reflection on practice can shape a teacher's working theory. Yvonne, like most teachers, began with an eclectic view. She used whatever seemed to work. She also used the language teaching methods being advocated at the time. However, with more experience and study, she found that by reflecting on her practice and basing it on current research and theory, she was able to move away from eclecticism and develop a principled approach to her teaching, which she now shares with other educators not only through her teaching but also through her writing and speaking.

Principled Teaching

Principled teaching involves implementing practices consistent with our beliefs about language, learning, teaching, and curriculum. These beliefs are what we refer to as our "orientation." A principled orientation is one in which beliefs are based on theory tested in practice.

Without being fully aware of it, Yvonne began her career as a Spanish high school teacher with a certain set of beliefs. She believed that language learning involved habit formation and that practice and memorization would result in language learning. She used the audio-lingual method (ALM), which was consistent with this orientation. In fact, her department chairperson insisted that she use only ALM materials from the assigned textbook. The techniques Yvonne used included memorization of dialogues and practice of language structures in controlled drills. However, she also used techniques that were not consistent with ALM, such as allowing the students to create their own interview questions and encouraging uncontrolled discussion on topics not included in the textbooks.

Yvonne found herself repeatedly struggling to follow the curriculum and materials she was given while trying to meet her students' needs. She was uncomfortable drilling students and teaching isolated grammar because she did not see how these activities were helping her students learn language. On the other hand, such techniques seemed to be accepted ways to teach language. Other teachers talked with confidence about doing "what works," and that seemed to be good advice. Yvonne tried several techniques but didn't totally trust her own instincts. After she had had a variety of teaching experiences and also had begun to read theory and research, Yvonne was able to develop a more consistent and principled orientation to teaching.

It is not always possible to determine a teacher's orientation simply by observing her teaching. For example, a teacher who structures the class around units of inquiry using literature and process writing may teach a minilesson on capital letters. That same lesson might also be taught by a teacher using a traditional grammar approach to language teaching. The technique, the lesson on capital letters, could be observed in classrooms of teachers with two quite different orientations. The first teacher teaches the minilesson because she has seen that students do not use capitals correctly in their writing. She understands that process writing includes attention to specific grammar points taught in context (Weaver 2008). In contrast, the second teacher teaches capitals on a particular day because that is the point in the curriculum where capitals are to be taught.

Our beliefs about language acquisition, about how people learn languages, and about how we should teach English language learners, all form our orientation. Our ideas are not fixed, and they change as we continue to learn and study. Nevertheless, they guide the methods and techniques we use. At any given time, we strive for consistency at the three levels——orientation, methods, and techniques.

When a teacher works in a school with a prescribed curriculum, the teacher's options are limited. While it is possible to make adaptations in implementing a fixed curriculum, there are limits on what a teacher can do. Schools that adopt programs for teaching reading, math, or other subjects to all their students—including their ELLs—rely on the expertise of the team that created the program rather than the needs of the students and the knowledge of individual teachers. Prescribed programs are applied to all students equally despite the great differences among them.

For that reason, it is better if groups of teachers, working with the administration, can adapt the curriculum to meet the needs of the students in their school. This curriculum should be based on the principles that teachers have developed through reading and discussing the theory and research that guides best practices for teaching ELLs.

Conclusion

A number of factors influence how teachers teach. These include their own experiences as students, their teacher education program, their school administrators and colleagues, the students, materials, and state and federal laws.

In response to these factors, teachers develop attitudes and beliefs about teaching second language students. Their beliefs often govern how they teach. However, when teachers read theory and research and reflect on their teaching in light of this knowledge, they develop principles that guide their teaching. New experiences can cause teachers to refine their principles to more effectively teach their students. A set of principles allows a teacher to evaluate new methods, techniques, and materials,

Yvonne's story shows how teachers become principled by reflecting on their teaching, theory, and current research. Yvonne first followed a method that was prescribed by her department chair. Her audio-lingual lessons, with their drills and dialogues, were based on a behaviorist view of language learning. She soon moved to a different view. With her adult ESL students, for example, she began to see her role as one of providing interesting materials and activities through which they could construct knowledge. She was still in control, but the students played a much more active role in their learning. Yvonne now investigates different aspects of teaching and learning second languages with her students, drawing on the principles she has come to understand.

KEY POINTS

→ A variety of factors influence how teachers teach.

→ Current legislative requirements such as English Only laws and NCLB have had the greatest impact on teachers of ELLs.

→ Teachers' attitudes, either positive or negative, toward teaching ELLs influence student success.

→ Yvonne's story shows how teachers can become principled by reflecting on their teaching as they increase their understanding of current research and theory.

APPLICATIONS

1. Think about a second or foreign language class you have taken or taught. (If you cannot identify a second language class, a first language reading, writing, literature, or language arts class would work.) Try to identify the orientation of the teacher and some of the techniques used to teach that class. Discuss this in pairs or groups.

2. Look back over Yvonne's story. Do any of her experiences make you think of something similar that you have experienced with teaching or learning? Discuss this with a partner or in a small group.

3. Interview a teacher who has had at least ten years of teaching experience. (Use yourself if you have taught for several years.) What has influenced that teacher's curriculum decisions?

4. In this chapter we have presented several scenarios illustrating different attitudes teachers develop. Which of these have you seen? Are there other common responses to teaching ELLs that you have observed? If so, try writing a scenario like the ones in the chapter and also write a short analysis and positive responses.

4

How Do People Learn and How Do They Acquire Language?

In the previous chapter we considered the factors that influence how teachers teach. Although a number of factors come into play, the teacher's view of how people learn ultimately guides teachers as they choose methods and techniques to use with their students. Principled teachers like Yvonne choose methods and techniques based on their understanding of the research and theory on learning and on second language acquisition. We begin this chapter by looking at theories of how people learn.

The model of learning we will present holds that learning, and especially language learning, must always be regarded as a social process. As Faltis and Hudelson (1998) point out, "learning and language acquisition overlap to a great extent in the sense that both are social, contextual, and goal-oriented. That is, individuals learn both content and language as they engage with others in a variety of settings to accomplish specific purposes" (85). While it is generally accepted that children go through a process of creative construction as they form and test hypotheses about academic content subjects and language, the learning they do is always social. According to Faltis and Hudelson, "learning does not happen exclusively inside the heads of learners; it results from social interactions with others that enable learners to participate by drawing on past and present experiences and relating them to the specific context at hand in some meaningful way" (87). We believe that this social view of learning applies to all learning, including learning a first or second language.

Vygotsky's Social View of Learning

Vygotsky (1962) developed a social theory of learning. Two concepts from his theory—the Zone of Proximal Development (ZPD) and the distinction between spontaneous and scientific concepts—contribute to a fuller understanding of how learning occurs. Vygotsky's work has been the basis for much of the current research in learning.

Zone of Proximal Development

For learning to take place, instruction must occur in a student's Zone of Proximal Development, which Vygotsky (1978) defines as "the distance between the actual developmental level as determined by independent problem solving and the level of potential development as determined through problem solving under adult guidance or in collaboration with more capable peers" (86). According to Vygotsky, learning results when we interact with someone else, an adult or a more capable peer, in the process of trying to solve a problem.

Vygotsky's research led him to theorize that for any kind of learning, the learner has a certain zone in which the next learning can take place. For example, a student might use the -*ing* forms of verbs to express progressive tense, as in "I studying English." The next area of learning for this student might be to add the auxiliary verb *am* to produce a more conventional sentence: "I am studying English." The teacher, recognizing a teachable moment, could point out the correct form, which could help the student begin to use the auxiliary. Or the student might notice auxiliaries as he interacts with more proficient English speakers and then incorporate them into his speech and writing. A student who already uses auxiliaries would not benefit from instruction on this topic, and a student who is just beginning to study English and uses only simple present tense, "I study English," would probably not notice the auxiliary and would not be ready for instruction on auxiliaries. The Zone of Proximal Development refers to the area that is just beyond what the student can currently do. Good teachers try to aim instruction at this zone.

Another way to think about the Zone of Proximal Development is to consider two students who both score 60 percent on a math test. This score would represent their independent level. A teacher might work with both students and then retest them. One student's score might rise to 70 percent while the other student might get an 80 on the second test. This would suggest that the two students had different zones of proximal development. One was ready to take a big leap with a little help while the other could make only a modest gain.

Mike, a graduate student who teaches fourth grade, provides us with an excellent example of how he works in his students' zones of proximal development during literature studies in his classroom. Mike teaches in an inner-city school, and many of his students are English language learners. He believes that literature studies are important for his students' learning. It is clear that Mike has found ways to support his students' growth:

> I continue to explore this exciting concept of literature study. Students self-select books and then meet in book groups to determine how many pages to read each day to complete the reading within a time frame I decide. The students are then invited to read, as a group, with a partner(s), or by themselves.
>
> As students read, I walk around, keeping anecdotal records of things students might be doing to make meaning from their texts. I have also joined in with groups as they have read, or even read with a group to provide some support and demonstrations of ways to approach reading and talk about it. Students are also encouraged to have a shared reading arrangement where they periodically stop and just do a "quick talk" with a partner about what they think is going on in their reading or to ask for clarification. This is to support the meaning-making process.
>
> I do wander in and out of groups and will ask them what they are finding, and then offer some direction as to things that I would like for them to be on the lookout for in the text. I base my comments on the kind of interests I see the readers having. I also will have readers give regular response (though not always written) on their reading. I want to get a look at how they are transacting with text.

It is important to note that Mike is not the only one in the classroom helping students learn within their zones of proximal development. The way literature studies are organized in Mike's classroom, more capable readers help their classmates understand and learn too.

Personal Invention and Social Convention

Central to the concept of the Zone of Proximal Development is the view of learning as a process of internalizing social experience. Vygotsky emphasized the role of social forces working on the individual. Goodman and Goodman (1990), however, argue that "language [and other aspects of learning] is as much personal invention as social convention" (231). The Goodmans present a view of learning that recognizes both the effects of social forces and the efforts of the individual learner: "Human learners are not passively manipulated by their social experiences; they are actively seeking sense in the world" (231). Social interaction is crucial. Individuals present their personal inventions to a group, which provides feedback the learners can use to make their inventions conform, to some degree, with social conventions.

We see this process occur when young children begin to write and invent spellings for the words they use. Over time, if teachers and peers respond to the messages they are attempting to express and if children are exposed to lots of print, their spellings change, moving steadily toward conventional usage. The key is to achieve a balance between the two forces of invention and convention. The Goodmans compare invention and convention with the centripetal and centrifugal forces that keep a satellite revolving around the Earth. Both forces are needed to keep the satellite in orbit. In the same way, in classrooms, if students are allowed to write any way they wish, they may produce spellings no one can read. On the other hand, if teachers insist on correct spelling, some students may choose not to write at all.

Helen was able to help her student, Magdalena, shape her personal inventions to move toward social conventions by engaging her in a writer's workshop:

> At the beginning of the year, Magdalena was not concerned if her work was readable or followed any of the conventions of standard English. She knew she was putting down her thoughts and ideas, and that was what I emphasized to her. I felt confident that her spelling and grammar would come along if she felt more comfortable in class, was allowed to write in a writer's workshop environment, and was exposed to more text. I decided to follow my instincts and only focus on one area with Magdalena. I wanted her to understand that writing is a process and that her misspellings were normal for a child who knew two languages. Recently, she started asking more questions about sentence structures and about the "right way" to spell. During a conference time with her group, she and I worked together to pick out the types of words she seemed to misspell or misuse most often. Then we problem solved the reasons why these words might cause her grief when writing. Most of the words we found were words she could spell correctly when she reread her writing.

Helen encouraged Magdalena to invent spellings to get her ideas down on paper. At first, Magdalena was not concerned with correct spellings. However, in the context of a writer's workshop Magdalena wanted her teacher and other students to be able to read what she had written, so she started to ask her teacher how to spell words. Helen helped Magdalena develop strategies that allowed this English learner to make her writing more conventional. If Helen had insisted on correct spelling from the beginning, Magdalena probably would not have developed the confidence to write. Helen took her cue from her student and helped her focus on spelling once Magdalena had produced writing she wanted others to read.

When English language learners first try to communicate in their new language, they often invent structures or words based on what they know about the language. For example, many students learning Spanish use *Yo gusto* instead of the irregular, conventional form, *Me gusta*, for "I like," since other verbs add *o* to form the first-person singular. Many students invent forms like *Yo gusto*. As they interact with more proficient speakers, they begin to notice the conventional form, *Me gusta,* and then they modify their personal invention to conform to conventional Spanish.

Yvonne's Venezuelan friends were amused when she used *coliflor*, the word for cauliflower, to refer to a hummingbird. Two conventional words for hummingbird are *colibrí* and *chupaflor*, and Yvonne combined these in her invention. In cases like this, when second language learners' inventions depart too far from social conventions, the feedback provided by native speakers helps learners seek a new way to express themselves. In the process, they learn a new language.

This process fits Selinker's (1972) characterization of acquiring a second language. He points out that in the process of acquiring a new language, learners go through a series of gradual approximations that move them from their native language to the new language through a series of interlanguages. These interlanguages are their personal inventions. Over time, these inventions come closer to the conventional forms of the language they are learning.

The Goodmans' theory of invention and convention claims that both personal and social forces influence the development of concepts. Their view fits well with Vygotsky's notion of the Zone of Proximal Development. Vygotsky says that we learn in social situations when others provide the help that shapes our inventions toward the social conventions of a particular society.

Spontaneous and Scientific Concepts

A second important theoretical construct that Vygotsky developed was the distinction between spontaneous and scientific concepts. Spontaneous concepts are ideas we develop fairly directly from everyday experience. For example, we know what "car" means if we live in a society in which people drive cars. We develop the concept for "car" by riding in cars and seeing cars. The word *car* becomes a label we can use to talk about this concept. We develop spontaneous concepts without any special help. They are simply part of our daily lives.

Scientific concepts, on the other hand, are abstract ideas that societies use to organize and categorize experiences. The concept of "transportation," for example, is a scientific concept. We use this term to categorize a number of different means of conveyance, whether the mode be a car, a bus, a boat, or an airplane. Children do not acquire scientific concepts from exposure to everyday events. Most often, they learn them in school.

Vygotsky conducted a number of experiments with adults in the eastern province of Uzbekistan a few years after schools had been built there. Some of the adults had attended schools while others from the same community had not. Vygotsky was interested in learning whether scientific concepts developed as a result of schooling. In one experiment, with adults who had not received schooling, he showed them pictures of objects such as a hammer, a saw, a log, and a hatchet, and asked which one didn't fit. These adults would say that all of them were needed. You need a hatchet to chop down a tree, a saw to cut it into logs, and a hammer to pound nails into the logs to build something. He presented the same pictures to a second group of adults who had received formal schooling. They would pick out the log as different. In order to pick out the log, the adults had to categorize the objects using abstraction (three of these things are tools) rather than focus on the functional properties of the objects.

In the same way, presented with pictures of a bird, a rifle, a dagger, and a bullet, the first group argued that you needed all of them (the bullet goes into the rifle to shoot the bird, and you use the knife to cut it up), and the second group said the bird was different because the other three were weapons. Both groups had developed the same spontaneous concepts. They all knew what birds and hammers were, but only those who had gone to school had developed the scientific concepts needed to categorize these objects. Vygotsky concluded that the development of scientific concepts reflected a change in the way people conceptualize the world. An important part of the learning that goes on in schools is the development of the ability to think in more abstract ways that go beyond everyday experience.

The ideas of spontaneous and scientific concepts are important in two ways when we apply them to language learning. Krashen (1982) makes a similar distinction between acquiring a language and learning one. We will discuss these concepts in the next chapter, but at this point we simply want to suggest that we acquire a language in the same way that we develop spontaneous concepts: in the course of daily living and without much conscious awareness of the process itself. On the other hand, if we study a language in school, we usually learn scientific concepts, such as "verb" or "present tense," that we can use to categorize aspects of the language. As Krashen points out, acquisition allows us to use language to communicate, while learning gives us abstract terms to talk about the language. Thus, there is a similarity between Vygotsky's ideas about spontaneous and scientific concepts and Krashen's ideas about acquisition and learning.

In the same way, Cummins (2000) makes a distinction between conversational language and academic language. This again is an important difference that we will discuss in more detail later. Here, we wish to suggest that conversational language is what we use to communicate spontaneous concepts and talk about daily events. On the other hand, academic language involves the use of terms and language forms we use to communicate scientific concepts that we learn in school.

Vygotsky argued that language is a tool for thought. As we develop scientific concepts in fields such as social studies or mathematics, we develop new ways to think and talk about the world. Spontaneous and scientific concepts are developed in the same way, but in different contexts. Spontaneous concepts are developed in settings outside the school, while scientific concepts are developed for the most part in schools.

Cognitive Apprenticeship

Vygotsky's theories are the basis of work by Brown, Collins, and Duguid (1989). According to Brown and his colleagues, the process of acquiring new concepts is through cognitive apprenticeship. Their research leads them to conclude that we learn new things as we carry out activities in particular situations. Examples of such activities are learning how to solve a quadratic equation or learning how to speak a new language. The key is for individuals to have a real purpose to engage in the activity. The motivation to acquire new concepts and skills comes from the context.

When we travel to a new country, for example, we want to be able to communicate with people there, so we are motivated to learn the language. To learn it, we must be actively engaged in speaking, listening, reading, and writing the language. We also need help from people who already know the language as we attempt to communicate. In this respect, we are like apprentices under the guidance of a more expert user of the language. Learning may be seen as a kind of enculturation, whether it be into the community of mathematicians or the community of Arabic speakers. We pick up language and concepts as we interact with other people in different contexts.

Gee (2008) makes much the same point as Brown and his colleagues. He refers to the practices of social groups, including the ways they use language, as Discourses (which he writes with a capital D). According to Gee, "Discourses are ways of behaving, interacting, valuing, thinking, believing, and often reading and writing, that are accepted as instantiations of particular identities (or 'types of people') by certain groups" (3). In other words, to communicate effectively in a new language requires knowledge of the language and knowledge of how to use the language in a particular cultural context. This knowledge can best be gained by becoming an apprentice member of the culture. This is true of language, and it is also true of academic "cultures" such as the culture of biologists and the culture of literary scholars. As apprentices, we engage in authentic activities within a culture. Brown and his colleagues (1989) define authentic activity as "the ordinary practices of the culture" (34).

Brown and his colleagues (1989) point out that one of the problems with learning in schools is that students are not engaged in authentic activities. For example, in foreign language classes, students often may learn about the language rather than using the language to communicate with other speakers of the language in everyday contexts. In the same way, students in math classes may learn certain terms and procedures for solving problems, but if they are not immersed in the culture of mathematicians they do not think, believe, value, and act as mathematicians do.

David provides a good example of how people learn through cognitive apprenticeship. As an undergraduate, he studied English literature and planned to be a high school English teacher. In college, he learned to read, analyze, write, and talk about literature as English professors or English teachers do. He was an apprentice learning the Discourse of English majors. After graduation from college, he taught high school English. He wanted his students to become part of a Discourse group of literary scholars, but because there was no such Discourse group already established at the high school for the students to join, he could not bring this about. Only if these same students went on to choose English literature as a major in college and interacted with professors and other majors would they be able to enter into such a Discourse.

Later, David went back to graduate school. When he entered the doctoral program in linguistics, he felt lost at first. The way linguists write and talk about language was completely different from anything he had experienced in his undergraduate English studies. In the first year, he often felt as if he was learning another language. As he read more and became engaged in linguistics problems, what linguists often call "doing linguistics," David began to acquire the Discourse of linguistics. He was engaged in authentic activities with other linguists, and he eventually became a member of the culture.

The Role of the Teacher

If learning is a process of enculturation into a particular Discourse and students may best be thought of as apprentices learning how to interact in a particular cultural context, just what is the role of the teacher? According to Vygotsky, the role of the teacher is one of *mediation*. A teacher (or other adult or more capable peer) mediates experience by helping the learner make sense out of it. Working in the learners' zones of proximal development, the teacher provides demonstrations, asks questions, or points out certain aspects of a situation. Teachers who mediate learning provide a *way* or *medium* that helps students gain new understandings. What students can first do with the help of a teacher, they can later do alone. The questions and suggestions of the teacher are a kind of learning tool that students can use. However, as Brown and colleagues point out, students often learn a procedure, an algorithm, or a definition, but fail to learn how to use it. This is why it is important to involve students in authentic learning activities.

Good instruction supports learning for as long as the learner needs it and then supports the student as he or she works independently. Many of us have had the experience of help that didn't last long enough. We go to the hardware store, and the

Type of Mediation	What the Teacher Does	What the Students Do
Direct Instruction	Tells students how or what to do or gives students information to learn and then apply	Follow directions, practice, or memorize information and then display the knowledge.
Model	Shows through actions or materials how students should do something	Follow the model provided to produce something similar.
Scaffold	*Verbal* Provides assistance to help students solve problems by asking questions, probing, pointing out aspects of a problem, or answering questions *Visual* Graphic organizers, charts, maps, timelines, videos, pictures, realia *Physical* Collaborative groups, bilingual pairs, hands-on activities with manipulatives	Use information provided to try to solve problems and accomplish tasks.

FIGURE 4–1. *Three types of mediation*

knowledgeable clerk explains very clearly how to install the equipment we are buying. Then, once we get home, we can't recall how to put the pieces together. We needed more mediation, more instruction within our zone of proximal development. The support for learning was withdrawn too quickly.

Cazden (1992) describes three ways a teacher can mediate learning: through direct instruction, by modeling, or by providing scaffolding. Figure 4–1 gives an overview of these three types of mediation.

Direct Instruction

One way teachers can support learning is through direct instruction. As Cazden explains, in direct instruction "the adult not only models a particular utterance but directs the child to say or tell or ask" (108). A parent might say "Bye-bye" and wave to a friend when leaving, and then tell the child, "Say bye-bye."

As Cazden explains, "direct instruction seems to focus on two aspects of language development: appropriate social language use and correct vocabulary" (108). Direct instruction is perhaps most often associated with the teaching of reading. For example, many standards for reading instruction call for explicit, direct instruction of phonics. Reading programs often include materials that instruct teachers to present lessons in a step-by-step manner. In a typical lesson, a teacher may direct students to produce each sound in a word and then blend the sounds to produce the complete word. Students then practice this skill with a series of words. Based on their review of research on reading for ELLs, Goldenberg and Coleman (2010) conclude that direct, explicit instruction is effective for teaching basic decoding skills. Research, however, has not shown that direct instruction for beginning readers leads to increased reading comprehension (Institute of Educational Services 2008).

In second language teaching, direct instruction is used extensively in the audio-lingual approach (ALM) that Yvonne first used. In ALM students often repeat after the teacher, and the teacher corrects any errors. Then the students practice in pairs or small groups. Current content-based second language teaching, however, makes limited use of direct instruction.

Modeling

Another way teachers can mediate learning is by modeling. Modeling is something a teacher can do with an individual, a small group, or an entire class. It is an intentional action by the teacher. For example, if a teacher wants to help students understand directionality in reading, she might decide to model directionality by reading a big book and moving her finger or a pointer under the print to indicate left-to-right movement. In doing this, the teacher models one aspect of reading.

An example of modeling comes from Sandra, a teacher of fourth-, fifth-, and sixth-grade newcomers who arrive with little previous schooling or with interrupted schooling. Most are migrant children with little background in English. As a prewriting activity, Sandra often writes on the overhead in front of the entire class, talking about conventions she uses in her writing. In an early writing lesson, Sandra's modeling is a prewriting activity in which she writes a description of her family on the overhead and offers a commentary such as the following:

> In the first sentence, I indent, and the first letter is a capital letter. "My family has five people." Notice that I put a period at the end of the sentence. "My husband's name is Alfredo." Notice that I have a capital letter at the beginning and for my husband's name.

As Sandra writes and talks, she models the kind of paragraph and the conventions she wants her students to write.

Sometimes materials can provide the model teachers need. When Sandra was working on a nutrition unit, she wanted to help her students answer the question, "Where does our food come from?" She read aloud a book, *Where Does Breakfast Come From?* (Flint 1998), which describes how products such as milk, cereal, pancakes, and bread come from the field or farm to the table. This book provided the model for Sandra's students. In groups students then chose children's literature books about foods, including *A Pizza the Size of the Sun* (Prelutsky 1996), *Too Many Tamales* (Soto 1993), *The Apple Pie Family* (Thompson 1997), and *If You Give a Mouse a Cookie* (Numeroff and Bond 1985). They worked in cooperative groups and drew posters of the food featured in the book of their choice, describing how it progressed from the field to the table. They interviewed adults at the school to find out what ingredients they needed for the recipes of the foods in the books and presented their posters to the class. These final projects included not only where products like flour and pizza sauce come from (wheat, tomatoes, peppers, cheese) but also the recipes for how to make the favorite dish. Sandra would never have gotten such excellent participation without the model she provided.

Scaffolding

A third type of mediation is scaffolding. Vygotsky argued that learning takes place when an adult or more capable peer asks questions, points out aspects of a problem, or makes suggestions, working in a learner's zone of proximal development. Bruner (1985) referred to this kind of help as *verbal scaffolds*. A scaffold is an appropriate metaphor for this kind of assistance. A scaffold supports the workers during a building's construction and then is taken down once the building is completed.

Cazden (1992) defines a scaffold as "a temporary framework for construction in progress" (103). A teacher, for example, might ask a student who has written a composition to expand on a certain point, to provide more information to support an argument. The teacher's comments provide the scaffold that allows the writer to move beyond what he or she produced by working alone. A native speaker might ask a nonnative speaker to rephrase or clarify a request, and in the process the nonnative speaker might start to develop the conventional forms needed for communication in the new language.

In addition to verbal scaffolds, teachers can provide visual scaffolds in the form of graphic organizers, maps, charts, or timelines. Gottlieb (2006) states that, "Visual or graphic support is a mainstay of the instructional repertoire of teachers working with English language learners" (134). She lists a number of reasons for teachers to use visual and graphic supports. As she notes, these scaffolds provide "multiple avenues for accessing content, constructing meaning, and communicating ideas" (134). She lists specific types of graphic organizers and shows how they can be used in different content areas. She also explains the kinds of language patterns that are associated with each graphic organizer. For example, a Venn diagram, which shows differences and similarities, is naturally associated with sentence patterns such as "One has . . . but the other doesn't have . . . ," or sentences beginning with "On the other hand" or "In contrast." Teachers can make effective use of graphic organizers to scaffold instruction for ELLs.

A teacher we observed who was working in a bilingual class provided excellent scaffolding for her students. After the students had read *Mañana Iguana* (Long 2004), a story about an iguana modeled on the Little Red Hen tale, the teacher put up a pocket web chart. In the center, she wrote the name of the story. Then, she divided her students into small groups. She gave each group a vocabulary word such as *frustrated* or *exhausted*. She also gave them a sentence frame, "Iguana was _____ because _____" and instructed them to work together to write a sentence with their word. The groups completed their sentences and inserted them into the pocket chart web. The pocket chart and sentence frame were important scaffolds that helped the students develop content knowledge and language. This activity provided a good review of the main ideas of the story. For example, one group wrote, "Iguana was exhausted because she did everything for the party." Another group added, "Iguana was frustrated because nobody helped her." The pocket chart web provided a visual scaffold to help the summarize the story using the cause–effect sentence pattern.

Another way that teachers can scaffold instruction is by grouping students heterogeneously. In many bilingual classes, teachers have students work in bilingual pairs. Depending on the language of instruction for a particular lesson, one of the students, who is more proficient in that language, helps scaffold the instruction for the less proficient student. When teachers use heterogeneous grouping for collaborative activities, more proficient students in the group can scaffold the instruction for their peers.

At times, teachers use homogeneous grouping to provide scaffolds. Marjorie, a fourth-grade teacher whose classroom has many second language learners, has found that when she uses other students as "teachers," all students are able to progress. At times, she groups students into same first language groups, especially when one of the students is more advanced in English. In a response to some reading in a graduate ESL methods course, Marjorie explained how students can provide a scaffold for one another:

> It's been interesting to watch the interaction this last week as my class has been reading the book *The Real Thief,* by Stieg. One group of three [Hmong] girls has especially caught my eye. One of the girls is one of my top students academically, having been on the honor roll all year. The other two girls have been in the United States for about two years and their independent reading level would be considered preprimer. As a team, all three are able to read and enjoy the book, even though many of the words are difficult. As one of the "lower" students reads along, every fourth or fifth word, she stops and asks, in Hmong, "Ab tsi?" (What?). The "top" student explains and on they move.

Scaffolds support learners by providing a structure they can rely on to build their competence. One role for a teacher is to provide scaffolds or to create situations where students can do this for each another.

A Model for Teaching

Fisher and Frey (2009) have worked extensively in schools with high concentrations of second language learners. They have developed a structured approach to teaching. In their approach the teacher models, provides scaffolds, and guides practice as students learn new material so that they can then work independently.

Each lesson consists of four stages. First, the teacher presents a focus lesson that sets a purpose and models what students are expected to do. During this stage the teacher thinks aloud as she reads a short text, sets up a science experiment, or solves a math problem. The students get to hear the mental steps the teacher takes so that, later, they can carry out these steps by themselves. Second language learners also get to hear the language the teacher uses as she thinks aloud. Fisher and Frey refer to this stage as the "I do it" part of a lesson since the teacher is doing all the work.

The next stage is guided instruction during which the teacher and the students work together to carry out an activity or solve a problem. This is the "We do it" stage. The activity is similar to but not the same as the one modeled by the teacher during the focus lesson. As the students attempt to carry out the process, the teacher is there to give support and guide the students. This stage is particularly important for ELLs in early stages of English language development. During this time, the teacher can provide extra help to be sure that the students understand exactly what is to be done and how to do it.

In the third stage, the students work in collaborative groups to carry out a task or solve a problem. This is the "We do it together" stage. This task builds on what the students have learned during the focus lesson and the guided instruction. Effective group work is designed so that there is both individual and group accountability. Students also need to be taught how to work together productively. Teachers can plan carefully to create heterogeneous groups so that ELLs receive support from more proficient English speakers as Marjorie did with her Hmong students.

In the last, "You do it alone" stage, students draw on what they have learned in earlier parts of the lesson to work independently to carry out an activity. The teacher is there to provide support to students who still need it, but students are encouraged to work on their own. At this point, they should have built the background knowledge and skills needed for independent work. The kind of work expected of the students would vary depending on their level of proficiency. For example, beginners might draw and label pictures to show a sequence of steps in a science activity while more advanced ELLs could write out the procedure as a series of steps.

Fisher and Frey's four-stage lesson structure has its theoretical base in the work of Vygotsky because the teacher continually works in the students' zones of proximal development to build scientific concepts. This model of teaching is also consistent with the cognitive apprenticeship theory Brown and his colleagues have developed. The role of the teacher is to mediate learning for students by providing scaffolds that enable them to solve problems and carry out activities independently.

Mary's Lesson on Idioms

Mary teaches high school English to beginning ELLs. She knows that they struggle to understand idioms in the stories they read. She followed a structured lesson format similar to the one used by Fisher and Frey. At each stage of the lesson her role changed. Mary began with a short focus lesson. She modeled how to determine an idiom's meaning from the context while she read the text aloud. Each time she came to an idiom such as, "Has the cat got your tongue?" she stopped to think aloud, "This doesn't make much sense. There's no cat in this story. I guess I can't take this literally. It must be an idiom." She went on to show how she could figure out the meaning of the idiom from the context.

Having introduced the idea that idioms express a nonliteral meaning, Mary passed out a list of idioms. Students chose one idiom. They drew a picture showing the literal meaning. For example, one student chose, "Killing two birds with one stone." He drew a picture of a boy throwing a rock at two birds on a tree branch. Then they wrote the nonliteral meaning at the bottom of the page. The students shared their drawings in small groups and then put them up on the bulletin board.

For the next phase of the lesson, the guided instruction, Mary worked with small groups of students. She read a short story to them that contained several idioms. Each time they came to an idiom, Mary helped guide the students to use their background knowledge and the context of the story to figure out the meaning. With Mary's support, students began to recognize idioms and to develop strategies for determining their meaning.

The third stage of the lesson on idioms involved the students in a collaborative learning activity. Mary divided the students into groups of four and gave each group a different short story that contained idioms. Students worked together to identify the idioms and to figure out what they meant. They made a list of the idioms they found. They also tried to think of a similar idiom in their first language, and if they discovered one, they wrote it down as well. The students enjoyed being "idiom detectives." After the groups all finished, they took turns sharing several of their idioms and the first language equivalents.

For the fourth stage, the independent learning phase, students were given a short play script with idioms underlined. They were directed to use the strategies they had learned to determine what each idiom meant. For example, Pedro used the context to decide that when one character was described as having kicked the bucket, it must mean that he had died. After figuring out the meanings of these idioms, the students tried writing their own short scripts using the same idioms or others they had studied earlier in the lesson.

Mary carefully scaffolded instruction in her lesson on idioms. She modeled how to think about idioms and how to determine their meaning during the focus phase. She provided students with practice in identifying and finding the nonliteral meaning of idioms during the guided instruction and the collaborative group work. She then gave her students an assignment that required them to put the skills they had learned into practice. This approach proved successful in teaching her beginning ELLs about idioms.

Learning a Language

To this point we have discussed generally how people learn and the role of the teacher in mediating learning. We now turn more directly to language learning. We begin by exploring the question, "What do people acquire when they acquire a first or second language?" Linguists such as Noam Chomsky have focused their work on this question. According to Radford (1981):

> Chomsky seeks to attain two parallel, interrelated goals in the study of language—namely to develop (i) a Theory of Language and (ii) a Theory of Language Acquisition. The Theory of Language will concern itself with what are the defining characteristics of natural (i.e. human) languages and the Theory of Language Acquisition with the question of how children acquire their native language(s). Of the two, the task (i) of developing a Theory of Language is—in Chomsky's view—logically prior to task (ii) of developing a Theory of Language Acquisition, since only if we know what language is can we develop theories of how it is acquired. (1)

Chomsky's claim, then, is that we need to decide on what language is before we can consider how people acquire languages. For Chomsky and other linguists, what we acquire is a grammar. The term *grammar* has several different meanings, but for linguists a grammar is a set of rules people use to produce and comprehend a language. Speakers of a language are not usually consciously aware of the rules they use. They can put sentences together and they can understand what others say, but they can't usually tell you how they do it. What Chomsky and other linguists attempt to discover is the nature of these subconscious rules.

Competence and Performance

Chomsky makes an important distinction in his study of language between competence and performance. He claims that "a grammar of a language is a model of the linguistic competence of the fluent native speaker of the language" (as cited in Radford 1981, 2). A speaker's competence is what a speaker can do under the best conditions. Our competence represents a kind of idealized best ability. As we all know, our performance seldom matches our competence. In most situations, we don't perform up to our full ability. We may be nervous, tired, bored, or simply careless.

Previously, linguists studied language by analyzing what speakers said or wrote. They based their descriptions on actual performance. Chomsky, on the other hand, wanted to look at underlying ability, so he ignored many slips of the tongue and described language by considering what speakers know is "right" when they have a chance to think about it—a kind of edited speech or writing. Chomsky felt that only by considering speakers' underlying competence could he get at the rules they use to produce and understand a language.

The concept of competence is important for teachers trying to determine how proficient a student is. We should remember that a student's actual performance may not fully show his or her underlying competence. For example, ten-year-old Alfredo, educated in both Mexico and the United States, understands, speaks, reads, and writes English well despite having an accent. When he arrives at a new school, his teacher first tries to engage him in friendly conversation and then calls on him to answer questions. He responds haltingly because he is nervous and is unaccustomed to the informal classroom atmosphere. Based on his performance, his teacher assumes Alfredo understands and speaks very little English. Actually, Alfredo's competence in English is much greater than his performance would suggest.

As this example shows, teachers need to be aware that students' performance in certain contexts may not be a good predictor of their competence in other contexts. For example, some students appear to be very proficient in everyday conversational English. They can joke with friends and talk about current events of interest. However, these same students may have great difficulty with the academic language of content-area textbooks and tests. Competence, then, is tied to particular functions of language use. We do not have a general language competence. Instead, we have (or lack) competence in using language for certain purposes.

Leny, a Dutch woman teaching English in Venezuela, provides a good example of a language learner whose performance in a specific context did not reflect her competence. She was learning Spanish and had developed good basic skills, but in one setting, she appeared to lack competence:

> There are many occasions when my performance in a foreign language does
> not reflect my competence in that language. One of those occasions was at the

hairdresser. The lady helping me did not seem to have the time or the interest to let me explain in my basic Spanish what I wanted, and on top of that, the whole shop was looking at me, the "gringa." I then tried to explain with gestures what I meant, with the result that I came out with a very different haircut than I wanted. This being the only decent hairdresser in town, I went back there a few times, but each time I wrote down beforehand what I wanted, although I was perfectly capable of saying it. But I knew that I just would draw a blank again as soon as I got into the shop.

Leny's story is instructive. The hairdresser did not really listen to her. Other customers began to stare at her. Even though she had developed some basic Spanish, she could not access it in that context. As language teachers, we need to remember that our reactions to students play an important role in their performance. For Leny, that one negative experience carried over to future visits. She was able to develop a strategy (writing things down) to overcome the problem, but many younger students lack the strategies they need to demonstrate their competence as they attempt to function in a new language.

Competence and Correctness

People acquire competence in one or more languages, but their ability to produce and comprehend the language or languages is not the same as their ability to use the conventional or standard forms of the languages. The competence we are describing is not the kind of conscious knowledge usually associated with school grammar lessons. It is not the ability to put commas in the right places or to use *different from* rather than *different than*. Those are matters of usage and are typically associated with standard written language.

The kinds of rules Chomsky and other linguists refer to when they speak of "grammar" are the rules that allow people to use language to communicate. It is our knowledge that something "sounds right" in the dialect we speak. Native speakers have this kind of competence but may lack the ability to produce standard (correct) speech or writing. School success depends on mastering the academic language of the different disciplines. This kind of language is usually learned in school or other formal settings. It is not something we normally acquire when we acquire a language.

Functions of Language and Kinds of Competence

One way to answer the question, "What do we acquire when we acquire a language?" is to say that we develop the language we need to do certain things. Smith (1983) points out that language can serve three functions: (1) the referential function, which speakers use to get and give basic information; (2) the expressive function, which speakers use to show their attitude toward what they are saying; and (3) the integrative function, which speakers use to mark their social identity. These three functions of language match with the two basic types of competence that someone acquiring a language needs to develop: grammatical competence and communicative competence. In the following sections, we explain each of the three functions and then describe the two kinds of competence related to these functions.

Referential Function

The most basic function of language is the referential function. We use language to refer to things in the world. This is the function that allows me to say, "My name is David" or, "I live in Texas." We need to be able to get and give basic information to survive, so the referential function is probably the first language function language learners develop.

In traditional ESL classes, teachers usually begin with basic vocabulary—classroom objects, clothing, food, transportation—and basic sentence types—simple statements with "be" or with action verbs in the present tense. This approach is designed to give students the tools to talk about everyday things. In other words, these classes begin by supplying students with the words and structures they need to perform the referential function of language.

Expressive Function

Just getting and giving basic information is not enough for someone to function fully in a language. We also need to be able to show our attitude toward what we are saying. This is the expressive function of language. Part of what we acquire when we acquire a language is this ability to show how we feel about the topic under discussion.

Gee (1988), explaining the expressive function, notes that "when we speak, we do not just talk about the world . . . we take a particular perspective or viewpoint on the information we communicate"(204). We reveal our viewpoints, our attitude, by stressing certain words, by pausing, even by choosing from among synonyms those words that carry the emotional tone we wish to communicate. Synonyms may have roughly the same referential meaning, but they differ in the emotions they trigger. There's a big difference between "I dislike cats" and "I abhor (despise) (detest) cats." Speakers signal their attitudes by the choices they make among synonyms such as these. When we acquire a language, then, we acquire not only the ability to communicate certain ideas, but also ways to express our attitudes toward those ideas. Often, second language students fail to communicate effectively because they lack the language skills needed to express these subtle differences in attitude.

Integrative Function

A third important function that speakers of a language need to develop is an ability to indicate their social status in relationship to the people they are speaking with. This is referred to as the integrative function. This function allows us to vary our language for social purposes. Often, second language speakers have not developed this function.

Gee (1988) suggests that two forces motivate language use. These are "the desire for status in regard to whatever reference group(s) one admires and the desire for solidarity with those one views as peers" (212). Our choice in language signals our relationship to the person we are speaking with or what Halliday and Hassan (1989) and other functional linguists analyze as the tenor of a conversation. Proficient language users are able to change from more to less formal registers depending on their audience and purpose for speaking. A *register* is a particular form of a language that includes choices of syntax, vocabulary, or pronunciation. We use different registers in different settings with different people.

While we were in Venezuela, for example, we noticed that our maid spoke more rapidly and dropped many endings when talking to members of her family. At first we thought she was speaking more slowly and clearly to us because we were foreigners. However, when other Venezuelan professors came to our home, we realized that she spoke the same way to them as she did to us. What we discovered is that she changed her register when speaking to people she perceived to be of a higher social status.

All of us do this in our native language, often without being aware of it. Politicians are often especially good at shifting to a "down home" variety of the language when trying to gain votes and achieve solidarity with the people they are speaking to. They speak quite differently in Washington, DC, where the goal is more often status. A tension always exists between solidarity and status. In many contexts, we have to choose language that achieves a connection with others or language that elevates us above them. In classrooms, teachers should realize that asking students to speak or write a certain way has definite social consequences for the students. At times, solidarity with their peers may be more important than the academic achievement that could come from using a higher-status variety of the language.

Part of what we acquire when we acquire a new language is this ability to choose language that reflects status or solidarity in appropriate ways. For example, when we taught at the university in Mérida, Venezuela, many of our interactions with other professors and with students took place in Spanish. We could communicate, but we did not always choose the right variety of language to achieve either status or solidarity.

The relationship in Latin America between students and professors is different from the relationship we have with our graduate students in the United States. In Venezuela professors maintain a position of such high respect that students do not expect their professors to treat them like friends. We came to realize that in interactions with students, we needed to remain rather formal and even demanding, if we wished to keep their respect as well as the respect of the other professors with whom we worked. This meant that the kind of language we used with students had to be different from the language we used with other professors.

Acquiring a language is complex. We need to know the words and how to put them together. Otherwise, we can't get and give basic information. But we also need to be aware that the particular words we choose and the way we combine and express them shows how we feel about what we are saying and also shows how we feel about the people with whom we are communicating. In order to use language to perform these three functions, we need two different kinds of competence: grammatical competence and sociolinguistic competence.

Grammatical Competence

Grammatical competence is knowledge of a language that allows us to get and give information about the world. It allows us to say, "Today is Monday," or "The man chased the dog." Linguists such as Chomsky have described grammatical competence. Their research focuses on the following areas: (1) phonology, (2) morphology, (3) syntax, and (4) semantics.

Phonology refers to the sound system of a language. Each language consists of a set of sounds (phonemes) that speakers use to indicate differences in meaning. Developing grammatical competence involves learning which sounds in a language make a difference in meaning, and being able to distinguish and produce those sounds. Phonology also includes other areas, such as intonation and stress.

Morphology is our knowledge of the structure of words. It involves knowing which prefixes or suffixes can be added to a root or base form. English morphology is fairly simple compared with that of other languages. English relies more on the order of the words (the syntax) than on prefixes and suffixes. Languages such as Turkish, on the other hand, have complex morphology, but there are fewer restrictions on the order of the words.

Syntax is the area most linguists working in English have focused on, since English relies heavily on the order of words to convey meanings. We know that there is a big difference between "The man chased the dog" and "The dog chased the man." This difference in meaning depends on the order of the words. Syntax is a study of the acquired rules that native speakers use to combine words into sentences.

Semantics is a fourth aspect of grammatical competence. Semantics has to do with word meanings. If we know English, we know that *dog* refers to a particular kind of animal, and *cat* refers to a different kind of animal. Meanings can be complex. Both *dog* and *cat* can have secondary meanings. You can *dog* it at work, and someone can be *catty*.

Semantics also has to do with the knowledge of words that commonly go together, or *collocate*. Words like *dog* and *cat* are usually associated with other words referring to animals. Words like *boat* might be connected with *water* or *lake*. We organize concepts into categories and use different terms to refer to more general or more specific ideas within the categories. *Cook* is a general term, and *bake* or *roast* are more specific. The three words are in the same semantic field. Grammatical competence involves a knowledge of how such fields are organized.

This is a very brief overview of some of the aspects of grammatical competence. We simply want to give you some idea of the kinds of knowledge speakers acquire as they acquire a language. In order to get and give basic information, speakers need phonological, morphological, syntactic, and semantic knowledge. That's what we all acquired as we picked up our native language, and it's what English learners need to develop as they acquire English. Grammatical competence allows us to talk about the world, but we need more than grammatical competence to function effectively in a new language. We also need communicative competence.

Communicative Competence

A second kind of competence that language learners need to function in a new language and culture is communicative competence. Hymes (1970) defines communicative competence as knowing what to say to whom, when, and in what circumstances. Learning a language, then, involves more than developing grammatical competence. Learners must also develop the knowledge of how to use the language appropriately in different social situations. The norms for communicative competence vary from one linguistic and sociocultural group to another, and part of what we acquire when we acquire a language is the ability to function effectively in different social settings. Often, second language learners have developed grammatical competence but still lack communicative competence.

We became more aware of the importance of helping students develop communicative competence while living in Venezuela. Both of us speak Spanish well enough to communicate (we have grammatical competence), but at times we found ourselves lacking in communicative competence. For example, in Mérida there is a very popular bakery where many people go to get fresh breads, rolls, and pastries. At certain times of the day, the long counter of the bakery is crowded with people two or three rows deep. We found ourselves avoiding these busy times because we had trouble getting the attention of the clerks. The orderly rules for taking turns that applied in the United States didn't apply at this bakery.

On one occasion Yvonne waited helplessly for twenty minutes as people came, called out their orders to the clerks, and left with their purchases. Finally, a man noticed how long she had been standing there, and he called to the clerk to help the *señora*. Yvonne knew what words to use, she could understand the Spanish, but she simply could not call out her order like all the Venezuelans who preceded her. She didn't want to appear rude, but what is interpreted as overly aggressive behavior in one country may be the norm in another. Yvonne lacked the communicative competence needed to buy bread in that situation.

Communicative competence is the ability to say the right thing in different social situations. This is hard enough in one's first language, and developing communicative competence in a second language is even more difficult. A professor friend of ours from Venezuela came to study with us in California. We took trips with her along the coast and to Yosemite with the dean of our graduate school and his wife. Both the dean and his wife are very religious people and also very proper. Even though the car trips were contexts for casual conversation, we maintained a fairly formal style of speech.

Our Venezuelan friend spoke excellent English, but she had not yet acquired some of the nuances needed for effective communication. As we drove into Yosemite National Park, she was very impressed with the views and continually exclaimed, "Oh, my God! That's so beautiful!" In Spanish, *Dios mío* (my God) is a very common expression that carries little emotional impact, but in English it is a much stronger expression and one we would not have used with the dean and his wife. Coming from this sophisticated professor in that company, the words sounded completely inappropriate. In other settings with other people, there would be nothing unusual about her words. One of the problems for second language learners is that teachers will seldom explain sociolinguistic gaffes. Instead, they interpret the inappropriate language as rudeness. However, students benefit when teachers help them develop both grammatical and communicative competence.

A second example from Spanish is the word *epa*. In Venezuela, that expression is used to get someone's attention. However, one must be careful not to use the word in certain social situations. It's fine, for example, for college students to use it to get a friend's attention around campus, but if a female in a nice restaurant used the expression to call a waiter, it would be considered very rude. Of course, there are hundreds of examples like this in every language, and as educators working with English language learners, we should be sensitive to our students when they use their new language inappropriately.

Even commonplace practices such as issuing and receiving invitations vary from one culture to another, so grammatical competence isn't all one needs to communicate effectively. After one month in Venezuela, we were feeling a bit hurt because we had not received any social invitations to homes, despite the fact that people were friendly at work. Several people had mentioned to us that we should stop by sometime, but we waited for a specific invitation. Luckily, we had a talk with a sociolinguist who was also new to Mérida. She too felt isolated so she decided to explore with her students how *la visita* (the social visit) was done in this town. The students explained that it is the obligation of the newcomer to visit first and that what we considered a casual comment, "Stop by sometime," had really been a definite invitation. She also discovered that if we, in turn, wanted people to visit us, we would need to specifically say, "Come by sometime and see where we live." That way people would feel free to visit us as newcomers. We needed to look at invitations in a new way to understand the social environment in which we lived.

Johnson (1995) points out that one specific social context in which our students need to function is the classroom. Classrooms have very clear (if typically unstated) rules that govern topics for conversation and writing and roles for participants in communicative exchanges. What students need, according to Johnson, is classroom communicative competence, which she defines as "the knowledge and competencies that second language students need in order to participate in, learn from, and acquire a second language in the classroom" (160). Teachers can help students acquire a new language by making the rules for classroom interactions explicit.

The TESOL (Teachers of English to Speakers of Other Languages) organization has developed English language proficiency standards (TESOL 2006). The first standard is that "English language learners communicate for social, intercultural, and instructional purposes within the school setting" (3). This standard clearly points to the need to help ELLs develop communicative competence for classroom contexts. Often, as teachers, we focus on the academic content we are teaching, but when classes include ELLs, it is important to also teach them how to use language for social purposes in culturally appropriate ways in the classroom.

For example, communicative competence also involves learning how to enter a conversation or to end one. In our native language, we seem to know instinctively the rules for contributing to an ongoing discussion. However, English language learners often have trouble knowing when to add to a classroom discussion. They may jump in at what seems to be an inappropriate time, or they may remain silent, even when called on. Classroom discussions may be particularly difficult if students have had previous schooling in other countries where the unwritten rules for discussion were quite different from the rules in their new country.

Competence and Learner Strategies

In the process of developing grammatical and communicative competence, effective language learners also develop a number of strategies that allow them to comprehend and produce language even when they lack the words, the structures, or the knowledge of appropriate social use. Part of what we acquire when we acquire a language is the ability to communicate even when we lack linguistic resources. Canale and Swain (1980) refer to this as *strategic competence*. They define strategic competence as "the verbal and nonverbal communication strategies that may be called into action to compensate for breakdowns in communication due to performance variables or due to insufficient competence" (30). Leny developed a strategy to communicate with her hairdresser. She wrote down what she wanted to say. Teachers can help English learners acquire English by making them aware of these strategies and encouraging their use.

The most natural response when we don't know how to say something is to use nonverbal strategies. We play a kind of charades, hoping that our actions will lead the listener to produce the desired word. We indicate *big* by spreading our hands apart and *small* by holding them close together. Nonverbal cues can include facial expressions, gestures, or movements. Good second language teachers often use these same kinds of cues to help make the target language more comprehensible, and English learners will often mimic the gestures when they can't remember a word.

A person acquiring a second language can also use different verbal strategies to express meanings. Most often, the strategies are used when the learner lacks a particular word. Figure 4–2 lists a number of these strategies.

One strategy language learners use is to make up a word to describe something in hopes that the person they are talking to will supply the target-language word. Wells and Chang-Wells (1992) recorded a conversation in which Marilda employs this strategy by coining the word *windfinder* for "weather vane." A teacher we work with reported that one of her English language learners asked if she could use the "pencil fixer." The teacher realized her student needed to use the pencil sharpener.

Language learners may also paraphrase, using a word or phrase that they hope is equivalent to the word they lack. Marilda, for example, could have referred to the weather vane as "the thing that helps us see which way the wind is blowing" rather than coining the term *windfinder*. While in Venezuela,

---

Strategy
1. Coins a word
2. Uses a paraphrase
3. Uses a cognate
4. Uses literal translation
5. Overgeneralizes
6. Asks for the word
7. Uses an L1 structure
8. Avoids a word, structure, or topic
9. Engages in conversations and activities

FIGURE 4–2. *Communication strategies*

Yvonne often found herself paraphrasing when talking to the maid about different kitchen objects and foods. When looking for the missing spatula, she asked for "the white thing that has rubber on the end to clean out the bowl," and when describing a fruit drink as opposed to pure juice, she asked for "the juice that you add water and sugar to."

When Christa, a student teacher, interviewed Moua for her case study, the Hmong student explained that his dad "puts in wind makers . . . cold wind makers" for a living. After a bit of probing, Christa figured out that Moua's father installs air conditioners. By using paraphrase, Moua was able to get his message across. Another teacher wrote about how her student used paraphrase. A small group of students were reading a book about what some children gave their mother for her birthday. The text did not name the gift, but the last page contained a colorful picture of a flower vase. One of the boys in the reading group asked, "What is that thing that you use to put flowers into?" This paraphrase allowed the teacher to help him find the word he wanted.

If a person is studying a language related to his or her native language, a good strategy is to use cognates. English and Spanish, for example, have many words in common derived from Latin roots. For example, the Spanish noun *parque* is a cognate for *park* in English. A good practice for English language learners when they come across an unknown word during reading is to stop to think whether it looks or sounds like a word they know in their native language. This is especially helpful in science, since for many scientific terms, such as *ecology* or *photosynthesis*, the English and Spanish are spelled almost the same. However, cognates also exist in other content areas like social studies where words like *government* and *contract* are very similar in the two languages.

Using cognates is not 100 percent foolproof. Sometimes a language learner assumes that words are cognates when they are not. ESL student teachers we worked with in Venezuela would ask, "Did you use a sweater when you went to the mountains?" They assumed that the Spanish word *usar* meaning "to wear" was the same as the English word *use*. Relying on cognates is a good strategy, but false cognates like this one can trip students up.

A variation on the strategy of using cognates is to use a word from the speaker's native language, assuming it might be a cognate, but adding a target-language ending. For example, an English speaker learning Spanish might claim that someone was *pusheando* her. She uses the English word that she knows, *push*, and adds the common Spanish ending equivalent to the English *-ing* form to express *pushing*. We know of one student who lost her wallet in Spain. Another American tried to help by asking some Spanish-speaking friends if they had seen Kim's *walleto*. She put an appropriate suffix on what she hoped was a Spanish word.

A very common strategy that many second language learners use is to assume that the language they are learning is completely regular. They then overgeneralize a rule and apply it to a word that does not follow the pattern. This strategy is used by young children acquiring a first language as well as by second language learners. For example, English-speaking children at a certain stage will often use a past-tense form like *goed* because they assume that all verbs form the past tense the same way. English learners use the same strategy. Moua used the word *becomed* as he talked with Christa. He also used *golds* for the plural of *gold*, overgeneralizing the rule to form plurals. Even though the forms may not be correct, they enable English learners to communicate.

A more direct strategy many students develop is to simply ask, "How do you say . . . ?" In fact, this is a handy phrase that most teachers give their students early in a language course. This strategy works very well in a language class in which the teacher is bilingual. It doesn't work as well in a setting in which the other people don't speak both languages. If a Spanish speaker asks, "How do you say *pensar* in English?" I can only help if I can translate *pensar* from Spanish to English. The other problem with using this strategy too much is that it interrupts the flow of conversation more than the other strategies we have described.

A strategy similar to using a cognate is to use an expression from the first language to convey an idea in the target language. This creates a kind of literal translation. This strategy may include a change in syntax. For example, a Spanish speaker might say, "I have a book blue" following the Spanish syntax, "*Tengo un libro azul.*" In other cases, a Spanish speaker might report, "I have ten years," translating directly the Spanish, "*Tengo diez años.*" This strategy works well when the two languages are closely related. Even though the expression is not conventional English, the listener can usually understand the sentence.

In addition to these specific strategies, learners can use more general strategies in the process of acquiring a second language. One strategy, avoidance, is not productive, while the other, engagement, is the mark of a successful acquirer. When specific strategies fail, language learners may simply avoid using a word, structure, or topic. For example, they may avoid a topic because they don't feel competent to talk about it in the target language, or they may stop in the middle of an explanation or story because the linguistic demands are simply too great.

Cohen and Olshtain (1993) describe examples of avoidance during an experiment in which second language speakers had to make requests in different social situations. For example, one student intended to form the sentence "I don't have any excuse," but stopped before the last word because, as he reported, he wasn't sure how to pronounce the x sound. In another case, a student wanted to explain her late arrival at a meeting by stating that the bus had not come, but she couldn't think of how to say that in English, so she changed her message to "I missed the bus." It is not always easy to tell if language learners are using avoidance. David recalls several times in Venezuela when he thought about bringing up an idea in a conversation but then decided not to when he realized that he simply didn't have the vocabulary he needed to explain his ideas.

Avoidance is different from the other strategies we have described. All the others allow a language learner to participate in a conversation or complete a written assignment. Avoidance removes the learner from the communicative event. Teachers can help students develop productive strategies so that they don't avoid using the target language to communicate. However, teachers should be aware of students' levels of language proficiency and plan activities in which the students can use their new language successfully. Further, teachers should not force beginning students to produce too much language too early, since students may become frustrated if they are asked to produce at levels beyond their current competence.

Rather than avoidance, successful language learners practice engagement. They find ways to interact with speakers of the target language. Belinda, for example, was able to enter into conversations in Arabic by relying heavily on a few all-purpose phrases, accompanied by appropriate intonation. She depended on the words for *yes*, *okay*, *thank God*, and *If God wills it*. These words and phrases allowed Belinda to participate in a conversation. It is this conversational interaction that results in acquisition.

Fillmore (1991, as cited in Grosjean 2010) reports that the successful second language learners she studied relied on three strategies:

> (1) join a group and act as if you know what is going on, even if you don't; (2) give the impression, with a few well-chosen words, that you can speak the language; and, (3) count on your friends for help. (187)

By using these three general strategies, the good language learners were more fully involved in the activities of the class, and, in the process, they acquired the language of instruction.

Conclusion

We began this chapter by examining theories of how people learn. Building on the work of Vygotsky, researchers such as Brown and his colleagues and sociolinguists like Gee have argued that learning is a process of cognitive apprenticeship. Learning takes place as teachers provide the support students need to carry out tasks independently. By working within students' zones of proximal development and providing scaffolding, an effective teacher helps students to acquire the academic language needed to communicate.

Cazden described three roles of the teacher: direct instruction ,modeling, and scaffolding. The teacher's role changes during different phases of a lesson. Fisher and Frey (2009) have developed a structured approach for lessons in which the teacher first models and then scaffolds by working with students, having students work together, and finally, having students work independently.

We then turned to the question of what people acquire when they acquire a language. We began by distinguishing between competence and performance. Competence is our underlying ability—what we can do under the best circumstances. Performance is what we actually do. Teachers recognize that students' performance may not reflect their competence. Competence should not be confused with correctness. Native speakers of a language can produce and comprehend the language, but they may not use the conventional, standard form of the language. When we say that someone acquires competence in English, we are not claiming that the person can punctuate sentences correctly. Instead, competence is the ability to understand native speakers of a language and to express ideas in the language.

There are three functions of language and two kinds of competence. When we acquire a language, we acquire the ability to get and give basic information (the referential function), show how we feel about what we are saying (the expressive function), and indicate our relationship to the people with whom we are communicating (the integrative function). To perform these three functions of language, we need both grammatical and communicative competence. Grammatical competence allows us to put together words and sentences to talk about the world. With grammatical competence, we can carry out the referential function of language. Communicative competence is the knowledge of how to use language in social situations. It is knowing when to say what to whom. We need communicative competence to carry out the expressive and integrative functions of language.

In the process of acquiring a language, learners develop strategies to compensate for their lack of linguistic and communicative competence. We described several strategies learners use, such as paraphrase and the use of cognates. These strategies help students communicate even when their competence is limited. One strategy that may impede language acquisition is avoidance. Students may not try to use the new language if instruction is not properly scaffolded. If learning is a process of cognitive apprenticeship, then the key for teachers is to find ways to engage ELLs in classroom activities so that they can acquire the English they need for academic success.

KEY POINTS

→ It is crucial that teachers understand learning theories.

→ Vygotsky claims that people learn when instruction is targeted to their zones of proximal development.

→ Goodman and Goodman argue that teachers should support personal invention in the context of social conventions.

→ Vygotsky distinguishes between spontaneous concepts acquired through everyday experience and scientific concepts developed in school.

→ Brown and his colleagues explain that learning is a kind of cognitive apprenticeship.

→ Teachers can mediate learning through direct instruction, modeling, and scaffolding.

→ Fisher and Frey's model of teaching includes four stages: teacher modeling, guided instruction, collaborative work, and independent practice.

→ Chomsky distinguishes between language competence and language performance.

→ Three functions of language are referential, expressive, and integrative.

→ Two types of linguistic competence are communicative competence and grammatical competence.

→ Language learners use various strategies to communicate in a second language.

APPLICATIONS

1. Think back to a learning experience where someone helped you to succeed. How does your experience fit in with Vygotsky's idea of a Zone of Proximal Development? Share your experience with others.

2. Think of examples you have seen of students' oral or written language use in which students have changed their personal inventions to conform more closely to social conventions. Be prepared to share your examples.

3. Cazden describes three types of assistance teachers can provide: direct instruction, modeling, and scaffolding. Think of examples of each that you have done in your teaching or have seen done with second language learners. Share the examples in a small group.

4. Fisher and Frey describe a structured approach to lesson planning. Plan a lesson or series of lessons you could teach that follow this structured approach.

5. In this chapter we talked about the difference between grammatical performance and grammatical competence, and gave a couple of examples. Can you think of some examples in your own learning or in the learning of students you work with where performance did not reflect competence? Discuss this with a small group.

6. Grammatical competence is not the same as grammatical correctness. Explain the difference to a classmate.

7. Communicative competence includes the ability to use language that is appropriate for the social situation. Have you been in any situations where you used a second language in ways that you later discovered were not appropriate? Share these with classmates.

8. Second language learners develop a number of strategies like paraphrase, literal translation, and the use of cognates. Think back on your own learning of a second language. Did you use any of these strategies? Have you noticed your students using them? List some examples to share.

5

What Are the Principal Theories of First and Second Language Acquisition?

We have looked generally at how learning takes place, and we have also considered what people acquire when they acquire a language. In this chapter we turn to the important questions, "How do people acquire a first language?" "Do people acquire a second language in the same way they acquire a first language?" and "Are the same processes involved in acquiring a language as in learning other things, such as how to solve a math problem?" To answer these questions we will examine theories of first and second language acquisition. A knowledge of these theories enables teachers to make informed decisions about how best to teach second language learners.

First Language Acquisition

When children begin to develop language, they start by babbling. Soon they utter their first word. Not long after that, they begin to produce two-word sentences like "Tommy go" or "Drink milk." And it isn't long before these two-word expressions evolve into full sentences. Parents hang on to every sound infants make. They marvel at how quickly their child learns to understand and speak. But parents aren't really surprised at the development of language in their child, because most children accomplish this incredible feat. How do children acquire language? What theory can best account for children's capacity for language development?

Researchers have focused on different aspects of language acquisition. Developmental psychologists have concentrated more on the child and the child's capacity for learning. Since language is the means by which humans communicate with one another, sociologists and anthropologists have studied the environmental setting to determine how the social context influences language development. Linguists have focused on language itself because language provides a window on the minds of those acquiring language. Although studies in these areas overlap and provide complementary information, it is helpful to look at them separately. In the following sections, we consider research in first language acquisition that has been centered on each of the three areas: the child, the environment, and the language.

Insights from Developmental Psychology—Focus on the Child

According to Rice (2002), "any satisfactory model of language development must be compatible with how children learn; their ability to perceive, conceptualize, store, and access information; and their motivations" (21). The question of how language learning is related to developmental psychology, then, might be, "Do children learn language in the same way they learn other things, such as how to tie their shoes or how to build with blocks, or do children have a special cognitive capacity for language learning?"

Much of the research in child language acquisition has focused on the early language that children produce. Since researchers can't directly observe what goes on in the brain, and since they can't ask one- or two-year-olds to reflect on how they are learning language, scientists have to rely on children's linguistic output. Researchers who have observed children over time and have transcribed children's speech have identified certain stages in normal language development. This work is very intensive, and the studies are longitudinal.

Brown (1973), for example, studied three children over time. He found that their earliest utterances referred to things of interest to the children (Mommy, ball). He discovered that there were strong parallels between children's language development and the stages of cognitive development identified by Piaget (1955). For example, at an early stage infants focus on objects and actions, and their early speech reflects this in sentences like "Mail come" or "See baby."

Although early studies, such as Brown's, were of middle-class white children, subsequent studies have looked at different ethnic and economic groups across a number of languages. The findings have been consistent with the earlier studies, suggesting that children's language development is a universal phenomenon.

Studies of child language development show consistency across children and across languages. During the first year, children develop the physical capacity for speech and begin to babble. Pinker (1994) notes that children's babbling undergoes a change at about seven or eight months. At this age, children begin to produce syllables with a consonant-vowel structure, like "ba" or "dee." At about one year, children start to produce individual words. Researchers have found that nearly all children

produce the same types of words. According to Pinker, about half the words are for
hold items, animals, and peo-
nportant to children. Brown's

l utterances at this stage, the
in (1997) reports on the lan-
nine months said "kaku" for
it "I want a cracker" or "I have
t appears that language devel-
m single words to complete
1g is that children are discov-
early stage, the whole idea is
1dd more words to express the
en start with the most impor-
resent actions. Over time they
tions (red ball, walk fast). The
ds like prepositions, conjunc-
referred to as telegraphic. Like
y words to express a message.
around eighteen months. At
ances. In English, simple sen-
en at this point are producing
syntax. That is, they are show-
1 sentences. Pinker reports on
stand the difference between
nd "Cookie Monster is wash-
video screens. On one screen
kie Monster washes Big Bird.
! Big Bird is washing Cookie
esearchers then record where
-word utterances, at an age
tently look at the video corre-
oung children are developing
ween two sentences like "Big
is washing Big Bird," a differ-

o begins to grow very rapidly.
vth jumps to the new-word-
aintain through adolescence"
idly along with the ability to

recognize and then produce sentences that reflect an understanding of syntax supports the idea that the capacity for language development is either innate or the reflection of a special cognitive processing capacity for language. Children don't learn other things nearly as rapidly as they learn language, and this ability seems to apply to almost all children.

Petitto (2000) discovered that infants exposed to sign language go through the same stages as babies exposed to oral language. Using a sophisticated computer visual graphic analysis system, Petitto and colleagues are able to record information from babies exposed to sign language and get the same kinds of detailed results that linguists can get by recording oral language on a spectrograph machine. Petitto observes "In order for signed and spoken languages to be acquired in the same manner, human infants at birth may not be sensitive to sound or speech per se" (1). Instead, it is certain characteristics of natural language that humans are able to learn, not just one modality of language, in this case speech. As Petitto states,

> One novel implication here is that language modality, be it spoken or signed, is highly plastic and may be neurologically set after birth. Put another way, babies are born with a propensity to acquire language. Whether the language comes as speech, sign language, or some other way of having language, it does not appear to matter to the brain. (1)

Petitto's research shows that any form of input that has the properties of language can be used to develop a form of language needed for communication. (A current website that summarizes Petitto's work on this topic can be found at: www.utsc.utoronto.ca/~petitto/lab-info-HowChildrenAcquireLanguages.php.)

Studies in child language development have concentrated on the early stages. The problem that researchers face is that beyond the two-word stage, language growth is incredibly rapid and complex. As Pinker (1994) writes, "Between the late two and the mid threes, children's language blooms into fluent grammatical conversation so rapidly that it overwhelms the researchers who study it, and no one has worked out the exact sequence" (269). Children's sentences become longer and more complex as their language approximates adult speech.

Insights from Sociology, Anthropology, and Education— Focus on the Environment

Sociologists and anthropologists have studied communication generally. Language always occurs in a social context, and the meaning of many utterances depends on the context. For example, "Excuse me" could be an apology, but it could also be a means of getting someone's attention. The meaning depends on the situation. Studies in this area look at the effects of the social context on language development.

Many studies of child language development have focused on the interactions between mothers or other caregivers and children. Researchers have analyzed the speech of adults as they interact with children using a kind of language, a register, often referred to as "motherese." Interestingly, adults adjust their language and speak to children in ways that they would never speak to adults. What mother would say to a friend "Time to go bye-bye"? Children hear this kind of language from their caregivers, and yet, over time, they develop speech that corresponds to adult norms.

Researchers have also looked at how children growing up in different speech communities develop the ability to function in those communities. Communicative competence is the ability to use the language appropriate to a particular social context. Heath (1983), for example, looked at differences in the language development of children in two different communities in the same area of the Carolinas. Roadville was a white working-class community. For four generations, people from Roadville had worked in the textile mills. Residents of Trackton also worked in the textile mills. Trackton residents were blacks who had previously been farmers. Children from both Roadville and Trackton attend school with mainstream whites and blacks. Heath shows differences between the ways Roadville and Trackton children use language to communicate. For example, Roadville children are taught to always tell the truth. Trackton children are encouraged to be imaginative and entertaining in their speech. Roadville children are only to speak when spoken to. Trackton children learn how to break into a conversation and hold the floor by their creative use of language. Heath points out many differences between these two groups' ways with words and also shows the problems both groups have in interacting appropriately in the school setting, where a different norm for appropriate language use exists. Heath's study of children's language use in different social contexts is one of many anthropological studies that examine how the social context affects language acquisition.

Insights from Linguistics—Focus on the Language

By the time they reach school, most children have mastered many of the features of their language and can use it effortlessly to comprehend and produce sentences. As Chomsky, a leading American linguist, comments, "A normal child acquires this knowledge [of language] on relatively slight exposure and without specific training. He can then quite effortlessly make use of an intricate structure of specific rules and guiding principles to convey his thoughts and feelings to others, arousing in them novel ideas and subtle perceptions and judgments" (Chomsky 1975). Humans continue to learn vocabulary throughout their life, but the basic structures of phonology and syntax are acquired early.

Chomsky noted that young children acquire the basic rules of language without formal instruction and without extensive exposure to models of the language. Parents, for example, usually respond to the message, not to whether the young child speaks correctly. For example, if the child produces a sentence like "Daddy go store," the mother is apt to answer, "Yes, Daddy went to buy some milk." Often young children pronounce words incorrectly, saying, for example, "pasketti" rather than "spaghetti." Parents seldom try correcting the way young children pronounce words or put sentences together, and if they do, it doesn't seem to have much effect. Parents know that fairly quickly children's language will become like the language of others in the speech community. If children can learn the rules of a language with such limited evidence and little correction, Chomsky reasoned, this must be because they are innately predisposed to do so.

Chomsky's claim is that humans have a language acquisition device, a specialized area of the brain designed for language. According to Chomsky, humans do not simply have a special cognitive capacity for figuring out language. Rather, humans are born with the basic structures of all human languages already present in the brain. Chomsky calls this innate knowledge of language Universal Grammar. Children are not born with knowledge of English or Japanese or any other human language. Instead, they are born with knowledge of those things that are common to all human languages.

As a result, the task facing the child is not to learn how language works, starting from scratch. Instead, since children are born with an implicit knowledge of language in general, they have to figure out how the particular language (or languages) they hear functions. For example, all languages have something like prepositions, words that show relationships among things ("The book is *on* the table"). In languages like English these words that show position come in front of the noun, so they are called *pre*positions. In other languages, these words follow the noun, so in those languages, a child would encounter sentences with the pattern ("The book is the table *on*"). In such languages, these words are called *post*positions because they come after (*post*), not before (*pre*).

Children are born with the built-in knowledge that the language they hear will have a word to show position. What children must figure out is whether the position word precedes the noun or follows it. This is a much easier task than starting without any knowledge and having to learn that there are some words that show position and also having to learn where those words go in the sentence.

Not all of language is innate. Certainly, children have to learn individual words. Vocabulary can't be built in because it is not completely systematic and predictable. There is no regular connection between the sounds of words and their meanings.

Even though there are patterns within vocabulary that enable children (and adults) to develop vocabulary knowledge fairly rapidly, learning vocabulary is different from acquiring the syntax (the basic structure) of a language. However, Chomsky's claim is that most of language is innate. He and other linguists base this claim on certain facts: (1) most children acquire a first language rapidly and without formal instruction, (2) they do this with only a limited amount of evidence, and (3) they do it with only limited feedback.

Perhaps the strongest evidence for Chomsky's claim that language is innate comes from the fact that there are certain kinds of errors that children never make. If learning language were like learning anything else, researchers would expect learners to make many different kinds of errors in the process of testing possible hypotheses. A child learning to tie his or her shoes might twist the strings in a number of different ways. Each attempt could be viewed as a test of the child's hypothesis about the right way to knot the shoe.

Close examination of language learners' errors shows something quite different. When children produce errors, the errors often represent an overgeneralization of a rule. The child who says "bringed" is applying the usual rule for past tense to an irregular verb. Children do make mistakes like this. But there are many other mistakes a child could logically make in testing hypotheses about language. The fact that children never make certain kinds of errors suggests that a child is born with some innate knowledge of the rules of language, and the child's language attempts never violate those basic rules. The child may make mistakes with the parts of language that are unpredictable, like irregular verbs. But children don't make mistakes in some areas where mistakes would be expected.

Pinker (1994) provides several examples from a number of areas of child language acquisition. For example, children seem to figure out how to divide up speech into words even though there is no physical separation of words in the speech stream. The few errors children make are considered cute because they are so rare. Pinker gives several examples including one in which a child responds to the adult statement, "We are going to Miami," with "I don't want to go to your ami."

Pinker reports on a study by Stromswald, who analyzed sentences containing auxiliaries (words like *do, is, will*) from the speech of thirteen preschoolers. Stromswald found that children never made the kinds of errors that would be logical. For example, an English sentence like "He is happy" can be changed to a question by moving *is* to the front ("Is he happy?"). Given another sentence, such as "He ate dinner," a child might be tempted to follow the same pattern and form the logical question, "Ate he dinner?" And yet children never make errors like this. Linguists argue that this evidence suggests that humans are born with an innate ability to acquire languages that is different from our ability to learn other things.

Although linguists, based on their studies of language, claim that much of language is innate, there is still the question of how much of language is built in and how much must be learned. In addition, the way language develops depends on the social context. Humans have a strong drive to communicate with others, so it is not surprising that normally developing children acquire language. If learning takes place through a kind of cognitive apprenticeship, as researchers such as Brown and his colleagues (1989) argue, then language learning can be seen as an instance of apprenticeship into social communities. Not all humans are motivated to join groups that specialize in mathematics or music, but nearly all humans are strongly motivated to join the group of people who speak the language that surrounds them. At the same time, only certain people seem to have a kind of innate ability to solve math problems or play music, but all humans seem to have an innate ability to learn languages.

Researchers from various fields continue to study first language acquisition. Investigations in child psychology, anthropology, and linguistics will continue to contribute to our understanding of how humans acquire language. Nevertheless, it is clear that first language acquisition is an almost universal phenomenon. What about second language acquisition?

Second Language Acquisition

Although nearly all humans develop a first language, fewer develop a second language. This raises the question of whether second language acquisition is different in some fundamental way from first language acquisition. For example, some researchers have argued that a first language is acquired, that is, it is picked up naturally without instruction, but second languages must be learned in the same way we learn history or biology.

For people living in the United States monolingualism is the norm, and bilingual people are often considered exceptional. Yet, this is not the case in most of the world. Grosjean (2010) defines bilinguals as "those who use two or more languages (or dialects) in their everyday lives" (4). As Baker (2006) tells us, "Children are born ready to become bilinguals, trilinguals, multilinguals" (116).

While in some countries, such as the United States, speakers of different languages are not in daily contact (although that is rapidly changing), in other countries it is the norm. For example, there are some 516 languages spoken in Nigeria, 427 in India, and 275 in Australia. Estimating the number of bilingual people in the world is difficult and imprecise. However, Grosjean cites data from studies in Europe showing that over half the people speak at least two languages. He estimates that about 35 percent of Canadians are bilingual. What about the United States? According to census data, about 17 percent speak at least two languages, and the number of bilinguals increases each year.

The data on the number of bilinguals in the world suggest strongly that second (and third) languages can be acquired. Baker (2006) distinguishes between two types of childhood bilingualism. When a child acquires two languages at the same time from birth, this is referred to as simultaneous childhood bilingualism or infant bilingualism. A more common scenario is sequential bilingualism, when children learn one language at home and then another language in preschool or elementary school. Studies of individual bilinguals shows that the process of second language acquisition is like first language acquisition. The keys to acquiring a second language are regular contact with people who speak other languages and a need to communicate with them. When those conditions are met, people acquire additional languages.

This kind of natural language acquisition does not usually happen, unfortunately, in most foreign language classes. Students studying another language in a foreign language class are not in regular contact with native speakers of the target language except for their teacher, and they do not have a need to communicate in that language other than to pass the class. That is why in many classes foreign languages are learned the same way other school subjects are learned rather than being acquired the way languages are naturally acquired.

Research in Second Language Acquisition (SLA)

Like first language acquisition, second language acquisition has been studied extensively by scientists from different fields. For example, psycholinguists have looked for insights into SLA from both linguistics and psychology. They examine the system of language the learner is developing. This system is referred to as the learner's interlanguage. An interlanguage is the version of English an English language learner speaks. It is different from the English of a native speaker, and yet it has consistent rules and a logic of its own. According to Seliger (1988), some questions that psycholinguists have investigated are:

1. How does the learner develop his or her second language system? What are thought to be the processes involved?

2.. What role does previous knowledge, such as the first language, play in second language acquisition?

3. What psychological characteristics contribute to successful second language acquisition? Are there good learners and bad learners? (20)

Neurolinguists are concerned with how language is represented in the brain. Advances in technology have increased our understanding of how the brain processes language. These are the kinds of questions that neurolinguists attempt to answer:

1. Where in the brain are first and second languages located?

2. What are the ways that languages with different characteristics are represented in the brain?

3. Is there a critical period for second language acquisition?

Sociolinguists consider the influences of social and cultural factors on language development. Beebe (1987) lists some of the major questions that sociolinguists attempt to answer:

1. Is interlanguage variation systematic or random and, if systematic, according to what social variables does it vary?

2. Does the learner's interlanguage change over time?

3. What is the role of sociolinguistic transfer in L2 development?

4. What is the nature of L2 communicative competence?

5. What is the "cause" of variation in interlanguage? (3–4)

All three areas of research—psycholinguistics, neurolinguistics, and socio-linguistics—have contributed to the development of current theories of second language acquisition.

Theory and Research

Research in SLA can contribute to a theory of second language acquisition. Examples of research would be a study of the natural order of acquisition of morphemes or a study of the relationship between intelligence and language aptitude. A theoretical researcher, for example, might develop a theory that the effects of reading in the second language will be reflected in students' second language writing. The researcher might then look at the writing of second language learners for evidence of the effects of reading.

Research always supports credible theories. However, attempts to apply research directly to practice have not been productive. In their research into the acquisition of morphemes by second language students, Dulay and Burt (1974) found that certain morphemes were acquired earlier than others. Morphemes are the smallest parts of words that carry meaning. So, for example, in a word like *unties* there are three morphemes: the prefix *un*, the base *tie*, and the suffix *s*. These researchers have found that certain kinds of morphemes appear before other morphemes in the speech of English learners. Krashen (1985) maintains that research findings such as these cannot be directly applied to practice. As he himself says, "I made this error several years ago when I suggested that the natural order of acquisition become the new grammatical syllabus" (47). He realized that he could not use the research to design a grammar textbook. Instead, the research helped him develop a theory of SLA that downplays the direct teaching of grammar.

Krashen believes that SLA theory acts to mediate between research and practice. Teachers can benefit from the knowledge they gain in their daily practice. However, they must always consider theory as they reflect on their practice. As Krashen asserts, "Methodologists are missing a rich source of information . . . if they neglect theory" (48), and "without theory, there is no way to distinguish effective teaching procedures from ritual, no way to determine which aspects of a method are and are not helpful" (52). A knowledge of SLA theory, then, allows a teacher to reflect on and to refine day-to-day practice. With that view in mind, we describe two important theories of second language acquisition.

Krashen's Monitor Model

Krashen's monitor model of second language acquisition is based on the theoretical linguistic research of Noam Chomsky. Chomsky's claims apply to children acquiring their first language. Krashen holds that concepts such as Universal Grammar and the Language Acquisition Device apply equally well to children or adults acquiring a second language. The process is the same for both first and second language acquisition.

Krashen's (1982) theory of SLA, the Monitor Model, has had a great impact on classroom practice. Even though Krashen's ideas have been debated and sometimes discounted by other researchers, they have been widely accepted by practitioners because they are understandable and because teachers can see positive results when they apply Krashen's ideas in the classroom. Krashen's Monitor Model consists of five interrelated hypotheses: (1) the acquisition/learning hypothesis, (2) the natural order hypothesis, (3) the monitor hypothesis, (4) the input hypothesis, and (5) the affective filter hypothesis. In the following sections, we explain each hypothesis and then provide examples and an analysis.

The Acquisition/Learning Hypothesis

Krashen begins by making an important distinction between two ways of getting a new language. The first of these is acquisition. According to Krashen we acquire a new language subconsciously as we receive messages we understand. For example, if we are living in a foreign country and go to the store to buy food, we may acquire new vocabulary or syntactic structures in the process of trying to understand what the clerk is saying. We are not focused on the language. Rather, we are using the language for real purposes, and acquisition occurs naturally as we attempt to conduct our business. Acquisition can also occur in classrooms in which teachers engage students in authentic communicative experiences. Krashen (2004a) has shown that we can acquire language as we read. In fact, since people are able to read more rapidly than they speak, written language is a better source for acquisition than oral language.

Krashen contrasts acquisition with learning. Learning is a conscious process in which we focus on various aspects of the language itself. It is what generally occurs in classrooms when teachers divide language up into chunks, present one chunk at a time, and provide students with feedback to indicate how well they have mastered the various aspects of language that have been taught. A teacher might present a lesson on regular verbs in the present tense, for example, giving attention to the s that is added to third-person forms in sentences such as "He walks." It is this structure that students are expected to learn. Learning is associated with classroom instruction and is usually tested. It is less common in the world beyond the classroom.

Although Krashen's theory focuses on individual psychological factors involved in second language acquisition, Gee (1992) offers a definition of acquisition that expands on Krashen's by including a social component:

> Acquisition is a process of acquiring something subconsciously by exposure to models, a process of trial and error, and practice within social groups, without formal teaching. It happens in natural settings that are meaningful and functional in the sense that acquirers know that they need to acquire the thing they are exposed to in order to function and that they in fact want to so function. (113)

This expanded definition of acquisition brings an important social element into the distinction between acquisition and learning. Acquisition occurs in social contexts as people attempt to communicate with others.

It appears that acquisition and learning lead to different kinds of abilities. As Gee (1992) puts it: "We are better at performing what we acquire, but we consciously know more about what we have learned" (114). In the case of second languages, acquisition allows us to speak and understand, read and write the language. Learning allows us to talk about (or pass exams on) the language. Many adults who have studied a foreign language in high school and/or college and received high grades never developed the ability to speak or understand the language they studied. Their performance on grammar and vocabulary tests determined their grades.

Yvonne's experiences studying French in college certainly proved this. She took four years of French, could translate French into English quite well, and knew French grammar. Her grades were always very high in the courses she took. However, her ability to communicate in French is severely limited. Recently, when Yvonne and David were in Costa Rica staying at a remote inn, the only other guests were from Paris. Although Yvonne had studied French extensively, she struggled to understand simple conversation and communicate basic ideas.

The difference between the effects of acquisition and learning is most evident in the case of second or foreign language learning. As Gee (1988) comments, "It appears that some substantive degree of incidental learning [acquisition] must take place before intentional learning is very efficacious" (217). Yvonne's foreign language French classes had not helped her acquire French because those classes focused on learning the grammar and vocabulary. Yvonne knew French grammar but could not converse with French speakers. Once someone has acquired a language, they may then want to learn more about the language, the grammar and vocabulary, to refine their knowledge.

A good example of the acquisition/learning distinction comes from the experiences of José Luis, Guillermo, and Patricia, who were discussed in Chapter 1. The teens studied English in El Salvador. This was a case of learning the rules and structures of the language. When they came to the United States, they did know some English, but it was very limited. In their new home in Tucson they were immersed in English and began to acquire the language as they used it daily.

Krashen argues that children acquire (they don't learn) their first language(s) as they use language to communicate and to make sense of the world. Krashen claims that both children and adults have the capacity to acquire additional languages because they possess a language acquisition device (LAD). He claims that acquisition accounts for almost all of our language development and that learning plays a minimal role. While second language classrooms should be places for acquisition, more often second and foreign language teachers focus on learning.

When teaching second language learners, Yvonne was constantly struggling with the difference between acquisition and learning, though she had not studied Krashen's theory and did not even know about it until graduate school. She was worried that students needed to learn the grammar, because that is how she had been taught language. However, she saw that students were more involved and more successful when they talked and read about things that were related to their lives. Discussions of music and television programs engaged students and got them involved in using language for authentic purposes, and they acquired language as they used it. Yet, the textbooks available for teaching all seemed to emphasize direct or indirect teaching of grammar and vocabulary. Yvonne had to depart from traditional approaches to change her classroom from a place for learning to a setting for acquisition.

EXAMPLE OF ACQUISITION/LEARNING—STAN

Stan studied three years of German in high school and two more years in college. After college he joined the army and was sent to Germany. He found that he could read signs and some newspaper articles, but he had a great deal of trouble in trying to communicate with native Germans. After he was discharged, he went to work for a company that assigned him to head a branch located in Mexico City. On arrival, he took a crash course in Spanish. At the same time, he had to try to communicate with his fellow workers, entertain important Mexican businessmen, and use Spanish for daily life transactions such as shopping. After only six months, Stan's spoken Spanish was much better than his German had ever been. What might account for this?

ANALYSIS

Stan learned German in school, but this learned knowledge was not very helpful to him in Germany. On the other hand, he both learned and acquired Spanish in the course of his studies and his daily interactions in Mexico. As a result, his ability to understand and speak Spanish was much better than his German proficiency.

EXAMPLE OF ACQUISITION/LEARNING—JOHN

John studied four years of high school Spanish. Despite lots of drill and practice with dialogues and exercises with grammar, he could not really understand the Spanish of Hispanics in his community. In college he met María and fell in love. Her family, who felt that maintaining their native language was very important, spoke only Spanish at home. John found that within a short period of time, he was able to understand the conversations at family get-togethers and even contribute at times in Spanish. What accounts for his rapid increase in Spanish proficiency?

ANALYSIS

This is another contrast between acquisition and learning. John had learned some Spanish in school, but with María and her family he was in an ideal situation for acquisition in a natural setting. Family discussions were on topics of interest to John, or the conversations were rich in context. For example, María and her mother would discuss a recipe while cooking, or John and his in-laws would watch a sports event on the Spanish television station. The Spanish input from María's family was comprehensible. As a result, John's proficiency improved rapidly.

The Natural Order Hypothesis

Krashen's second hypothesis is that language is acquired in a natural order. Some aspects of a language are picked up earlier than others. For example, the plural *s* morpheme added to a word like *girl* to form *girls* comes earlier than the third-person *s* added to the word *walk* in "He walks." Most parents are aware that phonemes like /p/ or /m/ are acquired earlier than others, like /r/. That's why English-speaking parents are called *papa* or *mama* by babies, not *roro*. In the area of syntax, statements generally precede questions. Children do not acquire the structure of questions early, so they often use statement structures with rising intonation such as "I go store, too?" or "You like teddy?" to pose questions. Krashen points out that all learners of a particular language, such as English, seem to acquire the language in the same order no matter what their first language may be.

Krashen bases this hypothesis on studies carried out by Dulay and Burt (1974). These researchers collected samples of speech from Chinese- and Spanish-speaking students learning English. They found that both groups acquired English morphemes in about the same order. They found, for example, that students acquired the plural *s* form fairly early, but the third-person *s* of "He walks" came much later. These early studies were subsequently confirmed by the work of a number of other researchers.

The natural order applies to language that is acquired, not language that is learned. In fact, students may be asked to learn aspects of language before they are ready to acquire them. The result may be good performance of the items on a test but inability to use the same items in a natural setting. In these cases, students' performance may exceed their competence.

In teaching Spanish, Yvonne found that the expression for *like* in Spanish was a late-acquired item. In Spanish, "I like" is *Me gusta* (It is pleasing to me). If the things I like are plural, I say *Me gustan* (They are pleasing to me). This structure caused no end of confusion for Yvonne's beginning students. She worked with them diligently, explaining how the structure worked and giving examples. Even those who did well on the department test that covered the structure, however, had not acquired the structure. When Yvonne asked her students to evaluate the course in their daily diary at the end of the semester, almost all the students incorrectly wrote *Yo gusto* for "I like." They knew that *yo* meant "I" and knew the verb *gustar* was "to like." So they simply conjugated the verb as a regular verb despite the emphasis on learning the expression *Me gusta*.

Most books used in language courses present grammar in a certain order, but since linguists have only a rudimentary understanding of the complete order of acquisition of phonemes, morphemes, syntax, and so on, no book can be written that can claim to mirror the natural order. Even if such a book were written, students would invariably be at different stages, and in a class of thirty students, no grammar lesson would be appropriate for everyone. Krashen, however, points out that if a teacher focuses on acquisition activities, rather than trying to get students to learn certain grammatical points, all students will acquire language in a natural order. The rate of acquisition of morphemes and structures will differ for different students, but the order will be the same.

EXAMPLE OF NATURAL ORDER—MRS. GÓMEZ

Mrs. Gómez is a bilingual second-grade teacher. She does lots of reading and writing with her students in Spanish. During ESL time, she believes that students need large doses of drill and practice to master English. She teaches her students how to use the *-ing* form of the verb with the auxiliary form of *be*. So the students practice "We are going to the library" and "I am studying math." What she cannot understand is that when her students ask her questions or tell her things in English informally, they consistently leave the *be* auxiliary out of the constructions: "Teacher, we going to the park"; "Look teacher, I swinging high!" What might be the reason for this?

ANALYSIS

Several different factors are at work here. Mrs. Gómez seems to feel that while first languages are acquired, second languages must be learned. As a result, she drills her students on parts of the language during ESL time. Mrs. Gómez doesn't recognize the difference between learning and acquisition, and may not be aware of the natural order of acquisition. Natural order studies show that verbs with *-ing* (*going*) come in early, but the auxiliary verb comes later, so students will first say "I going" and later add the *am*. She drills her students on the progressive forms with a *be* verb, but since they haven't acquired the *be* auxiliary yet, they don't use the progressive correctly in natural situations.

The Monitor Hypothesis

The monitor hypothesis helps explain the different functions that acquisition and learning play. Acquisition results in the phonology, vocabulary, and syntax we can draw on to produce utterances in a new language. Without acquisition, we could not produce anything. Learning, on the other hand, provides us with rules we can use to monitor our output as we speak or write. The monitor is like an editor, checking what we produce. The monitor can operate when we have time, when we focus on grammatical form, and when we know the rules.

Yvonne applied her monitor during her oral exams for her doctorate. Her committee of five had asked her several questions in English about language acquisition and bilingual education that she had answered fairly comfortably. Then, one of her committee members asked a question in Spanish, a clear suggestion that Yvonne should also answer in Spanish. Her most vivid memory of the incident was how much she was checking to be sure her Spanish was correct, how much she was applying her monitor. In particular, she was careful to watch for the correct use of the subjunctive mood, verb endings, and adjective agreement, all aspects of Spanish that she had learned rather than acquired. In this situation, Yvonne was focusing on form. She did not want members of her doctoral committee to judge her Spanish as substandard. It seemed especially important in this setting to speak "proper" Spanish. Of course, the content of what she actually said was secondary, and to this day she cannot even remember what the question was.

The problem with using the monitor during speaking is that one must sacrifice meaning for accuracy. A person can't concentrate on the form and the meaning at the same time. On the other hand, the monitor is useful in the editing stage of writing. At that point, a writer has time to focus on form, rather than meaning. In contrast, at the rough draft stage, writers who slow down and think about correct form may forget what they were going to write. Monitoring is helpful if the monitor is not over- or underused, but even then, the monitor can only check the output.

The teens from El Salvador differed in their use of the monitor. Guillermo in particular focused on communication. He seldom monitored his output and was at times difficult to understand. Nevertheless, he was enthusiastic and personable and used a number of strategies (gestures, tone of voice, and so on) to be sure his listener understood. Guillermo underused his monitor even though he had studied English grammar and knew many of the rules.

His brother, José Luis, on the other hand, was quiet and shy. He did not like to speak English unless he could produce language that was grammatically correct. He too knew the rules, and he applied them carefully. His focus on form kept him from expressing his ideas freely. He overused the monitor.

Patricia seemed less self-conscious than José Luis. She generally concentrated on what she wanted to say rather than how she would say it. At the same time, she did check her output to be sure she was producing understandable English. She also knew the rules and seemed to have found an optimal use of the monitor.

Teachers can help students become optimal monitor users. It does help to know the rules, but it's essential to know when to apply them and when to concentrate more on the meaning of a message. Sometimes teachers hope that by correcting their students' errors, they will increase students' proficiency. However, Krashen (1985) claims that while error correction in learning situations allows students to modify their knowledge of learned rules, it has no effect on their acquired language. "According to the theory, the practice of error correction affects learning, not acquisition. When our errors are corrected, we rethink and adjust our conscious rules" (8). Since the monitor can only be accessed under certain conditions, error correction has limited value. Learning, according to Krashen, has no effect on basic language competence.

EXAMPLE OF THE MONITOR—MISS SMITH

Miss Smith studied Spanish extensively in high school and college and spent a summer in Guadalajara, Mexico, where she lived with a Mexican family and spoke Spanish every day. After graduation, her company sent her to work in Spain. During her first meeting with local Spanish company representatives, she was conversing fluently in Spanish until she began to use an irregular verb in the subjunctive and couldn't remember the correct verb form. As she tried to decide what form to use, she paused and lost her train of thought. For the rest of the meeting her Spanish was halting and stilted. What could have accounted for her performance?

ANALYSIS

Miss Smith has acquired a good deal of Spanish. However, in a formal setting she begins to overuse her monitor. She tries to remember and apply the rules for the subjunctive and carry on a conversation at the same time. As a result, her rate of speech slows down. She can't focus on what she is saying and how to say it at the same time. She is overusing her monitor to the point that she can no longer communicate effectively.

EXAMPLE OF THE MONITOR—MARY

When Mary was in the first and second grade, she lived in Mexico City and attended a bilingual school where she and her sister were the only *gringas*. While there, she learned to speak Spanish fluently. After returning to the United States, she attended a bilingual school. She also made friends with some children recently arrived from El Salvador. When Mary conversed with her Salvadoran friends, her Spanish was fluent, but when she had to take a Spanish course in high school several years later, she was frustrated at times by the rules of grammar and accents. What might be causing Mary's frustration?

ANALYSIS

Mary has acquired Spanish, but the school puts an emphasis on rules that must be learned. Even though Mary can understand and speak Spanish, she has not studied the rules needed for formal written Spanish, so she does not have the tools to monitor her speech and writing.

The Input Hypothesis

The key to Krashen's theory of language acquisition is the input hypothesis. He claims that people acquire language in only one way—when they receive oral or written messages they understand. Krashen asserts that these messages provide comprehensible input. In order for acquisition to take place, learners must receive input that is slightly beyond their current ability level. Krashen calls this i + 1 (input plus one). If the input contains no structures beyond current competence (i + 0), no acquisition takes place. There is nothing new to pick up. On the other hand, if the input is too far beyond a person's current competence (i + 10), it becomes incomprehensible noise, and again no acquisition can take place.

According to Krashen, comprehensible input is the source of all acquired language. Students do not have to produce language in order to acquire it. Only input leads to acquisition, and so output—speaking or writing—does not contribute to acquisition, although it may result in cognitive development. As Krashen notes, output can help people learn academic content, or, as he puts it, output can make you smarter. In addition, through output, a person can engage others in conversation with the result that the person receives more input. Thus, output can lead to comprehensible input needed for acquisition.

Since comprehensible input is the key to language acquisition, the teacher's job is to find ways to make academic content comprehensible. This is why the theory is so important for teachers. Most current language methods for teaching a second language are designed to help teachers develop techniques for turning academic content matter into comprehensible input (Freeman and Freeman 1998, 2009).

Simplified Input

Studies by Hatch (1983) suggest that the kind of input that leads to language development is simplified input. According to Hatch, simplified input includes caregiver talk, teacher talk, and talk to nonnative speakers. Hatch identified some characteristics of simplified talk. The phonology includes fewer reduced vowels and contractions, and the rate of speech is slower, with longer pauses. The vocabulary is characterized by more high-frequency items, fewer idioms, and less slang. There are fewer pronouns, and speakers often use gestures and pictures. At the level of syntax, sentences are shorter, with more repetitions and restatements. Discourse includes more requests for clarification and fewer interruptions.

During our year in Venezuela, one thing we noticed in early interactions with colleagues was that they often tried to provide us with simplified input. When speaking directly to us in a meeting, for example, they obviously slowed their speech. In fact, if someone in the meeting used slang, the meeting would usually stop and everyone would try to explain the expression to us. Our landlord spoke no English at all and was nervous about talking to us. In our first meeting, she spoke slowly and used lots of gestures in an effort to make herself understood. She used all the techniques of an excellent language teacher, even though she is a lawyer by profession.

One problem with claiming that simplified input leads to acquisition is that simplified input may not contain new language structures or items. Krashen claims that we acquire language when we receive input that contains language *slightly beyond* our current level of competence.

A second problem with simplified input is that it may result in unnatural language with short sentences and short, everyday words. Language that is not natural is more difficult to acquire because it doesn't follow predictable language patterns. In addition, texts with short sentences and words do not prepare students for the academic language in school textbooks (Goodman and Freeman 1993).

EXAMPLE OF INPUT—MR. ROBERTS

The students in Mr. Roberts' first-year Spanish class do well in his structured program, although they seem bored at times. Mr. Roberts is careful to introduce only one new structure at a time and drill that structure until the students have mastered it. Although the students are making satisfactory progress, the class seems to lack animation, so to liven things up Mr. Roberts decides to bring in a guest speaker to talk about dating customs among Mexican teenagers. Despite the fact that Mr. Roberts warned his guest to limit his vocabulary and grammatical structures, the speaker gets carried away with his subject and uses the full range of Spanish. Surprisingly, although the students don't understand everything, they seem to be following most of the lecture. In addition, for the first time all year, they seem interested. What is going on here?

ANALYSIS

The speaker is using structures slightly beyond the students' current level of comprehension. Some of the input is comprehensible because of the students' background knowledge of dating. In addition, the students are interested in the topic and make an effort to understand it. As a result, this input has probably contributed to their Spanish acquisition. (See also "The Affective Filter Hypothesis," on the next page.)

EXAMPLE OF INPUT—JOSÉ

José is in the fifth grade and doing very well this year, despite the fact that his fourth-grade teacher, Mrs. Lynch, recommended him for special education. In Mrs. Lynch's class, students studied grammar rules and practiced accurate oral reading of basal reader selections during language arts. Mrs. Lynch contended that José was in the lowest reading group, had done poorly on standardized tests, and could not do the worksheets assigned to him. José's parents asked that he be given another chance. In fifth grade his teacher had students do lots of reading and writing and work on projects in groups. The children did not use the basal readers or worksheets but instead studied literature using drama, art, and music. In only one semester, José's English had improved noticeably, and he was enthusiastically reading and writing in English. When Mrs. Lynch insisted that he be tested with the basal reader tests, José's results showed a two-year gain despite the fact that he had not been working with worksheets or basal readers. What might be the reason for this dramatic progress?

ANALYSIS

Mrs. Lynch focused on grammar and accurate decoding of texts. This approach did not provide José with comprehensible input. The kinds of activities his new teacher uses make the English input comprehensible for José. Because of this, José has acquired a great deal of English in a short time, and this acquired language has increased his overall proficiency, as shown on the reading tests.

The Affective Filter Hypothesis

The affective filter hypothesis explains the role of affective factors in the process of language acquisition. Even if a teacher provides comprehensible input, acquisition may not take place. Affective factors such as anxiety or boredom may serve as a filter that blocks input. When the filter is up, input can't reach those parts of the brain (the LAD) where acquisition occurs. Many language learners realize that the reason they have trouble is because they are nervous or embarrassed and simply "can't concentrate." Lack of desire to learn can also "clog" the affective filter.

Yvonne's intern experience teaching high school Spanish to get her credential provides an example of the affective filter. Her class consisted of twenty-four boys, all on the junior varsity football team, and three girls. Most of the students had signed up for the "new intern" teacher mainly because they had failed Spanish 1 the year before. Positive affective factors such as high interest or motivation can help keep the filter down, but those students had neither. Yvonne's major job was to try to lower the students' filter by getting them interested and convincing them that they wanted to learn Spanish.

Since Krashen's theory of language acquisition is based on input, in his discussion of the affective filter he only refers to language that is coming in, not to language the person is attempting to produce. In other words, the affective filter can prevent a person from getting more comprehensible input.

This hypothesis does not apply to a person's output, only to the ability to acquire language. At times, students who have developed high levels of language proficiency may not perform up to their capacity. As we have explained, there are times when students are nervous, bored, or unmotivated, and their performance does not match their competence. This was the case for Leny, whom we described in Chapter 4. She became nervous trying to speak Spanish in the beauty parlor, and her performance did not reflect her competence. Students may not perform well in a new language if they overuse their monitor. However, when Krashen refers to an affective filter, he is referring only to affective factors that block input.

EXAMPLE OF AFFECTIVE FILTER—DAVID

David accepted a teaching job in Colombia, South America, even though he didn't speak any Spanish. Fortunately, his wife spoke good Spanish. David and his wife agreed that she would translate for the two of them and also teach him the language when they got there. For the first few months of their stay, the couple lived with a Colombian family that did not speak any English. During meals David was frustrated because he could understand little and say nothing. He started to resent being in this new culture. Besides, he was embarrassed by his inability to speak. After a few weeks he even refused to try to speak Spanish and discontinued the lessons with his wife. Despite being immersed in Spanish, he didn't seem to be learning anything. What might have been the reason for this?

ANALYSIS

Although David received comprehensible input, the input didn't contribute to acquisition because David's affective filter was high. He was suffering from culture shock, and he was frustrated at not being able to communicate and having to depend on his wife. The raised affective filter blocked the input from activating the LAD, and the result was a lack of language acquisition.

Summary

As these scenarios show, Krashen's theory helps explain a number of common situations in which second language learners find themselves. The five interrelated hypotheses constitute Krashen's Monitor Model of SLA. Krashen (1985) sums up his theory by stating, "We acquire when we obtain comprehensible input in a low-anxiety situation, when we are presented with interesting messages, and when we understand these messages" (10).

Kristene, a graduate student and a bilingual teacher, wrote the following reflection on her own acquisition of Spanish as a second language after studying Krashen's theory:

Perhaps my success in Spanish language classes in high school came about because my first exposure to Spanish was through communicative practice in real situations as Krashen suggests. I lived in Spain at the age of ten for six months. My parents hired a tutor who spoke only Spanish. She took us to the beach, to town on the bus, shopping at la plaza, to church, to the movies, to the park, to buy bread at the bread shop. (I can still remember the fabulous aroma and taste of freshly baked Spanish bread some thirty years later!) The input was comprehensible!

Krashen would take this example from Kristene to support his theory. Kristene acquired Spanish in a natural order because she was in a setting in which the input was comprehensible and her affective filter was low. Later, in high school, she drew on her acquired knowledge of Spanish. The result is that Kristene has developed a high level of proficiency in Spanish.

Schumann's Acculturation Model

A second theory of SLA comes from the sociolinguistic research of Schumann (1978), who claims that acquiring a new language is part of a more general process of acculturation. For Schumann, language acquisition can best be understood by looking at what happens when people from one cultural group are transplanted into a new setting.

The Hmong people provide a good example of how acquiring a new language is part of a more general process of acculturation. The Hmong who came to the United States from Southeast Asia moved not only across a great physical distance but across time. Many of the Hmong people who moved to the Central Valley of California chose to settle there because a Hmong leader told them that in Fresno there was lots of farming. In Laos, where they were part of a nomadic, agrarian society, they used only hand tools. They practiced slash-and-burn agriculture. Hmong farmers who moved to California had to learn new words and new concepts. In California, they were confronted with the idea of land ownership. In addition, farming in a highly technological society like the United States was very different. Here, farmers used scientific research as well as a variety of machines and chemicals to help them produce their crops. As a result the Hmong newcomers had to rethink the whole idea of farming.

Most of the Hmong adults who arrived from Laos did not acquire English. They continued to speak Hmong and follow Hmong customs, even after many years in the United States. Schumann would claim that their failure to acquire English could be explained by the fact that they did not acculturate to the new society.

In his model, Schumann focuses on sociocultural factors that act on the language learner. He bases his theory on studies of individuals acquiring a second language. He does not discuss any internal cognitive processing that might take place. Much of the theory can be understood by examining Schumann's analysis of one learner, Alberto.

Alberto, an adult from Costa Rica, acquired English without formal instruction. However, Alberto's English proficiency was much lower than might have been expected, and it improved little over the ten months Schumann studied him. Even though he was intelligent and interacted regularly with native speakers of English, Alberto's own English remained limited. Schumann's analysis was that Alberto's social and psychological distance from speakers of the target language accounted for his lack of proficiency. As Brown (1980) explains, "Schumann's hypothesis is that the greater the social distance between two cultures, the greater the difficulty the learner will have in learning the second language, and conversely, the smaller the social distance (the greater the social solidarity between the two cultures), the better will be the language learning situation" (133).

According to Schumann, eight factors influence social distance:

1. *Social dominance*. Social dominance refers to the power relationships between two groups. Social distance is greatest when one group dominates the other. Social distance diminishes if the two groups have roughly equal power in society.

2. *Integration pattern*. Social distance is greatest when there is a pattern of limited integration between the two cultures, and it decreases when there is greater integration.

3. *Enclosure*. Social distance is increased when the learner group is self-sufficient and doesn't need to interact with members of the target culture in daily activities. Social distance decreases when enclosure is lower.

4. *Cohesiveness*. Social distance is increased when the learner group is tight-knit, and social distance is reduced when the learner group is less united.

5. *Size*. When the learner group is big, there is more apt to be social distance from the target culture. A small learner group experiences less social distance.

6. *Cultural congruence*. Social distance is increased when the two groups are very different culturally, and the distance decreases when the two groups are more similar.

7. *Attitude*. Social distance is increased when the learner group has a negative attitude toward members of the target-language culture, and it is decreased when the attitude is positive.

8. *Intended length of residence*. Social distance is greatest when members of the group only intend to stay in the country a short time. Social distance decreases when they intend to stay in the country for a long time.

In almost every case, Alberto fell into a category that predicted limited acquisition. For example, in the area of social dominance, Alberto, who worked in a factory, was in a subordinate social group to those English speakers with whom he was in contact. This social distance limited the integration pattern. Factory workers like Alberto did not interact regularly with the native English speakers who managed the factory. Alberto's group had what Schumann refers to as high enclosure. They had their own churches and publications, including newspapers, and this kept them apart from the mainstream culture. He was part of a fairly large, cohesive group of Latin American immigrants, and this limited his contact with English speakers as well. His culture differed from that of the target culture in some respects, and attitudes between the groups were either neutral or negative. In addition, Alberto intended to stay in the United States only a short time, so he had little interest in becoming proficient in English.

In addition to social distance, which describes relationships among social groups, Schumann identifies a second factor that can be used to predict the degree of language acquisition: psychological distance. In situations in which social distance neither strongly promotes nor inhibits language acquisition, psychological distance may play a crucial role. There are three main factors that determine the psychological distance a second language learner has from the target language and culture.

1. *Motivation.* Those with a high motivation to learn the language are more likely to learn the language than those with low motivation.

2. *Attitude.* Those with a positive attitude toward the language and culture are more likely to learn the language than those who hold a negative attitude.

3. *Culture shock.* When a newcomer experiences culture shock, he experiences more difficulty in learning the new language.

An important component of psychological distance is a student's attitude toward members of the cultural group whose language he or she is learning. García (1999) reports on two studies that show the importance of attitude. In one, researchers found that the positive attitude of English-speaking Canadians toward French-speaking Canadians increased their motivation to learn French. In another study, the researcher found that Chinese, Japanese, and Chicano students who had a positive attitude toward English speakers developed high levels of English proficiency. Schumann's theory suggests that a positive attitude toward members of the target-language group decreases the psychological distance between the learner and the group whose language he or she is learning.

The example of Yvonne's intern teaching experience described earlier gives us a further example. The boys in the class had signed up for the intern teacher because they had failed Spanish 1 the year before with an older, strict, and very traditional teacher. Needless to say, Yvonne had students with low motivation (they preferred football to Spanish), and their attitudes toward learning Spanish were negative (they didn't really want to learn Spanish, and besides, last year's teacher proved to them that they couldn't learn it). In order to help her students learn Spanish, Yvonne first had to motivate them. This helped reduce the psychological distance between her students and the target language, Spanish.

Schumann found that a positive attitude reduces the psychological distance between learners and the target language. Yvonne also worked hard to help her students develop a positive attitude toward her class. She developed a good relationship with them, she engaged them in meaningful activities in which they used Spanish, and she showed them that they could, in fact, succeed in this new language. Even though most of the students still preferred football to Spanish, their attitude toward the Spanish class improved, and they learned much more Spanish than they had learned the previous year.

Culture shock also increases psychological distance. Recall David's story above. When he first moved to Colombia, David didn't speak any Spanish. He lived with a Colombian family who did not speak English. David found living in a new country very challenging, and it was difficult to be the only person who could not communicate. Everything was different from what he was used to, and he soon found that trying to learn a new language and adjust to the new culture was overwhelming. For a period, he did not even try to learn Spanish. He was suffering from culture shock, and this increased the psychological distance.

It might be helpful to look at several examples of language learners who reflect the kinds of social and psychological distance Schumann has identified. Amy, for example, a language learner with a positive attitude, was the subject of a case study that Kim, a graduate student, carried out. Amy went to Costa Rica to work with a local church. She wanted to be of service in the country she visited, and she wanted to learn Spanish for use with Spanish-speaking friends in California. During her time in Costa Rica she was in contact with only one other American. She interacted with local church members and lived with a Costa Rican family.

Several factors decreased the social and psychological distance for Amy. She was part of a very small group, and her living and work situation resulted in constant integration with members of the target-language culture. Enclosure was low and social dominance was not a factor, since Amy was a volunteer worker. Although there were cultural differences, the two cultures were somewhat congruent. In addition, Amy had a very positive attitude toward Spanish speakers and high motivation to communicate. All of these factors help account for her gains in Spanish proficiency.

Unlike Amy, Moua, a sixth-grade Hmong student, struggled with learning English in school. Several factors contributed to Moua's school performance. One of these was the social distance he experienced. He was part of a subordinate social group. The Hmong immigrants in California have generally worked in low-income jobs. He was part of a large, cohesive community. There are stores that specialize in Southeast Asian food, and there are Hmong radio and TV stations, so the enclosure was high. Moua was the second oldest of seven children, and there was a large extended family. Nearly all his friends were Hmong. As a result, there was little integration with members of the mainstream culture. Even in school, there were many other Hmong students. The Hmong culture is not at all congruent with mainstream U.S. culture. All these factors contributed to increased social distance. On the other hand, Moua had a positive attitude toward English speakers, and his family planned to remain in the United States permanently, so his motivation to learn was high. Nevertheless, as Schumann points out, psychological distance only becomes a factor if social distance is neither positive nor negative.

Another good example of a student who experienced great social distance from the community of English speakers was Nafa, a Lahu girl. Janie, Nafa's teacher, took a special interest in Nafa and her family. As Janie explained, the Lahu come from Laos, where they form a minority group that lives in the mountains. Nafa lives in a small farming community in California. Many other Lahu families have moved to this area. They represent a high-enclosure group, a cohesive community with a pattern of limited integration with the mainstream culture. Like Moua, Nafa is part of a large family, and most of her social activities are with extended family members. Nafa's parents work in low-paying jobs, as do many of the other Lahu. As a result, the Lahu are in a socially subordinate position. All these factors contribute to social distance and inhibit language acquisition. As Schumann's theory predicts, Nafa has had difficulty in learning English.

Schumann claims that for a learner to acquire full proficiency in a second language, he or she must be acculturated, because SLA is just one aspect of the larger process of acculturation. A learner who is socially distant from members of the target-language group might develop only limited grammatical and communicative competence in the target language.

It is important to note that acculturation is distinct from assimilation. A person can take on a new culture without giving up his or her primary culture. This is acculturation, and the result can be bilingualism and biculturalism. Many students are able to maintain their first language and culture and still learn English and succeed academically. Sharma, the Punjabi girl described in Chapter 1, for example, maintained her first language and many of her Indian customs and also adopted practices that allowed her to fit into mainstream American culture. Assimilation, on the other hand, involves losing one's primary culture and becoming "similar to" those of the target culture. Assimilation often results in loss of the native language and culture.

Schumann's theory has been attacked on several fronts. Larsen-Freeman and Long (1991) conclude their review of Schumann's theory by commenting:

> [B]oth group and individual social and psychological factors must surely have some role in a comprehensive theory of SLA, perhaps most obviously as variables conditioning the amount and type of target-language exposure the learner experiences. Equally clearly, on the other hand, it should come as no surprise if a mental process, (second) language learning, is not successfully explicable by any theory which ignores linguistic and cognitive variables. (266)

The objection to Schumann's theory is that it is not comprehensive because it does not take into account linguistic and cognitive differences among learners. Despite these limitations, Schumann's theory is useful. Concepts such as social and psychological distance help us understand why certain people succeed or fail to learn a new language, but the help is limited because Schumann says so little about language and cognitive processing.

What are the implications of Schumann's theory for teachers? The acculturation model highlights the importance of social and psychological factors on acquisition. Teachers should create a classroom environment in which students can interact with and develop positive attitudes toward speakers of the target language. Acculturation does not require that students give up their primary language and culture. Models of education such as dual-language bilingual programs, where speakers of two languages learn in both languages, becoming bilingual and biliterate, fit well with Schumann's model. However, his theory has little to say about how teachers can plan instruction that would promote language acquisition. Perhaps for this reason, Schumann's theory of SLA has not led to specific methods of second language teaching.

Schumann and Krashen

Schumann's acculturation theory complements Krashen's monitor model. Schumann focuses on external, social factors that lead to language acquisition. Krashen's theory explains the internal, psychological process that results in acquisition.

Krashen (1982) comments that Schumann's acculturation hypothesis "is easily expressible in terms of comprehensible input and low filter level. Acculturation can be viewed as a means of gaining comprehensible input and lowering the filter" (45). Krashen also notes that his theory accounts for acquisition in a wider range of settings. "Moreover, the comprehensible input hypothesis accounts for second language acquisition in situations that acculturation does not attempt to deal with" (45). For example, with good teaching, a student can acquire a foreign language in a school setting without ever traveling to another country.

Although Krashen's theory of second language acquisition has been the basis for methods used to teach second language students, two questions frequently come up. Teachers (and researchers) ask about (1) the importance of student output and (2) the value of teaching grammar. In the following sections, we discuss these two topics.

What About Output?

Krashen argues that acquisition occurs when learners receive comprehensible input, messages that they understand. Other researchers have given importance to output as well as input. Ellis (1990) refers to theories such as Krashen's as reception-based. Theories that include attention to output he classifies as production-based. According to Johnson (1995), "Reception-based theories contend that interaction contributes to second language acquisition via learners' reception and comprehension of the second language, whereas production-based theories credit this process to learners' attempts at actually producing the language" (82).

Long (1983) developed the interaction hypothesis, a theory of SLA that is reception-based. Long claims that learners make conversational adjustments as they interact with others and that these adjustments help make the input comprehensible. As Johnson (1995) points out, "Like Krashen, Long stresses the importance of comprehensible input but places more emphasis on the interaction that takes place in two-way communication and the adjustments that are made as a result of the negotiation of meaning" (83).

Swain (1985) argues that language learners need the opportunity for output. She noted that students in French immersion classes did not reach native-like proficiency in French. These students were in classes where teachers did most of the talking. Peer interaction was limited, and when interaction occurred, students spoke only with others learning French rather than with native speakers of French. Based on her observations of these students, Swain proposed that second language acquisition depends on output as well as input. According to Scarcella (1990), Swain's comprehensible output hypothesis

> suggests that students need tasks which elicit . . . talk at the student's $i + 1$, that is, a level of second language proficiency which is just a bit beyond the current second language proficiency level. She claims that such output provides opportunities for meaningful context-embedded use for the second language which allows students to test out their hypotheses about the language and "move the learner from a purely semantic analysis of the language to a syntactic analysis of it." (70)

EXPOSURE		
	receptivity	attention-focusing
INPUT		
	investment	apprehension/comprehension
INTAKE		
	practice	retention access
UPTAKE		
	authentic use	extension creativity
PROFICIENCY		

FIGURE 5–1. *Van Lier's model of SLA*

Swain's claim is that when we receive input that we understand, we focus on meaning—or the semantic level. However, in talking, we need to string sentences together, and that requires attention to syntax. Our syntactic analysis is probably not conscious, but producing output requires us to access parts of the language system different from that which we use to comprehend input.

One model of SLA that includes both input and output has been developed by Van Lier (1988) and is shown in Figure 5–1. Van Lier claims that certain conditions are necessary for certain outcomes. According to this model, if learners are receptive during exposure to a new language, their attention will be focused. If attention is focused, the language becomes input. If learners invest some mental energy in the input, they will begin to comprehend it. Language that is comprehended changes from input to intake. If learners practice with intake, they can retain the language and access it later. Language that can be accessed is considered uptake. Finally, with authentic use, learners can extend their language and use it creatively. It is the ability to use language creatively that is a measure of proficiency.

Problems with Forcing Output

Traditional approaches to language teaching often require students to produce language before they have received enough comprehensible input. While SLA theories such as Long's, Swain's, and Van Lier's point out the importance of output as well as input, requiring second language learners in early stages of English acquisition to produce language too soon can have negative consequences.

This became clear to us as we worked with student teachers in Venezuela. Because of their own experiences as students in English classes, the new teachers first asked their students to say everything in complete sentences and even asked them to stand and recite what they were learning. Use of visuals was minimal, and chalkboards were filled with vocabulary lists and language structures. Although the topics of the lessons were personally interesting to the students—explaining likes and dislikes, or discussing similarities and differences among classmates—the insistence on output raised the students' affective filters. These beginning-level English students expended so much energy trying to pronounce words, learn vocabulary, get verb endings right, and put sentences together that little real language acquisition took place.

The student teachers began to use a variety of visuals and other strategies to ensure that the input they were providing was comprehensible. They allowed students to show comprehension through gestures and one-word answers. The emphasis in the classroom moved from correct pronunciation, vocabulary, and sentence structures to comprehension and interaction. What was most exciting was that the teachers saw how much more English their students were acquiring and how much more positive they were about the class.

Production-based theories of SLA such as Van Lier's and Swain's recognize the importance of input but add output as an important component. Long argues that output is needed for social interaction. Krashen's argument is that output can't help us acquire new vocabulary or grammatical structures. One can't learn a new word simply by talking. At the same time, we learn language for communicative purposes, and no language teacher would feel successful if students never uttered a word of the new language. In effective classes for ELLs, students need opportunities for both comprehensible input and output at levels students are prepared to produce.

What About Grammar?

In our discussion of theories of second language acquisition, we have not addressed one issue that is central for many language teachers: grammar. Grammar is certainly an important component of most language classes. The reasons for this seem clear: Most people who become language teachers like grammar and know quite a bit about grammar. Besides, they probably received large doses of grammar when they were students. In addition, a person teaching a language has to teach something, and the grammar of the language is a natural candidate. These are all reasons that language teachers teach grammar, but are they good reasons?

Approach	Teaching Method
Language as Structure	Teach grammar rules explicitly and have students practice with decontextualized exercises.
Language as Mental Faculty	Teach only a few grammar rules that students can use to monitor output.
Language as Functional Resource	Following a curriculum cycle, teach grammar forms and functions through modeling, joint construction, and individual practice.

FIGURE 5–2. *Three approaches to grammar teaching for ELLs (based on Derewianka 2007)*

Derewianka (2007), in her review of teaching grammar to English language learners, identifies three approaches that have been used widely. Figure 5–2 provides an overview of these three approaches and the teaching method associated with each.

Language as Structure

The first approach, *language as structure*, involves identifying different parts of speech, such as nouns and verbs, and the rules for combining them into sentences. As Derewianka writes, "Traditionally grammar in the ELT [English language teaching] field has been conceived of in terms of identifying the parts of speech and the rules for combining them into structures" (2007, 844). Structures refers to subjects, predicates, and other parts of a sentence. Traditional approaches to second language teaching, such as the grammar translation method, use this approach. This method consists of explicit teaching of rules followed by decontextualized exercises designed to give students practice with the rule. For example, students might learn the proper forms for the present perfect tense in English and then be given an exercise in which they convert past-tense sentences, such as "He studied English" to present perfect, "He has studied English."

Derewianka comments that a traditional approach to teaching grammar is still the most widely used model of English language teaching. However, this applies primarily to teaching English in countries where English is not the native language. Traditional approaches to grammar teaching result in students learning about the language (they can tell you how to form the present perfect tense), but this approach has not been shown to help students develop the ability to communicate in the language. For that reason, in English as a second language (as opposed to English as a foreign language) and bilingual classes, traditional grammar is not the basis for the language teaching method.

Although traditional grammar-based approaches to teaching a second language are outdated and are not supported by research, within more current second language teaching methods, some aspects of grammar continue to be taught. That is, there is still what Long (2001) refers to as a "focus on form." The question is whether the rules should be taught explicitly or incidentally.

Ellis (1998), for example, looked at four ways of presenting form-focused instruction. One way is to *structure the input*. "This option asks learners to process input that has been specially contrived to induce comprehension of the target structure" (44). Learners are not required to produce the structure, but they are exposed to large amounts of the structure and asked to attend to it. For example, students often say things like "I am boring" when they mean "I am bored," so structured input might focus on the difference between these two grammatical forms. For example, the teacher might give a series of sentences such as "The book is boring, so I am bored."

A second possibility is *explicit instruction*. Such instruction can be direct (the teacher teaches the rule and the students must practice it) or indirect. In indirect explicit instruction, students look at some sample of language and try to figure out the rule. That is, explicit instruction can be deductive or inductive. Explicit instruction is designed to raise students' consciousness of the grammatical form.

A third approach to incorporate grammar into second language teaching is what Ellis calls *production practice*. This approach involves students in practicing certain grammatical forms. For example, a student might do a worksheet in which the task is to put the words *in*, *on*, or *at* into the appropriate blanks in a sentence. Finally, teachers can teach grammar by *providing negative feedback*. When a student makes an error, the teacher can correct it, usually by providing the correct form. If the student says, "I have been here since two days," the teacher might respond, "Oh, so you have been here *for* two days. What have you been doing?" Figure 5–3 presents an overview of the different ways teachers can focus on form.

As Ellis points out, most language teaching includes a combination of these methods, so it is difficult to know which one works best. Working with native speakers, Weaver (2008) has shown that teaching specific grammatical forms in the context of a student's writing can improve student performance. This would also hold true for second language learners. In general though, most current approaches to teaching English learners in this country include only limited teaching of grammar.

Language as Mental Faculty

The second general approach to teaching grammar to ELLs that Derewianka identifies is *language as mental faculty*. This approach is based on the work of Chomsky, who views language as a built-in mental ability. Chomsky's linguistic theories have developed over

Focus on Form (Language as Structure)	Description
Structure the input	Teachers structure the input to teach particular forms. Students are asked to notice, but are not asked to produce forms.
Explicit instruction (direct and indirect)	In direct explicit instruction, the teacher teaches the rule and students practice. In indirect explicit instruction, students look at structures and figure out the rule.
Production practice	Students practice specific grammar forms.
Providing negative feedback	Teacher corrects incorrect grammar structures that students produce.

FIGURE 5–3. *Focus on form (based on Ellis 1998)*

time, but the basic ideas of a language acquisition device and Universal Grammar still are central to his research. Chomsky argues that humans have an innate ability to construct rules that allow them to comprehend and produce utterances in any language. What they need is exposure to specific languages to refine general rules to fit those languages. Given that this is a subconscious process that functions without the need for teaching of the rules, this view of language leads to a belief that explicit grammar teaching does not lead to language acquisition. Clearly, this is the case for babies acquiring their first language.

For second language teaching, the basic question is whether second language learners can still acquire language the same way that children acquire their first language. Sociolinguists such as Grosjean (2010) provide numerous examples of how adolescents and adults can acquire a second language. Krashen's theory of second language acquisition is based on Chomsky's theory of language. Within Krashen's theory, grammar teaching is limited. Krashen's claim is that knowledge of grammar can be used to monitor output, but that direct teaching of grammar has little or no effect on language acquisition. As a result of Krashen's work, many second language teachers have limited or eliminated teaching of grammar and, instead, focused on providing comprehensible input to promote acquisition.

Language as Functional Resource

The third approach to grammar discussed by Derewianka is what she refers to as *language as functional resource*. This approach is based on linguistic studies by Michael Halliday and his colleagues (1989). Halliday explains language "not in terms of a genetic blueprint located in the individual brain, but as the result of countless social interactions over the millennia" (1989, 849). Halliday sees language use as a series of choices based on the context of situation, which he explains as being made up of three components: the *field* (what we are talking about), the *tenor* (who we are talking to), and the *mode* (the means of communication such as speech or writing). We constantly make choices in each of these areas in order to carry out social functions, such as explaining or describing. Each context of situation occurs in a context of culture since different cultural groups have different ways of carrying out the functions of language.

In Australia, Halliday's approach to language has been translated into a method of second language teaching called the *curriculum cycle*. The cycle involves building up the field (providing students with basic concepts for a subject), modeling and deconstruction (for example, showing students how to write a science report and analyzing the report so that students understand each part), joint construction (students and teacher work together to create a text or carry out a project), and independent construction (students work independently to write their own text or solve problems).

The curriculum cycle is similar to Fisher and Frey's lesson plan discussed earlier. Explicit attention is given to how language works to convey and construct meaning in the curriculum cycle. Although this approach has been widely used in Australia, it has not yet gained popularity in the United States.

Gibbons (2002, 2009) has analyzed English language teaching from a Hallidayan perspective. She has shown how successful teachers scaffold instruction to help second language learners develop the language functions they need to communicate successfully in classroom settings. Her work illustrates the importance of scaffolding both the academic content and the language students need to learn in order to comprehend and produce academic knowledge.

Conclusion

Studies in first language acquisition by developmental psychologists, sociologists, and linguists all help explain how children naturally acquire a first language, moving through stages of development, as they learn to use language for the different functions needed to communicate in the social groups they are part of. Studies in second language acquisition also show that both children and older learners can acquire second languages in much the same way that they acquire first languages. Krashen's theory attempts to explain the different factors involved in second language acquisition. According to Krashen, we acquire language in a natural order when we receive comprehensible input under conditions in which we have a low affective filter.

Learning rules of grammar, from Krashen's perspective, contributes very little to acquisition, but learned rules can be used to monitor output. Gee suggests that Krashen's theory can be expanded to include a social dimension since we acquire language to communicate with others in social settings both in and outside of school.

Schumann and others have studied social factors that affect language acquisition. When there is social and psychological distance between the learner and the target language, there is limited acquisition. Other researchers have looked at the role of output in language acquisition. During output, teachers can scaffold language teaching and provide corrective feedback that helps learners acquire different aspects of a language.

A key question is whether the teaching of grammar improves students' ability in a new language. Traditional second language teaching focused on presenting language structures and having students practice those structures. Krashen and others who view humans as having an innate ability to acquire language hold that explicit grammar teaching has very limited value. More recently, linguists and teachers working from Halliday's conception of grammar as functional resource have emphasized the importance of teaching language functions in context. They argue that academic content is constructed through language, and so teachers should scaffold both language and content as they teach.

KEY POINTS

→ Child psychologists, sociologists, and linguists all provide different insights into first language acquisition.

→ Psycholinguists, neurolinguists, and sociolinguists pose different questions about second language acquisition and have contributed different theories of second language acquisition.

→ Krashen's monitor model consists of five hypotheses: the acquisition/learning, natural order, monitor, input, and affective filter hypotheses.

→ Schumann's acculturation model claims that acquiring a second language is part of a general process of acculturation and depends on the social and psychological distance between the learner group and the target language group.

KEY POINTS

→ Swain has proposed that output plays a key role in second language acquisition.

→ Van Lier's model includes both input and output.

→ Derewianka has identified three approaches to teaching grammar: language as structure, language as mental faculty, and language as functional resource. Each approach sees a different role for the teaching of grammar.

APPLICATIONS

1. Listen to a very young child (between eighteen- and twenty-four months old). Write down the child's speech and note the context of the talking. Does what you observed and heard fit into the discussion of first language acquisition?

2. Whether we are learning a language or something else, we all have experienced the difference between learning and acquisition. Share a personal example.

3. Schumann's Acculturation Model suggests that the social and psychological distance a second language learner has from speakers of the target language affects language learning. Think of two second language learners you know who represent different social and psychological distances. Use the questions provided below to determine the factors that influence the two learners. Share with a partner.

Social Distance
- *Social dominance.* Whose social group is more dominant?
- *Integration pattern.* How much do learners integrate, or do they do most things apart from the mainstream?
- *Enclosure.* To what extent does the learner's group have its own resources for interaction, such as church, publications, clubs?

- *Size*. How large is the group?
- *Cohesiveness*. How much does the group "stick together"?
- *Cultural congruence*. How are the cultural patterns and customs of the home culture and the target culture alike or different?
- *Attitude*. What attitudes do the home and target cultural groups have toward one another?
- *Intended length of residence*. How long does the member of the group intend to stay in the new country?

Psychological Distance

- *Motivation*. Does the learner want to learn the new language?
- *Attitude*. How does the learner feel toward the target-culture group?
- *Culture shock*. Is the learner suffering culture shock?

4. Observe a young child who is acquiring his or her native language or an English language learner acquiring English. Pick out examples where the learner has overgeneralized language rules, such as adding *-ed* to *go* to form the past tense. Write down the examples and bring them to your group for discussion.

5. Share a second language learning experience that you (or someone you know) had when you applied your monitor (your learned rules) to your output.

6. Krashen claims that input alone results in language acquisition. Swain disagrees, citing examples of the importance of "comprehensible output." Do you agree with Krashen or Swain? Can you find any evidence to support your position? Discuss with a group.

7. What is your opinion of the direct teaching of grammar? Are there situations in which you think teaching grammar helps students develop a new language? Write down your opinions and share them with the group.

What Are Key Concepts, Theories, and Models of Bilingual Education?

¿Por qué soy tonto?	**Why am I dumb?**
En mi país	**In my country**
Yo era listo.	**I was smart.**

These lines from Jane Medina's poem (1999) echo the feelings of many children who enter schools speaking a language other than English. It is unfortunate that children perceive themselves this way when we, as educators, could help them view themselves differently. What we call students makes a difference. García (2009, 2010) and colleagues (García, Kleifgen, and Flachi 2008) have proposed that instead of labeling our children as limited English proficient, culturally and linguistically diverse, language minority, or even calling them English language learners, we refer to these students as *emergent bilinguals*. This term signals that we acknowledge that we value the language they already know as well as the language they are learning.

In school children acquire English, and if we educate them appropriately, they become bilingual. Unfortunately, too often educators and the general public discount the languages students bring to school and value only their acquisition of English. Rather than thinking globally, many in our education system rarely look beyond local concerns.

World Bilingualism and Globalization

Although estimates vary, there are around 7,000 languages found in the 192 countries in the world (Grosjean 2010). Most of these countries are bilingual or multilingual. Grosjean, looking at the numbers of countries and the numbers of languages in the world, estimates that at least half the world's population must be bilingual. In fact, with the exception of Iceland and possibly North Korea, the world's countries have almost always been inhabited by people who speak two or more languages.

Most of us think of countries and connect them to a language. For example, we say that in Sweden, people speak Swedish; in Mexico, people speak Spanish; or in Brazil, people speak Portuguese. However, in these countries there are people who speak many different languages. Languages really do not belong to specific countries; "Rather, languages belong to the people who speak them, who are in different geographical spaces" (García 2009, 26). Linguists tell us that language cannot be defined without considering the people who use it and the context in which it is used.

Interestingly, few people around the world view bilingualism and multilingualism this way despite the fact that within almost all countries, many languages are spoken daily. For example, less than 25 percent of the world's 192 countries recognize two or more languages officially. The United States is no exception. Many English-only advocates in this country proclaim that "This is America; we speak English here," despite the hundreds of different languages spoken in the United States. What educators working with emergent bilinguals must come to understand is that English learners draw on their different languages frequently and that in a multilingual world it is monolingualism, not bilingualism, that should be considered a problem.

Perhaps looking at the changing global society will help make this point clearer. In the twenty-first century, geopolitical and technological changes impact the view of languages and language use. New economic trading blocs and new sociopolitical and socioeconomic organizations, including the European Union, Mercosur in Latin America, and the North American Free Trade Area, create a climate where multilingualism is the norm. The formation of these groups has caused population changes doubling the numbers of international migrants to 175 million. What is so interesting about these migrants is that, with improved technology and transportation, they move back and forth frequently, creating a kind of transnationalism. In fact, as we mentioned in Chapter 2, many long-term English language learners are transnationals moving back and forth between the United States and their native countries. This movement of transnationals across the globe creates an even greater use of many different languages.

Language Death

Even with its large immigrant population and a long history of immigration, the general public in the United States does not support the use of multiple languages. Not only is bilingualism devalued, it is also misunderstood. English-only advocates, for example, do not understand the importance of maintaining language diversity. Crystal

(2000) points out that languages express identity, they are repositories of history, and they contribute to the sum of human knowledge. Languages contain different understandings of the world, ways of thinking, and ways of viewing the past, present, and future. When a language dies, so does a culture.

Harrison (2010), a linguist studying vanishing languages around the world, reports that "key insights of biology, pharmacology, genetics, and navigation arose and persisted solely by word of mouth, in small, unwritten tongues" (1). Harrison points out that what the "Kallowaya of Bolivia know about medicinal plants, how the Yupik of Alaska name 99 distinct sea ice formations, and how the Tofa of Siberia classify reindeer" (1) could be lost as people shift to speaking global tongues. He cites the example of Johnny Hill Jr., the last known speaker of the Chemehuevi tribe in Arizona, who told the linguist, "I have to talk to myself. There's nobody left to talk to, all the elders have passed on" (2). With the death of the elders, traditions and ceremonies conducted through Chemehuevi will also certainly be lost.

What is happening to indigenous languages like those of the Kollowaya, Tofa, Yupik, and Chemehuevi is called *language shift*. Language shift happens to both indigenous and immigrant language groups. In language shift, the forms and uses of these minoritized languages change and are reduced, and eventually, the speakers of these languages shift to using the dominant language. This can lead then to language death. Skutnabb-Kangas (2008) speaks passionately about this phenomenon and claims that education that excludes students' mother tongues violates their right to education, and "it can sociologically and educationally be termed genocide" (1) as children lose their language and their culture.

English as a Global Language

English is one of the world's languages that is partially to blame for the death of other languages. English and other powerful languages like Mandarin Chinese have spread in different ways including through political domination, subordination of minority languages, colonization, trade, education, religion, emigration, and mass media (Baker 2006). English speakers are viewed as first language speakers if the majority of the population speaks English and English enjoys official status. So, for example, the United States, Australia, Canada, Ireland, and New Zealand have first language speakers of English.

In many other countries, including India and South Africa, English co-exists with other languages and has remained the official language or one of the official languages of the country. Since English is viewed as important for economic and political reasons, millions of other people around the world study English. In China, Japan, and many Latin American countries, almost everyone who can afford to study English does. Around the world, English has about 375 million first language speakers, from 100 million to 400 million second language speakers, and from 100 million to one billion foreign language speakers, depending on whether one counts who is simply studying the language and who actually has learned it quite well (Baker 2006).

Because of its prestige and the use of English around the world in areas such as international communication, science, technology, medicine, computers, research, tourism, advertising, and youth culture, English dominates as the world's global language. For example, Crystal (2000) explains that 80 percent of the information on the World Wide Web is stored in English. Over 50 million elementary children around the world study English, and over 80 million study it at the secondary level.

In much of the world English is associated with prestige. Certainly, in the United States those who speak English well have *linguistic capital* (Bordieu and Passeron 1977), a kind of power that those who do not speak the language well do not have. There are other kinds of capital. Students from the dominant culture who understand how things are done within a culture have *cultural capital.* Students coming to school with a native language other than English have neither linguistic nor cultural capital when they begin school. As they are learning English, they lack this power because they are not yet proficient in either the language or the cultural practices. Even people who speak two or three languages other than English daily may lack linguistic capital because the languages they are using are not valued, and their skills at using language are not appreciated.

English and other major languages are so predominant that minority language speakers come to see the dominant languages as more important than their own languages. Many speakers shift from their native tongues to the power language, giving up not only their language but also their culture in the process. Skutnabb-Kangas claims that when schools do not value students' first languages or their languaging practices, the dominant languages, like English, actually become what she calls "killer languages" (Skutnabb-Kangas 2008). They commit murder on the less powerful languages of the world. Educators need to consider how their decisions about language use affect students who come to school speaking languages other than the majority language.

Languaging and Translanguaging

Our native language gives us the critical abilities to communicate basic information, express our point of view, and establish social relationships. As García points out about emergent bilinguals, "whether born abroad or in the United States, most of the children have a rich family life with abundant *languaging* in languages other than English" (2010, 3). García's use of the word *languaging* makes *language* into a verb.

People language as they communicate; that is, they use language in different settings with different people in order to accomplish different purposes.

When bilingual and multilingual students use language, they often *translanguage*. García (2009) defines *translanguaging* as the "process of going back and forth from one language to the other" (49). She points out bilinguals in everyday use often "code switch." They translanguage with different people for different reasons as they communicate.

Code switching (or translanguaging) has a negative connotation for many people who assume that English learners may insert a word or phrase from their native language because they don't have full command of English. While it is true that one strategy English learners can use is to rely on their first language as they communicate in a second language, most code switching is done for other purposes.

Grosjean (2010) lists several other reasons that bilinguals code switch. One reason is that some concepts are better expressed in one language than in another. For example, Yvonne learned that the Spanish word that refers to her son-in-law's mother is *consuegra*. This one word in Spanish replaces what needs to be expressed by an entire phrase in English. When the use of a word from another language becomes widespread, such as the Spanish word *taco*, in English, we say the word is borrowed. Code switching can be a more temporary borrowing by an individual. As Grosjean notes, if the person you are speaking to is also bilingual, bringing in words from both languages enriches the conversation in the same way that having a large vocabulary in one language allows a person to express herself more fully.

A third reason that people code switch is to establish social solidarity. As Grosjean writes, "Code-switching is also used as a communicative or social strategy to show speaker involvement, mark group identity, exclude someone, raise one's status, show expertise, and so on" (54–55). In South Texas along the border, bilinguals often code switch to identify themselves as part of the Mexican American community. On the other hand, parents who speak a second language may use that language to exclude their monolingual child from the conversation.

A good example of code switching to raise one's status comes from Zentella (2000), who describes in detail language use in *el bloque*, a Puerto Rican neighborhood of New York City. Adults and children constantly communicate in both Spanish and English. "They form part of dense and multiplex networks that provide a wide variety of linguistic input in many multi-party conversations" (268). Because community members move back and forth between languages in order to communicate, they are "accused of ruining 'pure Spanish' and of corrupting Spanish and English" (269). It is proficiency in English that is valued, and students' abilities to translanguage, or move back and forth between English and Spanish, is seen negatively. In fact, even among the Puerto Ricans in *el bloque*, it was the acquisition of English that was usually valued and raised the social status of the speaker who used English well.

Both Grosjean (2010) and Baker (2006) list a number of other purposes for code switching. Where we live on the border between Texas and Mexico, code switching is very common but often looked down on as an inability to speak either language well. After reading about code switching, our students listed reasons and examples of code switching they had observed. Krishtel and Monica provided a number of examples that are listed in Figure 6–1.

Linguistic studies show that "instead of being a haphazard and ungrammatical mixture of two languages, code-switching follows very strict constraints and is implemented by bilinguals who are competent in their languages" (Grosjean 2010, 56–57). Grosjean has studied the phonology of code switching. He has shown that not only do bilinguals shift the pronunciation of sounds as they move from one language to another, they also shift their intonation patterns to match the native patterns of each language. Other linguists investigating the syntax of code switching have found that bilinguals will only code switch at natural phrase boundaries in a language. These studies show clearly that code switching, or translanguaging, is governed by precise language rules and is not careless or haphazard.

Balanced Bilinguals or Not?

One commonly held assumption is that the goal of bilingual education is to produce balanced bilinguals. A balanced bilingual is someone who is equally competent in two languages. This would mean that if a bilingual Spanish–English program did its job well, a student should be able to speak, read, and write both English and Spanish equally well in all settings.

However, since the 1960s with the emergence of the study of sociolinguistics, linguists have come to understand that "most bilinguals use their languages for different purposes, in different situations, with different people" (Grosjean 2010). Grosjean refers to this phenomenon as the *complementarity principle*. Rather than developing equal abilities in each language, bilinguals develop the languages they need to speak to different people in different settings when discussing different subjects. One language complements the other.

Grosjean points out three consequences of the complementarity principle. First, most bilinguals are more fluent in one language than the other. As Grosjean (2010) explains, "In general, if a language is spoken in a reduced number of domains and with a limited number of people, then it will not be developed as much as a language used in more domains with more people" (31). Many bilinguals report, for example, that they can do mental math more easily in one language than the other. Someone

Purpose	English–Spanish Example
1. To emphasize a particular point in conversation.	*Andale*, go do your homework.
2. To substitute an unknown word in another language.	Voy a hacer mi trabajo en la *laptop*. La *teacher* nos dejo mucha tarea.
3. To express a concept that has no equivalent in the culture of the other language.	There was a *piñata* at the party. That lunch looks good, *bon appétit*.
4. To reinforce a request.	Get to work—*pónganse a trabajar*. Come, come! *Córrele!*
5. To clarify a point.	Animals adapt to their environment— *los animals se adaptan a su medio ambiente, es decir, se acostumbran al lugar donde viven.* For this exercise you are going to do three circles, *tres círculos*.
6. To express identity, communicate friendship or family bonding.	Come here, *mijito*. *Así es, amor*, good job!
7. To report a conversation held previously.	Holding a conversation in English, but retelling it to someone else in Spanish: When he came into the room, we all yelled, *¡Feliz cumpleaños!*
8. To interject into a conversation.	If two people are having a conversation in Spanish, and you interject by saying, "Excuse me."
9. To indicate a change of attitude or relationship.	People code switch when there is less social distance, more solidarity, and growing rapport: Angela telling me, "*Dra. Freeman, Ud. Me conoce. No soy así.*"
10. To exclude people from a conversation.	Grandparents speak in a language their grandson does not understand.
11. To refer to certain topics, such as money.	*Fui al* dealership *y el* car *costaba* five thousand dollars.

FIGURE 6–1. *Purposes for code switching (adapted from Baker 2006)*

What Are Key Concepts, Theories, and Models of Bilingual Education?

teaching English as a foreign language may not acquire full fluency in the native language of the country simply because he spends most of the day speaking English to his students. This teacher may only develop the native language in limited domains, such as speaking to clerks in stores about purchases. He may live in another country for several years without becoming equally fluent in two languages.

This leads to a second consequence. The language that bilinguals are more fluent in is their dominant language. Since bilinguals tend to use one language more often with more people in more situations than the other language, they don't use the two languages equally. For that reason, very few bilinguals are "balanced." For example, in the South Texas university where we teach, many students use Spanish with their peers, at home, at church, and in social functions. Even though they study almost exclusively in English, they are more dominant in Spanish.

The lack of balance shows up in a third consequence of the complementarity principle: the difficulty bilinguals have in translation. Since bilinguals develop fluency in different domains rather than an equal ability in each domain, they often find it difficult to translate. For example, many bilingual teachers have been asked to explain in Spanish the rationale for bilingual education to parents or other community members. Even though these teachers speak Spanish, they may not have developed the vocabulary needed to translate these complex concepts into Spanish.

Grosjean concludes his discussion of the complementarity principle by stating that most bilinguals "simply do not need to be equally competent in all their languages. The level of fluency they attain in a language . . . will depend on their need for that language and will be domain specific" (21). Because bilinguals develop their two languages differently, very few are completely balanced.

Perhaps the reason that people assume that the ideal bilingual is balanced results from thinking of a bilingual as the sum of two fully developed monolinguals. In contrast, Grosjean takes a holistic or bilingual view of bilingualism. He argues that "the bilingual is an integrated whole who cannot easily be decomposed into two separate parts . . . he has a unique and specific linguistic configuration" (75). Grosjean compares a bilingual to a hurdler in track and field. The hurdler has to have the skills of a high jumper and the skills of a sprinter, but combines both jumping high and running fast into a new and different skill. That is, the hurdler does not have to be the highest jumper or the fastest sprinter to be a very proficient hurdler. A problem with conceptualizing a bilingual as two monolinguals is that we test the two languages separately, expecting equal proficiency in each one in the academic language domain. As a result, bilinguals are generally found to be deficient in one or both of their languages.

Our eight-year-old granddaughter, Maya, provides an example of a typical bilingual. When she is with us, she almost always speaks in English. No one told her to speak English to us, she just figured out that that was our stronger language even though we often speak Spanish to others around her.

When Carmen, a monolingual Spanish speaker, comes to the house, Yvonne speaks Spanish to her, and so does Maya. If Carmen and Yvonne are in conversation, Maya will often join the conversation in Spanish and code switch for Yvonne to clarify something she has said in Spanish to be sure Yvonne understands. Maya also speaks Spanish to her godparents from Argentina who do speak English, but are native speakers of Spanish and always make a point of speaking to her in Spanish.

At her birthday party, Maya called to one friend who was a newcomer to the country in Spanish, and turned and spoke in English to another friend who only speaks English. Maya was translanguaging. No one taught her to do this, she just naturally translanguaged in order to communicate.

Like most bilinguals, Maya is not completely balanced. She uses English more often than Spanish in more settings with more people. As a result, she is more fluent in English than in Spanish. However, her language dominance could change. If her parents moved to a Spanish-speaking country and Maya attended school where all the classes were taught in Spanish and if she developed Spanish-speaking friends, her language dominance would shift. Her fluency in Spanish would naturally increase as she used Spanish more often in more settings with more people.

A goal of bilingual dual-language education is to help students build academic proficiency in *both* languages. When students are schooled in two languages on a daily basis, they can gain increased proficiency in both languages although their overall fluency in the two languages may never be completely balanced. Even though bilingual dual-language approaches to teaching emergent bilinguals has been shown to be more effective than English-only approaches, even though in most of the world bilingualism is the norm, and even though there are clear advantages to bilingualism, in many schools in the United States emergent bilinguals are only instructed in English.

English-Only Approaches

Teachers working with English language learners recognize the importance of helping them develop competence in English. It seems logical that the best way to develop English proficiency is to immerse learners in an environment in which they hear, speak, read, and write English all day. Although the idea that "more English leads to more English" is logical, it is not the best approach for working with bilingual students.

Cummins (2007) encourages us to rethink monolingual strategies for teaching multilingual students. He discusses three misconceptions commonly held by educators of ELLs, including the idea that instruction should be carried out exclusively in the target language without recourse to the student's L1, that translation between L1 and L2 has no place in the teaching of language or literacy, and that in bilingual programs the two languages should be kept separate. These misconceptions arise when teachers or researchers ignore the reality of bilingual communities and everyday language use as bilinguals translanguage. Figure 6–2 lists these three misconceptions and the realities of effective teaching for emergent bilinguals.

The first misconception Cummins discusses, what he calls the direct method assumption, is that second language students should be taught entirely in the target language. For English language learners, this means that all instruction should be given in English. Cummins cites several researchers who have concluded that the use of the first language in classes for ELLs actually enhances their acquisition of English. For example, he describes a study by Lucas and Katz (1994, as cited in Cummins 2007) of nine exemplary programs in which English was the primary language of instruction. Nevertheless, as the researchers explain, in these classes teachers found multiple ways to use students' first languages for useful purposes. Later in this chapter we list some strategies for incorporating the first language during instruction in English.

A second misconception Cummins discusses is the belief that translation has no place in the classroom—what he calls the "no translation" assumption. Like the direct teaching assumption, excluding translation ignores what happens in bilingual households and communities. Zentella's (2000) case studies of children in *el bloque* revealed example after example of how skilled the children were at translating back and forth between English and Spanish as they played with friends or interacted with the adult community. They often served as language brokers, helping adults with important business transactions.

Misconceptions	Reality
All teaching should be in the target language.	Research shows that judicious use of the first language promotes second language acquisition.
Translation should not be allowed in the ESL or bilingual classroom.	Emergent bilinguals are often asked to translate outside the school. Teachers can draw on this skill in school.
In dual-language bilingual programs, the two languages should be kept strictly separate.	There are times to keep the two languages separate, but there are also times to bring them together for instructional purposes.

FIGURE 6–2. *Misconceptions and realities*

Cummins (2007) suggests that using translation in the classroom recognizes skills children bring to school as language brokers, and it promotes the acquisition of English. Cummins is not referring to concurrent translation, in which the teacher translates each thing she says. This practice is ineffective because students only pay attention to the language they understand. However, judicious translation can allow students to better comprehend key concepts during activities like morning message. The teacher can have a more advanced bilingual translate the message so that a beginning English learner can understand what has been written. Translation also promotes biliteracy development as students write and translate their own books. When bilinguals can show monolingual peers their translanguaging abilities, they are more valued by their classmates, and they develop a sense of self-esteem. As Cummins notes, allowing translation in the classroom helps bilinguals develop "identities of competence" (228).

The third misconception, which Cummins terms the Two Solitudes, is that the two languages should be kept rigidly separated in bilingual classrooms. However, many effective practices are excluded when instruction is limited to one language at a time. For example, having students access cognates depends on using both languages simultaneously. Teachers can have students read bilingual books. Students can carry out linguistic investigations and compare and contrast their languages. Teachers can arrange exchanges with sister classes in other countries where one of their languages is used.

Cummins writes:

> [I]t does seem reasonable to create largely separate spaces for each language within a bilingual or immersion program. However, there are also compelling arguments to be made for creating a shared or interdependent space for the promotion of language awareness and cross-language cognitive processing. The reality is that students are making cross-linguistic connections throughout the course of their learning in a bilingual or immersion program, so why not nurture this learning strategy and help students to apply it more efficiently? (229)

Supporting Students' First Languages

Cummins encourages teachers to rethink monolingual instruction for emergent bilinguals. An important point that he makes is that accessing both their languages helps emergent bilinguals develop identities of competence. In some settings, ELLs are made to feel incompetent. Skutnabb-Kangas (1983) describes how newcomers to English feel when immersed in English-only instruction:

> [T]he child sits in a submersion classroom (where many of the students have L2, the language of instruction, as their mother tongue), listening to the teacher explaining something that the child is then supposed to use for problem solving . . . the child gets less information than a child listening to her mother tongue. (116)

Not only does the child learn less; the child may also come to view herself as not being competent in school tasks. This is the attitude reflected in the poem at the beginning of the chapter where the narrator asks, "Why am I dumb?"

Krashen (1996) has reviewed research on the importance of using the first language for instruction. He argues that we acquire language when we receive comprehensible input, messages that we understand. For second language students, use of the primary language is the best way to make input comprehensible. To learn a second language, students need to have an understanding of what they hear or read. If students enter school speaking languages other than English, and if English is the only language of instruction, then the students may simply not understand enough English to acquire the language or to learn any subjects taught in the language.

While bilingual education may not be possible in some schools for a variety of reasons, teachers in monolingual teaching settings can find ways to use their bilingual students' first languages to promote academic success. We have developed a list of strategies that teachers we have worked with have used to support their students' primary languages as they teach:

1. Ensure that environmental print in the classroom reflects students' first languages.

2. Supply school and classroom libraries with books, magazines, and other resources in languages in addition to English.

3. Have bilingual students read and write with aides, parents, and other students who speak their first language.

4. Encourage bilingual students to publish books and share their stories in languages other than English or produce bilingual books in English and the students' first languages.

5. Allow bilingual students to respond in their primary languages to demonstrate comprehension of content taught in English.

6. Use DVDs or videotapes in other languages produced professionally or by the students to support academic learning and raise self-esteem.

One other strategy that draws on students' first languages that we suggest is *preview, view, review*. If the teacher, a bilingual peer, a bilingual cross-age tutor, a bilingual aide, or a parent can simply tell the English learners in their native language what the upcoming lesson is about, the students are provided with a preview. During the view, the teacher conducts the lesson using strategies to make the input comprehensible. With the help of the preview, the students can follow the English better and acquire both English and academic content. Finally, it is good to have a short time of review during which students can use their native language. For example, students who speak the same first language could meet in groups to review the main ideas of the lesson and then report back in English. Figure 6–3 outlines the preview, view, review technique.

The preview, view, review technique provides a structured way to alternate English and native-language instruction. Using preview, view, review can help teachers avoid concurrent translation. Preview, view, review can also motivate students to stay engaged in the lesson. Listening to a second language is more tiring than listening to one's native language. Second language learners may appear to have shorter attention spans than native speakers, but in reality those students may be suffering from the fatigue of trying to make sense out of their new language. Often teachers complain that their English learners misbehave and don't pay attention, or they think their second language learners may have some learning problems because they do not

---

Preview

first language

The teacher or a bilingual helper gives an overview of the lesson or activity in the students' first language. This could be giving an oral summary, reading a book, showing a film, asking a key question, or leading a short discussion. If several language groups are in the class, students could work in same language groups to answer a question and report back in English.

View

second or target language [English]

The teacher teaches the lesson or directs the activity in the students' second language using strategies for making the input comprehensible.

Review

first language

The teacher or the students summarize key ideas and raise questions about the lesson in their first language. Students can work in same language groups to do this and report back in English.

FIGURE 6–3. *Preview/view/review*

seem to be learning. The first language preview and review can help them understand and stay engaged in their lessons.

Yvonne recalls an experience she had in an elementary classroom when she was asked to give a demonstration lesson. The teachers had not had much experience with English language learners who were now appearing in their school. The principal had tried to explain to the teachers the importance of drawing on students' first languages and thought bringing in someone from the outside might help.

Yvonne taught a reading/science lesson on seed growth to a class of second graders with primarily native English speakers and five native Spanish speakers, one of whom had been in the country only three months. She explained to the native English speakers that some of the lesson would be in Spanish, but that she would do things to help them understand. She previewed the lesson in Spanish by showing some seeds and talking about them and then reading a very comprehensible big book in Spanish, *Una semilla nada más* (Ada 1990).

Native English speakers got restless almost immediately and complained, "I don't understand!" and "Speak English!" However, the native Spanish speakers participated eagerly. The newcomer, José, answered and commented so much that Yvonne had to tell him to let others talk. Yvonne followed the preview, view, review model and did the view in English with lots of comprehensible input and a hands-on activity where students classified seeds according to shape, size, texture, and color. All the students, including the Spanish speakers, participated during the view. During the review, Spanish speakers participated again while English speakers were beginning to understand some and listened more carefully, but did not really participate.

At the end of the lesson Yvonne approached the classroom teacher, who had tears in her eyes. She told Yvonne:

> I thought José had serious learning and behavioral problems. Seeing him today helped me see that he wants to learn, he just doesn't understand! Look at how my English speakers responded! They were acting like José does when I teach in English all day long!

Allowing translation when it serves a pedagogical purpose, using preview, view, and review, and including different strategies to support students' first languages can promote academic success for emergent bilinguals. It is important to understand, however, that the most effective way for second language students to develop both academic concepts and English language proficiency is through the full development of their first language (Thomas and Collier 2002; August and Shanahan 2006; Cummins 2001; Rolstad, Mahoney, and Glass 2005; Krashen 1999; Crawford 2007).

Academic proficiency in the first language supports both language and content learning in the second language.

Francisco's Teaching Journey

Ser bilingüe es como vivir en dos mundos. Uno puede hablar con personas en español y entrar en su mundo. Lo mismo pasa cuando hablas, escribes y lees en inglés. Ahora que empecé el programa de educación bilingüe, puedo ver que tan valioso es ser bilingüe porque hay tantos niños que puedo ayudar en su primer idioma.

Translation

To be bilingual is like living in two worlds. One can speak to people in Spanish and enter into their world. The same thing happens when you speak, write, and read in English. Now that I have begun the bilingual education program, I can see how valuable it is to be bilingual because there are so many children that I can help in their first language.

This quote comes from Francisco, a college student who was just entering a teacher-education program to become a bilingual teacher. Yvonne was his university advisor and instructor. Francisco came to the United States from El Salvador when he was fourteen. His mother, a migrant worker, had lived and worked for several years in the United States before she could bring Francisco and her other children to join her. She wanted a better life for them than was possible in their native country. By the time Francisco arrived in the United States, he was high school age. Like most students who come at the secondary level, Francisco received no first language support. He was submersed in classes given only in English. His English as a second language classes focused on conversational language and did not prepare him for the academic demands of college.

Fortunately, Francisco was an outstanding soccer player. He attended a local Christian university on a soccer scholarship. He nearly dropped out of college because earning good grades was so difficult. Nevertheless, he persisted with encouragement from his mother and his coach. Because he struggled with English, he remained quiet in his college classes. When, as a senior, he did some observations in a first-grade bilingual classroom, Francisco saw for the first time how English language learners in a bilingual setting were able to participate fully in the classroom activities. He noted that the children felt good about themselves as learners because they could draw on their first language strengths as they studied school subjects. Francisco was inspired to use his bilingualism to help others so that they would not have to struggle as much as he had.

Theoretical Rationale for Bilingual Education

Francisco had studied about bilingual theory, but it was when he saw the positive results in a classroom and compared those results to his English-only schooling that the theory became real to him. What theory can explain the consistently positive results of bilingual education? The key concept is Cummins' (1981) Interdependence Hypothesis:

> To the extent that instruction in L_X is effective in promoting proficiency in L_X, transfer of this proficiency to L_Y will occur provided there is adequate exposure to L_Y (either in school or the environment) and adequate motivation to learn L_Y. (29)

In other words, when students are taught in and develop proficiency in their first language, L_X, that proficiency will transfer to the second language, L_Y, assuming they are given enough exposure to the second language and are motivated to learn it. Cummins explains that the reason that proficiency transfers from one language to another is that there is a common proficiency that underlies an emergent bilingual's languages. Because of this common underlying proficiency (CUP), there is an "interdependence of concepts, skills, and linguistic knowledge that makes transfer possible" (191). Cummins cites extensive research showing that there is a common proficiency that underlies specific languages.

According to Cummins (2000), the common underlying proficiency can be thought of as "a *central processing system* comprising (1) attributes of the individual such as cognitive and linguistic abilities (memory, auditory discrimination, abstract reasoning, etc.) and (2) specific conceptual and linguistic knowledge derived from experience and learning (e.g., vocabulary knowledge)" (191). As a result of this interdependence, an emergent bilingual can draw on a common pool of cognitive and linguistic abilities and skills as she develops literacy in two languages. In addition, there is a transfer of background knowledge and related linguistic features, such as cognates or similar syntactic patterns.

To take a simple example of how CUP operates, David learned about linguistics by studying in English. He knows about phonemes and syntax. David has also acquired a high intermediate level of Spanish. Even though he didn't study linguistics in Spanish, he can draw on his underlying knowledge of linguistics when discussing linguistics in Spanish.

Cummins' CUP theory can help account for the difference in academic performance of students with similar levels of English proficiency. Consider José and Felipe, who arrived in Mrs. Enns' third-grade classroom in September. Both boys had just come from Mexico and did not speak any English. By April, Mrs. Enns wanted to refer

Felipe to be tested for learning disabilities, as he was doing poorly in her class. José, on the other hand, was doing very well.

When the bilingual specialist conferred with Mrs. Enns, they looked at the previous schooling of the two boys. Felipe had lived in a rural area and had had interrupted schooling. He had never learned to read or write in Spanish and missed most of the content instruction of the early grades. José, in contrast, came from Monterrey, a large city, and had attended school since preschool. His report card from Mexico showed that he had received 8's, 9's, and 10's, high grades in the Mexican system. The difference in the boys' academic performance in English can be accounted for by the difference in their primary-language schooling.

In another case, Francisca arrived in Mr. Churchill's class from Mexico City to attend sixth grade in a school that is 85 percent Hispanic. After eight months, Francisca was doing better academically than many of her Mexican American classmates who had attended school in the United States all their lives. Mr. Churchill thought Francisca was more motivated and tried harder. However, when he began to study bilingual education, he investigated Francisca's past educational history. He discovered that Francisca had studied in Mexico City and was a top student in all subject areas there. Mr. Churchill could see that her schooling in Mexico had provided the literacy and content-area knowledge she needed to succeed in English. She already knew how to read, and she knew the concepts in Spanish, so her literacy and academic knowledge transferred to her second language. In contrast, many of her U.S. born classmates who had come to school speaking Spanish had never had instruction in their primary language to build the kind of knowledge base that Francisca had.

Cummins (2000) contrasts the idea of a common underlying proficiency with that of a separate underlying proficiency (SUP). Those who hold to the SUP theory must believe that what we learn in one language goes to one part of our brain and cannot be accessed when we are learning and speaking another language. This must be what opponents of bilingual education believe when they say that students learning in their first language are wasting time. They should only be learning in English. However, students in programs that build their first language as they acquire English develop higher levels of academic English proficiency than students schooled only in English.

Cummins' Dual Iceberg Image

Cummins uses the image of a dual iceberg to characterize his CUP model. The two peaks of the iceberg that are above the waterline represent the surface features (oral and written) of the two languages. The very compact ice core is relatively heavier and keeps a large percentage of the iceberg under water. When an iceberg tumbles over

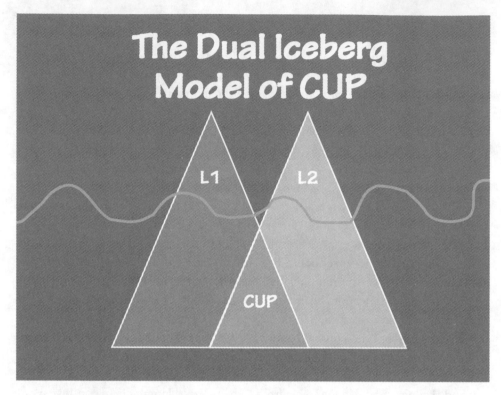

FIGURE 6–4. *Dual iceberg*

several times, its light snow layers on the surface are compacted. Thus, even more of the iceberg is submerged under water. As those who studied the *Titanic* disaster of 1912 discovered, what is seen on the surface is not the whole story. Figure 6–4 represents the dual iceberg.

If the two tips of the iceberg are thought of as the surface proficiency that speakers have in their first and second languages, then what is below the surface is the common underlying proficiency that has built up in the two languages and can transfer from one language to the other. Students who have more schooling in their first language can draw upon that as they are learning their second language. However, that proficiency may not always be apparent in the surface abilities they show in the second language. It is over time that students with greater total underlying proficiency show that proficiency in both their L1 and their L2. Students without the underlying academic proficiency in their first language, however, struggle because they have nothing to draw upon as they are learning academic content in a second language.

Schooling Models for Emergent Bilinguals

Cummins' theoretical research is supported by the applied research carried out by Collier and Thomas (2009) and Thomas and Collier (2002), who analyzed data for over 210,000 language minority students in five urban and rural school districts in various regions of the United States. Students were in different types of support programs, and both quantitative and qualitative data were collected. Eighty language groups were represented in the study, although the majority of the students were Spanish speakers.

Collier and Thomas (2009) identify six characteristics of effective programs for English language learners:

1. long term

2. instruction through the first language

3. instruction through the second language

4. sociocultural support

5. interactive, cognitively challenging discovery learning, and

6. integration with the mainstream. (47)

Of these characteristics, the most important were that students be given an extended period of support, six or more years, and that this support includes instruction through the first language. Collier and Thomas state that "all linguistically diverse groups benefit enormously in the long-term from on-grade-level academic work in their first language, for as many years as possible" (48). In programs that provide this support, English language learners are able to succeed academically.

The researchers analyzed English learners' standardized test scores in reading and math in English from kindergarten through high school. Students who had received strong cognitive and academic development through their first language at least through grade 5 or 6 score higher on tests in English through the high school years than students who received more limited first language instruction. More dropouts came from students who had been given English-only instruction in districts with neither ESL nor bilingual support. Thomas and Collier conclude:

> Enrichment 90/10 and 50/50 one-way and two-way developmental bilingual education (DBE) programs (or dual language, bilingual immersion) are the only programs we have found to date that assist students to fully reach the 50th percentile in both L1 and L2 in all subjects and to maintain that level of high achievement, or reach even higher levels through the end of schooling. The fewest dropouts come from these programs. (333)

Collier and Thomas contrast enrichment programs with English-only programs. In enrichment bilingual programs, students study in conditions that promote first and second language academic, cognitive, and language development in a supportive sociocultural context. In contrast, in English-only programs, students develop a second language, but they do not continue to develop their first language. As a result, they fall behind their native-English-speaking peers in their academic and cognitive development and receive no sociocultural support. A brief review of the types of programs offered ELLs in the United States will help readers understand better the conclusions of the Thomas and Collier report.

Types of Programs Serving ELLs

Although there are tremendous variations in the implementation of programs serving ELLs in the United States, there are several basic program models that are widely used. Part of the controversy that surrounds programs for emergent bilinguals stems from confusion about programs that have been called *immersion* and those called *submersion.*

Submersion Versus Immersion Programs

Advocates of the English Only movement propose an immersion program for language minority students. Often, they claim that their proposals are for programs similar to the successful French immersion programs in Canada. Their reasoning is that French immersion worked in Canada, so why can't this model work in the United States? In some school districts in the United States, immersion programs have been implemented. However, because of key differences between U.S. and Canadian contexts, the immersion education that many language minority students in the United States have received really amounts to "sink-or-swim" or submersion education.

The goals and results of the French immersion programs in Canada are very different from the immersion programs offered to language minority students in the United States (Hernández-Chávez 1984). In the original St. Lambert French Immersion program, middle-class, educated parents of English-speaking Canadian children requested French immersion so that their children would become bilingual and bicultural. In kindergarten the children in the French immersion programs were put in an all-French classroom with other English-speaking peers. There were no native speakers of French to compete with them. Teachers were bilingual and allowed the children to ask questions and give answers in English. The teachers received special training in using techniques to make the content of the classes comprehensible to the children. These techniques helped them teach academic content through the French language. As students progressed through school, their first language, English, was added to the curriculum, until in the sixth grade 40 percent of the curriculum was in French and 60 percent in English (Genesee 1984). Research on the first fifteen years of the implementation of the program showed that French immersion students achieved on a par with students in the regular English programs except that the French immersion students achieved in both French and English.

The success of the Canadian programs can be attributed to several factors. Parents initiated and supported the programs. Bilingual teachers were carefully prepared to work with the children. They taught the new language through content, not as a foreign language. All the children in a class were at about the same level of French ability. They did not have to compete with native speakers of French. At the same time, there was no danger of students losing their English, since that was the language spoken in the home, and it was the prestige language of the larger community. Further, more English was added to the curriculum each year so that by sixth grade more teaching time was given in English than in French. The goal was to produce students who were bilingual and bicultural in both French and English.

In the United States, English language learners face a very different situation when they are put into an immersion program. In the first place, they are minority, not majority, students, and they are in direct competition from the beginning with native-English-speaking peers. While the teachers receive some training in teaching content through a second language, the training in many cases is minimal. Structured immersion teachers are not usually bilingual, so at the early stages, the teachers can't answer questions the students ask in their primary languages or respond when students speak in their first languages. There is no provision for the students' primary language to be added to the curriculum as they advance through school. Their parents have not chosen the immersion program to make them bilingual and bicultural. In fact, since their parents are often from a disempowered segment of society, they have little voice in what happens in the school program. The first language and culture of the language minority students is not valued by the larger community, and it is clear from the beginning that the goal is not to produce bilingual, bicultural students but to produce students who can speak English. Many of the students lose their first language in the process of learning English. Figure 6–5 shows the differences between French and English immersion programs.

Immersion programs in the United States are really submersion programs, where students are more likely to "drown" in the English they receive. Since no first language support is given, and teachers may or may not have received training in the

French Immersion	English Immersion
Parents initiated and supported the programs.	Parents do not choose the program.
Teachers were bilingual.	Most teachers are not bilingual.
In lower grades, students could respond or ask questions in their L1.	Students can only use English.
Teachers were trained to teach academic content through a second language (French).	Teachers are trained to teach academic content through English.
All children started at the same level of French proficiency.	Students start at different levels of English proficiency.
There were no native French speakers in the program, so children learning French did not compete with native speakers.	From the beginning, second language speakers compete with native English speakers.
English was the prestige language of the community.	The students' first language is not the prestige language of the community.
English was added to the curriculum so that by sixth grade, 60 percent of the instruction was in English.	The students' first languages are not added to the curriculum.
Children became bilingual and biliterate.	Students often lose their first language in the process of learning English.

FIGURE 6–5. *French vs. English immersion programs*

techniques to use with English language learners, students may not receive comprehensible input and soon fall behind academically. Unlike the Canadian program, which is additive in that students come out of the programs with proficiency in two languages, immersion programs in the United States are subtractive because students lose their first language as they learn English. Not only do these programs fail to develop students' primary languages, especially the written forms, but students rarely come out of the programs with a level of English proficiency that allows them to achieve at the same level as the native English speakers. We can further distinguish between two types of English immersion programs: English immersion and structured English immersion (SEI).

ENGLISH IMMERSION

English immersion is not really a program for ELLs. English immersion occurs when ELLs are taught in mainstream classes with native speakers of English and given no special services. Although this approach is not legal, it still happens in parts of the country, especially where having English language learners in schools is a fairly new phenomenon. Parents can also refuse ESL services for their children, and some immigrant parents believe that immersion in English is the best way for their children to learn English. English immersion is subtractive, as students' first languages are not acknowledged or developed. Research by Thomas and Collier (1997) and others has shown this group has the highest number of dropouts.

STRUCTURED ENGLISH IMMERSION

In structured English immersion (SEI) programs, students are taught only in English by teachers who have received some training in strategies for teaching non-English speakers. This program is one that has been mandated in California and in Arizona, but the understanding of and implementation of SEI varies widely. Generally, students receive all instruction in English. In a study of California's SEI program, the investigators concluded that after five years of implementation:

> Very little evidence can be found in the empirical analyses conducted during this study that its basic premise was correct (i.e., that immersion methods of instruction are uniformly superior to bilingual methods in enhancing educational outcomes for ELs) . . . the best analyses we have been able to conduct given data limitations indicate that differences across models of instruction—holding constant such critical factors as student demographics—are minimal or nonexistent. (Parrish et al. 2006, vii–2)

Despite the generally negative results of structured English immersion programs in California, newspapers have periodically reported strong test gains for ELLs in the program. Krashen (2004b) investigated newspaper claims that test scores had skyrocketed. In California all ELLs are placed in structured English programs unless their parents sign a waiver allowing them to be in bilingual classes. Krashen found that test scores had gone up (*skyrocketed*, to use the newspaper's term) for all students as the result of the introduction of a new state test. As he explains:

> There were no significant differences in gains between districts that kept bilingual education and those that dropped it. . . . Missing from nearly all discussions of the effectiveness of bilingual education is the fact that controlled studies consistently show that bilingual education works. The Skyrocket Legend is false. (39)

Krashen's assertion is supported by Collier and Thomas (2009), who studied the test results of students in structured English immersion programs in California following the passage of Proposition 227. They found that even in the early grades ELLs were not making gains compared to native speakers. These students started behind due to their lack of English and did not catch up despite intensive instruction in English. Collier and Thomas concluded that "this program type has resulted in the lowest achievement for English learners of any program in the U.S." (61).

Similarly, reporting on results of a study of ELLs in SEI programs mandated by Proposition 203 in Arizona, Mahoney and her colleagues (2005) concluded that "[a] review of the state's English language proficiency data suggests that students are not achieving English fluency at the rate anticipated by proponents of Proposition 203 and that the theory underlying the model is false" (319).

In both California and Arizona, structured English immersion was touted as the solution to the low academic achievement of ELLs. However, after several years of implementation, these programs have not produced positive results. In fact, in Arizona, where ELLs are segregated for instruction in grammar, vocabulary, and pronunciation in English for four hours each day, there is growing concern that most ELLs will not be able to graduate from high school.

ESL Pullout Traditional Instruction

Unlike immersion programs, ESL programs provide specific support for ELLs. In ESL pullout programs ELLs are pulled out of their mainstream classes for ESL support. The traditional ESL pullout classes teach basic vocabulary and grammar. This instruction is not connected to the content ELLs are studying in their regular classes. Students study in English only and usually lose their first language abilities. Thomas and Collier (1997, 2002) have identified this program as the least effective of ESL programs, yet it is the program that is most often implemented in U.S. schools. Students in pullout programs miss the instruction that goes on in the regular class, and they lose instructional time as they transition to a new classroom and later return. This is also one of the most expensive programs, since an additional teacher is hired to teach the ELLs.

ESL Pullout or Pull-in Content Instruction

Students in these programs are pulled out of mainstream classes, or an ESL specialist is pulled into mainstream classrooms to work with students. This differs from ESL traditional pullout in that what the ESL students study is connected to the content they are learning in their classrooms. The ESL specialists use strategies to make the regular classroom content comprehensible to ELLs. While this program is more effective than traditional ESL pullout, Thomas and Collier (1997, 2002) found that students who had this type of ESL support usually dropped out in high school or were doing poorly when compared to their high school peers. In fact, none of the English-only models has been shown to be as effective as bilingual models for emergent bilinguals.

The Place of English in Bilingual Programs

Both immersion and ESL programs deliver all instruction in English. Although the key component of any bilingual program is primary-language instruction, bilingual programs that are successful always include effective English instruction as well. Often, people think that in bilingual programs, students spend the whole day receiving instruction in their first language. In fact, they also receive instruction in English.

Effective English instruction is meaningful, functional, and context-rich so that it meets the needs of bilingual students. In other words, it contains large amounts of comprehensible input. Krashen (1992) has shown that it is comprehensible input that counts in language acquisition, not just exposure to a second language. That is the reason that students receiving only one or two hours of English a day in a bilingual program may actually acquire English more rapidly than students who are in an English environment all day long. The students in the bilingual program with good English instruction are receiving greater amounts of comprehensible input.

Models of Bilingual Education

There are several models of bilingual education. The main difference among the models is the amount of time students receive primary-language instruction. Students in transitional programs typically receive some primary-language instruction for two or three years, while students in maintenance or dual-language bilingual programs are taught in their primary language for at least six years. Baker (2006) classifies the short-term transitional programs as *weak* bilingual programs and the long-term maintenance or dual language programs as *strong* programs. He points out that students in strong bilingual programs consistently outperform students in weak programs. Baker's claim is supported by a large body of research.

Early–Exit Bilingual Education

Early-exit or transitional programs are the most widely implemented of all the bilingual models. In early-exit programs students are prepared to transition into all-English classrooms within three years of beginning school as non-English speakers. The rationale for these programs is that they provide students with understandable instruction in their first language until they have developed enough English proficiency to be instructed in English. The first language serves as a bridge that helps students move into English-only instruction. Theoretically, non-English-speaking students who enter school in second grade (or later) should also receive three years of primary-language support. However, in practice older learners usually receive less than three years of first language instruction. There are fewer bilingual upper-grade teachers, and often even those teachers are encouraged to get students into English as quickly as possible.

Early-exit programs appeal to those who want to see children in all-English classes as soon as possible. Since most children develop conversational proficiency in about two years, teachers and administrators often use this as an indication that the children are ready for all-English instruction. Many tests used to determine whether students are ready to transition to the mainstream only test oral proficiency, so students who have developed conversational English are exited out of bilingual programs before they have developed primary-language literacy and academic content knowledge that can transfer into English-only instruction.

Thomas and Collier (2002) found that students in early-exit programs usually lose their first language proficiency as they do not develop it beyond the two to three years of instruction. High school students in their study who had been in early-exit programs generally scored below the fiftieth percentile in tests of reading in English.

Late–Exit or Maintenance Bilingual Programs

In late-exit programs, students receive instruction in their first language through at least sixth grade. Late-exit is a one-way model because all of the students in a class are ELLs, so their language learning is going one way, toward English; but at the same time, their first language is maintained. In the early grades, late-exit students usually receive more first language support, but once they get into third and fourth grades, they study subject matter and do reading and writing in English as well as in their first language. Throughout their program, English is taught through academic content.

Usually, students in late-exit programs develop proficiency in their first language and in English. Ramírez (1991) found that late-exit students scored better in math and reading in English than students in English-only or early-exit programs. Collier and Thomas found these students scored above the fiftieth percentile in reading in English by sixth or seventh grade. Although late-exit programs are fairly successful, they are the least often implemented model. One problem with maintenance bilingual programs is that the ELLs are segregated from native English speakers. A second problem is that this program is often seen as remedial.

Bilingual Enrichment Programs: Some Distinctions

> Enriched educational programs emphasize challenging standards in the core curriculum domains while enriching students' development in both their first and second languages. These programs aim for full proficiency in two languages, an understanding and appreciation of the cultures associated with those languages, and high levels of achievement in all core academic domains. (Cloud et al. 2000)

Dual-language bilingual programs are a type of enriched education. Enrichment education, however, could refer to programs that are not dual language. The French immersion programs in Canada are enrichment programs because they do all of the above: they aim at full proficiency in two languages, an understanding and appreciation of two cultures, and high levels of academic achievement. However, all the students are English speakers learning in French and English. The students do very well academically in both languages. In addition, because they do not interact in school with native French speakers other than their teacher, research has shown their French is not entirely native-like. Swain (1985) found that the grammatical competence of grade 6 French immersion students was not equivalent to that of native speakers, "in spite of 7 years of comprehensible input in the target language" (251).

In the United States there has been a recent growth in enrichment programs where students develop two languages. Unlike the French immersion programs, students in dual language enrichment programs do not all have the same first language. Some are native English speakers and some are not. Students are usually integrated for content instruction in two languages. Usually, students come from both low-income and middle-class or upper-middle-class families. The students learn together in each other's languages and become competent in both. They also build important friendships and come to appreciate one another's languages and cultures. Researchers have shown that the achievement of students in dual language programs in English is equal to or better than that of native English speakers schooled all in English (Thomas and Collier 2002; Lindholm-Leary 2001).

For areas with high Hispanic populations where most students have some Spanish in their linguistic background and many enter school only speaking Spanish, a kind of one-way immersion program has become popular (Cloud et al. 2000). In these programs content is taught in both English and Spanish throughout the day, both languages are valued equally, and students become proficient biliterates. This model differs from a two-way program, but test results show that Latinos in these programs succeed academically (Gómez, Freeman, and Freeman 2005).

Figure 6–6 shows the similarities and differences among the types of programs that serve English language learners: English immersion, structured English immersion,

Type of Program	Description	Language Result	Academic Result
English Immersion	English language learners are taught with mainstream students and given no special services.	Subtractive— Students learn to communicate in English but lose most or all of their native language proficiency.	Show less progress in math and reading than students in ESL/ bilingual programs. Highest number of dropouts is in this group.
Structured English Immersion	English language learners are taught only in English and teachers are trained to make the input comprehensible.	Subtractive— Students develop literacy and learn to communicate in English. Students lose most or all of their ability to use their native language.	In California after five years of structured English students have limited conversational English and have difficulty reading and understanding grade-level texts.
ESL Pullout Traditional Instruction	English language learners are given ESL support. They are taught basic vocabulary and language structure (grammar) and then integrated into all English instruction.	Subtractive— Students develop literacy and learn to communicate in English. Students lose most or all of their ability to use their native language.	These students show little academic progress and once mainstreamed rarely catch up. Many students drop out before graduation.
ESL Pullout or Push-in Content Instruction	English language learners are given 2–3 years ESL content support services and then integrated into all English instruction.	Subtractive— Students develop literacy and learn to communicate in English. They lose most or all of their ability to use their native language.	By the end of high school many of these students drop out or are in the lowest fourth of their class.

FIGURE 6–6. *Programs for English language learners*

Type of Program	Description	Language Result	Academic Result
Early Exit or Transitional Bilingual Education	English language learners receive a portion of their content instruction in their primary language for 2–3 years and then are integrated into all-English instruction.	Subtractive—Students learn to communicate and study in English only. They usually lose their first language.	At the end of high school these students score below the 50th percentile in tests of reading in English.
Late Exit or Maintenance Programs	English language learners receive content instruction in both L1 and L2 for four to six years.	Additive—ELLs become bilingual and biliterate.	ELLs outperform students in English-only programs. Students achieve above the 50th percentile on standardized tests.
Enriched Immersion (example: French Immersion in Canada)	Native English speakers are taught language through content instruction in a second language. English is introduced in second grade or later.	Additive—Students become bilingual and biliterate.	Students acquire a second language and achieve the same levels of competence in academic subjects as peers taught all in English.
Bilingual Dual-Language Education (One-way and Two-way)	English language learners and native speakers of English learn language through content in both English and the first language of the English learners.	Additive—Native English speakers and English learners become bilingual and biliterate.	Students from both language groups outperform students in transitional and developmental bilingual education and score above the 50th percentile on standardized tests.

FIGURE 6–6. *Continued*

ESL pullout taught traditionally, ESL pullout or push-in taught through content, early-exit or transitional bilingual education, late-exit or maintenance bilingual education, and dual-immersion programs.

Monoglossic and Heteroglossic Models of Bilingualism

Traditionally, programs for bilingual students have been categorized as subtractive, when children go to school and lose their first language in the process of learning the language of school; or additive, when children go to school, maintain and develop their first language, and learn the second language. The images that have been used to depict these programs are a unicycle and a bicycle. In subtractive programs, students begin and end school with just one language, so these students can be represented by the unicycle with just one wheel. Students in additive programs are like a bicycle with its two wheels. As we discussed earlier, a balanced bilingual is like a bicycle with two equal wheels.

Rather than viewing programs for ELLs as additive or subtractive, García (2009, 2010) asks us to look at bilingualism through a new lens. She argues that views of bilinguals and bilingual education programs are better considered as monoglossic or heteroglossic. Instead of picturing the languages of a bilingual as a unicycle or a bicycle, Garcia suggests that a better image is an all-terrain vehicle. The wheels may be of different sizes, they can move up and down independently, and they can move in different directions as the vehicle negotiates an uneven landscape. This perspective fits with Grosjean's (2010) contention that bilinguals use their different languages in different contexts and for different purposes.

Monoglossic Views and Models

Monoglossic comes from the prefix *mono* meaning *one*, and the root *glossic* meaning *tongue* or *voice*. Monoglossic views of bilinguals and bilingual education consider that each language is one separate entity. García considers subtractive programs, such as early-exit and ESL programs, to be monoglossic because students enter school with one language, lose that language, and add a second. The goal of subtractive programs is to create proficient speakers of English, and in the process, children frequently begin and end as monolinguals.

García would also say that programs usually labeled as additive, including dual-language and maintenance bilingual education, come from a monoglossic view because the goal of these programs is to develop a person who is the equivalent of two monolinguals. During instruction and assessment, the two languages are kept separate. In García's (2009) words, "bilinguals are expected to be and do with each of their languages the same thing as monolinguals" (52). For example, in a bilingual dual-language program students are expected to perform like English monolinguals during English time and like Spanish monolinguals during Spanish time. Monoglossic views of bilinguals and of programs for emergent bilinguals have predominated in schools.

Heteroglossic Views and Models of Bilingualism

Instead of operating from a monoglossic perspective, García asks us to think of bilingualism from a heteroglossic perspective. The prefix *hetero* comes from the Greek meaning *other*. The term *heteroglossic* comes from the writing of the Russian literary critic, Bakhtin. He used the term to refer to the multiple or other voices that co-exist within a novel, the voices of the characters and of the narrator. García uses the term to refer to the two or more languages that exist in a bilingual speaker. These two languages cannot be strictly separated because both are always present.

This view is a better reflection of how bilinguals really use their languages. Recall our discussion of translanguaging earlier when we described Maya's language use and the language use of the people in *el bloque*, Zentella's study of Puerto Ricans in New York City. García argues that strict separation of languages is not natural. It does not reflect the normal use of language by bilinguals. Instead of keeping languages apart, bilingual programs in schools should draw on the translanguaging practices of bilingual children as Cummins (2007) suggests.

García discusses two models of bilingualism that are heteroglossic: recursive bilingualism and dynamic bilingualism. Recursive bilingualism occurs when a community whose language is being lost makes an effort to revitalize that language. García uses the example of the Maori of New Zealand. The Maori language had been marginalized and was dying out, but now it is being taught in the schools. García explains that as they regain their language, the Maori people are drawing on past knowledge. They move back and forth between Maori and English as they reconstitute the heritage language, using it for new functions as well as old. This reconstitution is not simply a new language being added. It is a drawing from what was known to develop the language more fully to meet the present needs of the speakers.

Dynamic bilingualism for García is how we must come to look at bilingualism in our globalized society. From a dynamic perspective, bilinguals and multilinguals use their languages for a variety of purposes and in a variety of settings. They are more or less proficient in the different contexts where they use the languages and are more or less proficient in different modalities (visual, print, and sound). García draws on the Language Policy Division of the Council of Europe's definition of bilingualism to set a goal for students in U.S. schools: "The ability to use several languages to varying degrees and for distinct purposes" (54).

García (2009) challenges us to look at bilingual education in a new way, taking a heteroglossic view of dynamic bilingualism. She argues that this new view of bilingual education is needed because bilingual education in the United States has been built on four misconceptions or what García calls misconstructions.

1. The first misconstruction is to think of second language students as English language learners. She suggests the term *emergent bilinguals*, because "[w]hen educators speak about English language learners, they often forget that there is more to these students than simply learning English" (3).

2. The second misconstruction is the view that bilingualism is linear. Students speak one language, and they add another. Instead, she suggests that educators view bilingual education as a dynamic blending and mixing of languages that enables students to develop different language practices to meet the needs of increasingly multilingual communities.

3. The third misconstruction that García challenges is the conception of ESL and bilingual models of education. Instead, she urges educators "to build on students' complex bilingualism and plurilingualism and respond to and validate their multiple bilingual practices" (4).

4. The final misconstruction that García challenges is the use of the term *dual language* to describe the enriched immersion programs we discussed above. García believes that we must at all times remind educators and the public that these programs are *bilingual* dual-language enrichment programs and not remedial programs for students who do not speak English. If we take out the word *bilingual*, we are silencing not only the word but also the goal.

If educators adopt García's ideas of a heteroglossic view of dynamic bilingualism and reject the misconstructions that predominate in programs for emergent bilinguals, this would help to move education for bilinguals into the twenty-first century and the globalized society we live in. The theory and research we have reviewed in this chapter support the view of education García calls for. No students should ever ask, *¿Por qué soy tonto?* Their language should be embraced, and they should be enabled to develop as dynamic bilinguals.

KEY POINTS

→ In the modern world, monolingualism, not bilingualism, should be considered a problem.

→ Crystal lists several reasons that languages should be preserved; however, many languages have died and many more will die in the near future.

→ English has become a global language.

→ García uses the term *translanguaging* to describe how bilinguals communicate using both their languages.

→ Code switching requires competence in two languages, and people code switch for a variety of reasons.

→ Most bilinguals are not balanced. Instead they use their two or more languages for different functions with different people in different contexts.

→ Cummins refutes three assumptions about using monolingual strategies for bilingual and second language teaching programs.

→ Teachers can support students' first languages in a number of ways, including using preview/view/review.

→ The theoretical base for bilingual education includes Cummins' Common Underlying Proficiency theory and his Interdependence Hypothesis.

→ French immersion programs in Canada have important differences from structured English immersion programs in the United States.

→ English-only models for the instruction of ELLs include English immersion and ESL pullout or push-in.

→ Models of bilingual education include early-exit transitional programs, late-exit maintenance programs, and bilingual dual-language enrichment programs.

KEY POINTS

➜ García argues for a heteroglossic view of bilingualism rather than a monoglossic view that sees the bilingual as two monolinguals in one person.

➜ García lists four misconstructions of bilingual education. She contends that the labels we give bilinguals matter; bilingualism is dynamic, not linear; teachers should validate students' multiple bilingual practices; and the name we give bilingual programs matters.

APPLICATIONS

1. In this chapter we discussed language death. Why is it important not to allow languages to die? Consider the minority languages in your community. Are they in danger of becoming dying languages? Why or why not?

2. Think about the emergent bilinguals in your school. Do they have linguistic and cultural capital? Why or why not? Do you have linguistic and cultural capital? Why or why not?

3. García discusses *languaging* and *translanguaging*. Explain to a partner what you understand these two concepts to mean. Do you translanguage? Do your second language students translanguage? How do you feel about translanguaging? Have your opinions changed after reading this chapter?

4. We discussed Cummins' interdependence hypothesis and the concept of a common underlying proficiency. Think of your students. Do you see differences in their academic performance in English because of differences in their first language proficiency? Explain.

5. García contrasts different images of programs for ELLs. She discusses the unicycle, the bicycle, and the all-terrain vehicle. Connect each image to a type of program and explain what each image means from a language-use perspective.

6. We described different models for teaching English language learners. Which of these models is used in your school or district? After reading this chapter, do you think it is the best model? Why? Why not?

7. In planning a lesson this week, use preview, view, review as you teach. How did this work? Be prepared to share with your classmates.

8. García (2010) describes four misconstructions of bilingualism. Do you think teachers and administrators at your school would agree? Comment on each misconstruction.

7

How Can Schools Develop an Intercultural Orientation?

Ruíz—Three Orientations Toward Language

The various programs that have been developed to teach English to language minority students reflect different ways of conceptualizing a second language. Ruíz (1984) has described the historical development of three orientations toward language: *language-as-a-handicap*, *language-as-a-right*, and *language-as-a-resource*. He defines an orientation as a "complex of dispositions toward language and its role, and toward languages and their role in society" (16). Attitudes people hold about language come from their orientation. Figure 7–1 defines the three orientations.

During the fifties and sixties, *language-as-handicap* was the prevalent orientation. Ruíz points out that at this time educators saw ELLs as having a problem, even a handicap, so that "teaching English, even at the expense of the first language, became the objective of school programs" (19). In other words, educators with this orientation believed that to overcome the handicap they had, ELLs must transition into English as quickly as possible. While most ELLs were simply mainstreamed and left to sink or swim in English, ESL programs were started in parts of the country with significant numbers of ELLs.

Ruíz explains that in the seventies, the *language-as-a-right* orientation emerged. As a part of the Civil Rights Movement, bilingual educators called for the rights of non-native English speakers to bilingual education. Students in bilingual programs could exercise their right to maintain their native language while learning a second language. Those who held this orientation demanded freedom from discrimination on the basis of language and the right to use one's first language in daily living. While this *language-as-a-right* orientation is positive, Ruíz notes that many people were

Orientation Toward an ELL's First Language	Description	Type of Program Schools Offer
Language as a handicap	Language is seen as a problem that must be overcome for school success.	Submersion, structured English immersion, or ESL
Language as a right	ELLs have a right to use their language, but schools do not need to develop it.	Transitional or maintenance bilingual education
Language as a resource	ELLs' first languages are resources that should be developed fully.	Maintenance or dual-language enrichment bilingual education

FIGURE 7–1. *Orientations toward language (based on Ruíz 1984)*

resentful, especially when language rights were enforced. This orientation led to the establishment of transitional and maintenance bilingual programs.

More recently, a third orientation, *language-as-a-resource*, has developed in some parts of the country. Ruíz sees this orientation as a better approach to language planning for several reasons:

> [I]t can have a direct impact on enhancing the language status of subordinate languages; it can help to ease tensions between majority and minority communities; it can serve as a more consistent way of viewing the role of non-English languages in U.S. society; and it highlights the importance of cooperative language planning. (25–26)

The best examples presently of the *language-as-a-resource* perspective are bilingual dual-language programs. In these programs students' primary languages are developed as well as English, and native English learners also learn another language. These are enrichment education programs. Bilingualism and cross-cultural understanding are valued and promoted by all those involved.

At the same time that bilingual dual-language programs are promoted in some communities, there is a widespread movement in the United States calling for English only. There seems to be a return to the *language-as-a-handicap* orientation as many educators blame the lack of academic success of many immigrant children on their lack of English and their reliance on their first language. Structured English immersion programs reflect the *language-as-a-handicap* orientation.

Cummins—Educational Orientations

Ruíz discusses general orientations toward language. These orientations have led to the establishment of different kinds of programs for ELLs. Cummins (2001) also looks at orientations, but rather than focusing strictly on language, he points to language policies as just one of the areas to consider in analyzing how schools respond to second language students.

Cummins defines two orientations that schools can develop: intercultural or assimilationist. These two orientations differ in four areas: use of students' primary languages and cultures in the curriculum, relationships with minority community members, approach to teaching, and methods of assessment. Figure 7–2 outlines the key points of differences between the two orientations.

As Figure 7–2 shows, when schools take an intercultural orientation, they include students' primary languages and cultures, they involve minority parents in school activities, they encourage the use of current methods of collaborative critical inquiry, and they design assessments that allow students to demonstrate their competence. In contrast, when schools take an assimilationist orientation, they exclude students' primary languages and pay little attention to students' cultures, they discourage minority community members from active involvement in the schools, they teach using traditional methods, and they use forms of assessment, such as tests and quizzes, that help teachers justify the grades they give students.

Generally, schools that take an intercultural orientation see student diversity as an asset. Such schools find ways to incorporate diverse students into the institution and to provide programs that promote their success. On the other hand, some schools have as their goal the assimilation of diverse students into the mainstream. In the

	Intercultural Orientation	Assimilationist Orientation
Students' languages and cultures	Add them to the curriculum	Exclude them from the curriculum
Minority community members	Involve them in the school	Exclude them from the school
Teaching	Use transformative methods	Use traditional methods
Assessment	Help students show what they know	Use measures to justify grades

FIGURE 7–2. *Intercultural orientations*

attempt to assimilate students, such schools often have programs that disempower and marginalize second language students and the minority communities they come from.

Including Students' Languages and Cultures

In schools that adopt an intercultural orientation, students' primary languages and cultures are included in the curriculum. For example, schools may develop bilingual programs. This is an additive approach because new students add "a second language to their repertory of skills at no cost to the development of their first language" (Cummins 1996). Schools can also incorporate students' cultures into the curriculum through both classroom and whole school projects. In Chapter 6 we discussed several ways schools can include students' languages, even when the school does not have a bilingual program.

Moll and his colleagues (Moll 1994; González et al. 1993), working in Tucson, Arizona, have engaged both university researchers and classroom teachers in projects aimed at discovering students' funds of knowledge. Sometimes, teachers do not realize the rich background that language minority students bring with them to the classroom. In the research that Moll, González, and their colleagues have conducted, teachers make home visits, not to teach the parents something or discuss discipline problems, but to learn from the parents, to discover their funds of knowledge.

These funds of knowledge are the strategies and skills each family develops to function effectively. For example, families know who to call for medical advice or who to talk to if their car needs repair. As González and her colleagues explain:

> A key finding from our research is that these funds of knowledge are abundant and diverse and may include information about, for example, farming and animal husbandry (associated with households' rural origins), construction and building (related to urban occupations), and many other matters, such as trade, business, and finance on both sides of the U.S. Mexican border. (3)

Anthropologists from the university work with the teachers on how to conduct ethnographic research. Then the teachers visit their students' homes and also interview their students to discover the strategies and skills their family has developed. Teachers meet to discuss their findings and use this information to develop curriculum units that build on the knowledge their students bring with them.

Students are more engaged in school when the curriculum connects to their background and culture. A good example of how teachers can build on what students know and are interested in comes from Denise's unit on Pilgrims.

Denise's Hmong Pilgrims Unit

Denise, a third-grade teacher, developed a unit that drew on her students' cultural backgrounds. Denise was a bilingual teacher at a school with a high Latino population. However, the area the school served underwent a drastic change. Many of the Latino families moved out, and a large number of Southeast Asian immigrants moved into the area. As a result, Denise's class included many Hmong students whose families were refugees who had been living in camps in Thailand.

Denise found creative ways to include the Hmong culture in her curriculum. She felt strongly that, in studying the Pilgrims, her students should not only learn about the traditional American Thanksgiving Pilgrims and Indians. She decided to center her curriculum around the question, "What or who is a pilgrim?" She began with a literature book identified by the district for her grade level, *Molly's Pilgrim* (Cohen 1983). This book tells the story of a Russian refugee girl who teaches others in her class that recent immigrants are today's pilgrims.

Denise believed that it was important for all the students in her class to develop a better understanding of what a pilgrim was and the ways they themselves were pilgrims. The class then read and discussed *Sara Morton's Day: A Day in the Life of a Pilgrim* (Waters 1989) to get an idea of the typical daily life of a Pilgrim in colonial times. The class also read and discussed a book about two immigrant children sailing to America, *Watch the Stars Come Out* (Levinson 1985).

Next, Denise read *How Many Days to America?* (Bunting 1988). She knew that most of her Hmong and Laotian students, like the family in that book, were in the United States because they had had to flee their own countries. The students and teacher discussed the difference between immigrants and refugees. Denise drew a Venn diagram and helped the students decide on how immigrants and refugees are alike and how they are different.

Denise helped her students understand that refugees are immigrants who come to a new country to escape civil unrest and political or religious oppression in their own country. They also discussed other reasons that people immigrate. The students decided that some immigrants come to a new country because they want a better way of life. Others come to join relatives who had immigrated earlier. As a homework assignment, the children interviewed their families, asking three questions: "Where did our ancestors come from?" "Where did they settle?" and "When did they come to the United States and why?" Students could conduct the interview in their first language or in English.

Denise was well aware that many of her Hmong students' parents, like many recent refugees, were sensitive about this type of interview. Because of the terrible memories of the war and the persecutions they have suffered, many refugee parents will not discuss their past with their children. However, older siblings who know what happened typically believe that it is important for the younger generation to understand their history. Denise found that these brothers and sisters or older cousins were usually glad to answer the interview questions.

After conducting the interviews, the children shared in small groups what they had learned about their past. Denise knew that ELLs often are hesitant to share with the whole class and are more comfortable in a small group. For her beginner ELLs, Denise placed them in same-language groups so they could discuss their interviews in their first language, rather than having to report to a large group.

After the readings, the discussions, and the interviews, the whole class watched the video of *Molly's Pilgrim*. In the story and the video, Molly's mother made and dressed a pilgrim doll in a typical Russian outfit. Denise invited her students to make and dress a paper doll in traditional clothing from their cultural group. Denise explained how she organized this activity:

> Many mothers sew, and the children bring in fabulous pieces of fabric from Thailand and other countries. I put out all the scraps, give students a template of a doll run off on tag board, and with scissors and glue they make a pilgrim.

After the students made their dolls, Denise asked them to write a story. The children typed their stories; Figure 7–3 shows two dolls and the stories students wrote about these dolls. The students' pilgrims and stories were put on a bulletin board, which, Denise said, "truly reflected the diverse cultures in my classroom."

Denise explained how exciting this unit was for her and for her students:

> I wanted to move away from the basal reader, so I decided to try to extend a piece of quality literature that was relevant to my students. I had no idea this would be so successful. The bulletin board display attracted a lot of attention, and this was a positive learning experience not only for my students but for many others at the school.

Denise found creative ways to expand her Pilgrim unit to include the cultures of her students. As a result, all her students developed a better concept of pilgrims. At the same time, their own languages and cultural backgrounds were validated.

Involving Minority Community Members in the School

A second characteristic of schools that adopt an intercultural orientation is that minority community members are involved in school activities. These schools develop programs that encourage collaboration between the school and the minority

The Pilgrims

The pilgrim came from Laos to Fresno. And his name is John he really come for freedom he come to American over there. They have lots of people kill lots of people. So he come they Country to are Country. He wear short and t-shirt and pants he like to play restling.

My Doll

My doll came from Thailand because she came to have freedom. She came to have her own church and have her own place to live and get freedom. The soldiers were killing them. She did not want to be hurt so she came to have freedom in America.

FIGURE 7–3. *Hmong pilgrim dolls*

community. Schools that take an intercultural orientation foster strong home-school relationships with all parents, including parents of English language learners.

Our basic assumption is that all parents want their children to be successful. However, some parents of English language learners do not appear to show interest in their children's school lives. Francisco, whom we introduced in Chapter 6, provides us with some insights into why teachers and administrators might develop the impression that the parents of emergent bilinguals just don't care.

Francisco came to the United States in 1989 at age fourteen from El Salvador during the period of civil war there. Francisco, like may young men his age, was in danger of being conscripted by the army of either side and forced to fight. Concepción, his mother, viewed his arrival in Fresno as the end of her long struggle to get him to the United States legally. Concepción spoke no English and had not been·educated in El Salvador. She saw her responsibility as providing food and shelter for her children.

Now that Francisco was in the United States, his job was to succeed here—to accomplish the American Dream. His mother certainly cared about his schooling, but she was not prepared to approach his teachers to discuss his schoolwork and progress. The large inner-city high school of more than three thousand students intimidated her.

In his first year in college, Francisco found the course work overwhelming and was on the point of giving up when his college soccer coach, who could speak Spanish, came to Francisco's home to talk to Concepción about Francisco's academic struggles. After this visit, Concepción talked to her son long and hard about the sacrifices she had made to give him this opportunity for an education. Francisco still remembers thinking, *You don't know how hard it is. You have no idea*. He did not lack respect for his mother. He was simply living in a world that she was not part of and could never be part of. She was not a negligent parent. She was just not able to help him with his academic school subjects. Instead, she saw her role as providing strong encouragement for him to continue his education.

Tou, the Hmong student we describe in Chapter 1, came from an immigrant family that had suffered greatly because of the move from Southeast Asia to the United States. Tou's parents had separated, and he lived with his father, who could not find work and who did not speak English. His father only came to school for a conference at the request of school personnel. He would probably not have felt comfortable coming to parent meetings or participating in parent groups.

José Luis, Guillermo, and Patricia, the three teens from El Salvador, lived by themselves. Their only relative in the United States was their aunt. Unlike Francisco's mother, she was very well educated, studying for a doctorate. She was a wife, a graduate student, and a teacher of Spanish at both the university where she studied and at the local community college. Like Tou's father, she would come to a school meeting, but only if a serious problem arose. She provided the teens with family love and shelter. Her nieces and nephews knew what they needed to do to succeed, and it was up to them to do it. Even though she was involved in education, she had not attended public schools in the United States. In El Salvador, where she had been educated, parents were not expected to be involved in their children's schooling. As a result, she did not see her role as becoming involved in parent organizations.

Caretakers of English language learners like Francisco, Tou, and the three siblings from El Salvador realize that school may be the only road to success for young people. Sometimes they do not know how to help their relatives succeed, especially if they do not speak English and have had very little schooling themselves. Even if they have received an education, it may have been in a school system very different from the system in this country, and they do not understand the roles expected of them here.

Research on Teacher Attitudes

In many cases, teachers do not realize that parents of ELLs may not see their role as becoming involved in their children's schooling. In their research, Suárez-Orozco, Suárez-Orozco, and Todorova (2008) found that teachers believed that parents were not concerned about their children's academic success. The research team conducted interviews with seventy-five teachers in seven school districts in different areas of the country to determine their perception of the parents of immigrant adolescents. They asked questions such as, "How do you expect parents to support their children's education?" They found that many teachers felt that most immigrant parents were not as involved as they should be and that they held low expectations for their children's academic future. The researchers sum up their findings by commenting:

> Parents who came to school and helped with homework were viewed as concerned parents, whereas parents who did neither were thought to be disinterested and parents of poor students. A teacher shared with us: "Only a minimum percentage of parents get involved in their kid's education and usually the parents that are concerned and get involved are the parents of the students that are doing well in school. Parents that have kids with problems prefer to hide and not get involved." (77)

While the Suárez-Orozco team found that teachers perceived that parents held low expectations for their children, interviews with the students painted a different picture. As the researchers write:

> While overall teachers' assessments of immigrant parents were often patronizing at best and hostile at worst, looking into the eyes of immigrant youth, we found a very different perspective. The vast majority of the children had internalized very high parental expectations for their students' performance. (77)

The researchers asked students to complete the question, "For my parents, getting good grades is . . . ?" (77). Seventy-one percent of the students responded "very important" and another 22 percent responded "important."

Even though their children's academic success is important for parents of emergent bilinguals, often, they do not understand how school works and how to help their children with school. Gándara and Contreras (2009) in their study of Latinos and education found this to be the case, even when parents were middle or upper class:

Latino parents also have less access to information about schooling and other social resources because of more limited social networks and language differences, even when they are ostensibly from the same social class as white parents. And if they are undocumented, they have much less access to social and health services than a similarly low-income white family. (83)

Valdés (1996), in her study of ten migrant families over a three-year period, found that the gap between home and school was, indeed, wide. The school did not understand the families, and the families did not understand the school. She explains the problems in communication from the school's perspective:

> Schools expected a "standard" family, a family whose members were educated, who were familiar with how schools worked, and who saw their role as complementing the teacher's in developing children's academic abilities. It did not occur to school personnel that parents might not know the appropriate ways to communicate with the teachers, that they might feel embarrassed about writing notes filled with errors, and that they might not even understand how to interpret their children's report cards. (167)

The lack of communication between home and school was further complicated by the parents' lack of understanding of the school. In fact, not only did the parents not understand the expectations of the school, they did not conceive of a worldview different from theirs. Therefore, when teachers or administrators responded in ways they found insulting or uncaring, they took those responses at face value and were angry or hurt. While the school thought the parents were indifferent, Valdés found the parents were very concerned about their children's education:

> The parents, on the other hand, were living lives that required large amounts of energy just to survive. They had little formal schooling and few notions about what schools expected of them and their children. And yet, they valued education. The collective family wisdom had already instilled in them a sense of the importance of high school graduation. They wanted their children to have good jobs, and they wanted them to have whatever education they would need in order to get such jobs. (167)

Parent Education Programs

Valdés (1996) concludes her book about the ten migrant families with a chapter titled "Changing Families." She expresses some concerns with traditional parent education and parent involvement programs, which do not take the cultures and values of families into consideration. For example, parent education programs typically provide parents with information on how best to raise their children. Parents receive information about topics such as nutrition, discipline, and early-learning activities. These programs are well intentioned, but they may not be culturally sensitive. Parents from different cultural backgrounds have definite opinions about topics like proper eating and the best way to discipline children.

A second type of program that Valdés discusses is parent involvement programs. These programs emphasize the importance of parents helping children with homework, volunteering in school, and attending school functions. While most mainstream parents would find these suggestions reasonable, parents from some cultural groups may view their role as ensuring that their children are well behaved. For parents from some groups, it would be disrespectful to take on the role of the teacher. Although both parent education and parent involvement programs can be successful with language minority parents, it is important that the programs be culturally sensitive and that the school take an attitude that they can learn from the community members as well as teach them.

Based on their review of programs designed to help Latino students succeed academically, Gándara and Contreras (2009) state:

> Even though parent involvement has been shown to be correlated with higher academic achievement in students, schools are notoriously ineffective at connecting with parents, especially in communities of color and where a language other than English is spoken. Our research shows that this is one of the areas in which teachers feel they have the fewest skills. (295)

Some programs for parents are operated by social agencies in the community rather than by schools. One program that Gándara and Contreras describe has been successful in increasing parents' skills in helping their children. The Parent Institute for Quality Education (PIQUE) has worked with over 180,000 participants in several states over the last twenty years. Through this program:

> Parents are taught how to establish and maintain supportive home learning environments; communicate and collaborate with teachers, counselors, and principals; navigate the school system and access its resources; encourage college attendance; identify and avoid obstacles to school success; and support children's emotional and social development. (296)

This program has been found to improve parents' ability to help their students succeed in school. For example, one research group found that parents who had gone through the program increased the time that they read to their young students at home and more carefully monitored their homework. The PIQUE program is an example of the kind of program that does have positive effects in their work with parents.

A Successful Approach to Working with Parents

Individual teachers can also make a big difference in involving the parents of language minority students. Claudia, a Spanish/English bilingual teacher at a charter school with a high immigrant population, was concerned with the lack of parent involvement. She observed:

> Though the teaching staff at the school had made considerable efforts to bring parents into the life of the school, few Spanish-speaking parents played an active role in the school. My belief was that in order to bring Spanish-speaking parents into the life of the school, we would have to give them the opportunity to participate in a way that was personally meaningful.

At that time, Claudia was doing graduate work in bilingual education and beginning to work on her master's thesis. She was interested in parent involvement and had read about workshops for Hispanic parents (Vopat 1994), which validated parents and families. She had read the work of Freire as well and decided to develop a family program for the Spanish-speaking parents at her school and report on the results for her thesis.

The first night the *Los padres como socios* (Parents as Members) met, Claudia welcomed the parents and started the meeting by asking in Spanish: "What are the questions you have about how you can best help your children?" Claudia described what happened next:

> With hardly a pause, the questions flowed from parents, reflecting the depth of their concerns and worries about their children. They had questions about bilingual education and repeating grades. They wanted to know if they should encourage their children to speak English or Spanish at home, how they could help their children in math when they learned math differently, how to motivate their children to do their homework and chores. They also wanted to know how they could learn more English.

At the end of the evening, not only did Claudia have more questions than could be answered in the six weeks of planned workshops, but she had learned wonderful things about her students and a community of parents had been formed. They were excited about coming the next time to share and get answers to the questions they had had for some time.

Based on the questions raised that first night, Claudia invited guest speakers and planned discussions to deal with parents' concerns. Over a period of six weeks, meeting each week, the community grew. Because there was free discussion, the parents told stories of their children and school. In their time together parents shared information and supported one another in their efforts to help their children grow and learn.

Toward the end of the year, the parents got involved in the same kind of writing process their children were doing in school. Volpat suggested having the parents write poetry, and Claudia decided to try this with her parents. "The parents were a little nervous about writing and others seeing their writing, but as they went through the process of writing, editing, and then sharing, they were more confident and got excited." The parents wrote poems about their children's learning at home and at school. The poems were typed up, and the children illustrated them. Then the poems were assembled into a book, which was spiral-bound. Each family received a book to take home. Figures 7–4 and 7–5 are examples of two of the poems. The first was written about Alvaro by his mother and the second is an acrostic about Robert, written by his father, Roberto.

Finding ways to involve parents of emergent bilinguals can be a special challenge for teachers who are not bilingual themselves or who have students from several language backgrounds. Nevertheless the effort is well worth it.

Gayleen, a first-grade teacher, set up a schedule for her bilingual parents to come into her classroom and participate in class events. She had children whose first languages included Spanish and several Southeast Asian languages. She was especially excited about the involvement of one husband-and-wife team. The father of a Spanish-speaking child agreed to come into the class and read books to Spanish-speaking children in Spanish.

Gayleen encouraged the father to read the books in Spanish to the entire class. At first he was reluctant to do this, but when Gayleen let him choose the book ahead of time and take it home to practice first, both the father and the children had a positive experience with the reading. The wife was not comfortable reading in Spanish, but she also wanted to do something in the classroom. Gayleen asked her to help with cooking and crafts and encouraged her to speak Spanish with the children as she did this. All of the students in Gayleen's class benefited from these experiences, even though only a few spoke Spanish.

Gayleen also had a Southeast Asian grandfather who was literate in Hmong come into her classroom as a volunteer. He worked with the Southeast Asian children as they published bilingual books in Hmong and English. This increased Gayleen's resources in Hmong and helped her Hmong students take pride in their first language.

At times, whole schools work together to create projects that involve parents. An example of a schoolwide project that involved Spanish-speaking parents was the *Math Story Book* (Zanger 1996) project in Boston, Massachusetts. In an effort to help parents understand and participate in the math curriculum, the school produced a book of math story problems in Spanish and English. School administrators, classified personnel, teachers, students, and parents were encouraged to write math problems to be included in the book. Sample problems were sent home and children and parents wrote problems together. The results were exciting. The math word

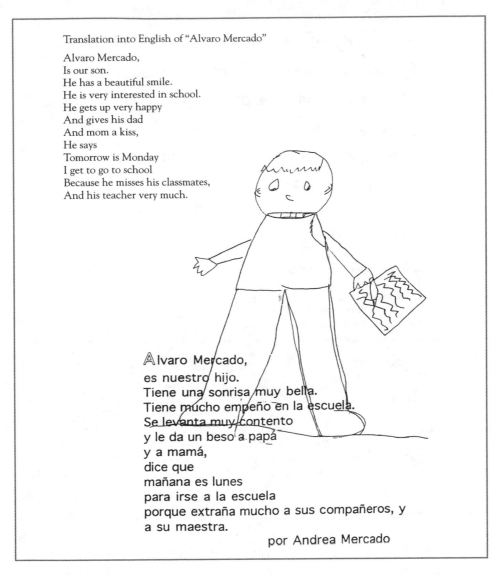

Translation into English of "Alvaro Mercado"

Alvaro Mercado,
Is our son.
He has a beautiful smile.
He is very interested in school.
He gets up very happy
And gives his dad
And mom a kiss,
He says
Tomorrow is Monday
I get to go to school
Because he misses his classmates,
And his teacher very much.

Alvaro Mercado,
es nuestro hijo.
Tiene una sonrisa muy bella.
Tiene mucho empeño en la escuela.
Se levanta muy contento
y le da un beso a papá
y a mamá,
dice que
mañana es lunes
para irse a la escuela
porque extraña mucho a sus compañeros, y
a su maestra.

por Andrea Mercado

FIGURE 7–4. *Alvaro Mercado poem*

problems reflected not only the bilingualism of the school community but also biculturalism. For example, one boy and his mother wrote and illustrated a math problem about a family baptism, an important social event in the Hispanic community. They listed who brought how many items and included the very important cake in the problem and illustration. No baptism is complete without an official bakery cake. Problem solvers were asked to count up the total number of items.

How Can Schools Develop an Intercultural Orientation?

Robert es mi niño más pequeño

Obediente aveces, a veces travieso

Bueno es con nosotros

En todo momento

Revisa sus libros y nos encuentra cuentos

Terminando, todas quedamos contentos.

por Roberto Jimenez

Translation of "ROBERT"

Robert is my youngest son
Obedient at times, sometimes naughty
Good with us
All the time
He looks over his books and finds us stories
In the end, we are all happy.

FIGURE 7–5. *Roberto's poem*

Home Visits

The home and the school can really be two different worlds. What can teachers and other school personnel do to bridge the gap? Valdés, in her study, spent a great deal of time in the homes of the families. It was only through these home visits that she came to understand their worldview. One way teachers can begin to understand the world of their immigrant students is to visit their homes. Power (1999) comments, "While home visits are time-consuming, in homes where English is the second language a visit can provide more information than any other experience" (24). Because of the insights that home visits provide, some school districts have made it mandatory for teachers to visit their students in their homes either before school starts or at the end of the first grading period.

Kristi was in her first year of teaching when she visited her students' homes at the end of the first grading period. Before she went, she complained about the time and effort the visit was going to take. Afterward, however, she realized how much she had learned. Her students' homes were modest, located around the small farming community where she taught. She came away from each visit with respect for both the parents and the children. She saw that many parents were struggling to get food on the table for their children. She found out that many of her first-grade children often took on responsibilities at home while parents and older siblings worked extra hours to make ends meet. Perhaps what touched her most, however, was the eagerness and respect with which she was received in the homes, and the interest, pride, and hope the parents showed for their children's futures.

Even when it is not a school requirement, several teachers we work with have made home visits because this has helped them understand their students and parents so much better. Peter sends an introductory letter to all the children in his class, and their parents, two weeks before school starts. He tells them in the letter that he will be visiting their home to get to know them in the following week. Then he makes short visits to as many homes as possible. Even though he does not speak the first languages of many of his students, he is welcomed into the homes and has a chance to see something of his students' home lives.

Peter has found that those visits have a made a big difference for students during their first days of school, and that after meeting their children's teacher, parents are much more comfortable with both him and the school. The visits have often given him ideas about how parents can become involved in his class. One parent, for instance, played a musical instrument, and another did wood carving. Peter would never have known this had he not been in the students' homes, and since the parents have met him, they are more responsive to his invitations to come and share their skills. This personal contact, undertaken before school even starts, has made a big difference for Peter in the home-school relationship.

Encouraging First Language Literacy

In the past, some schools have encouraged parents to speak English to their children at home. However, when parents talk to their children and read and write with them in their first language at home, communication is more natural. During these inter-actions, children build important background that leads to school success.

Yvonne has often been asked to present to parent groups in Spanish. She has developed some practical suggestions of what parents can do with their children in their first language. Not all parents are literate, even in their native language. How-ever, these suggestions can be worded in ways that give parents ideas for what they can do with their children to support their children's literacy development.

Parents can support their children's school success in the following ways:

1. *Talking.* Parents who have conversations with their children help them to think and to explore their world. In this process children learn to use language for a variety of purposes.

2. *Reading*. Parents who read with their children and take them to the library give them experiences with books that they need for school success. If parents are not confident readers, they can ask their children to do the reading, or parents and children can follow a story while listening together to a tape-recorded reading. If the children read a book in English to their parents or if the children and parents listen to an English book on tape, the children can then explain the story to the parents, and they can discuss it in their first language as they look at the pictures.

3. *Writing*. Parents who encourage their children to draw and write teach them to express themselves in writing. Parents can also make children aware that adults use writing for a variety of purposes every day, including writing letters, making out checks, jotting notes, and making shopping lists. If parents do not write frequently themselves, they can have writing materials including paper and marking pens around for children during play time.

These three suggestions are supported by research conducted by Goldenberg and Gallimore (1991), who worked over several years on a project to improve reading achievement of Spanish-speaking children. One of the aspects of the study included parent involvement. The teachers at the school where the research was conducted were hesitant about parent involvement because they believed that there was no literacy in the home, that parents were not interested in the children's achievements, and that because of their minimal academic background, parents could not help their children. However, Goldenberg and Gallimore found these assumptions to be false. They write:

> Although literacy did not occupy a prominent place in most homes, it was not entirely absent. Virtually all homes, for example, sent and received letters to Mexico or Central America. All homes received printed flyers or advertisements . . . most parents reported (and subsequent studies have confirmed) that children consistently asked about signs, other "environmental print," or the contents of letters to or from relatives. None of this would be possible if literacy did not exist in the homes, at least at some level. (8–9)

In interviews with parents, Goldenberg and Gallimore found that parents "saw themselves as playing a key role in their children's school success, particularly while their children were young" (9). In addition, when asked, parents expressed great interest in helping their students at home, though many "expressed fear of confusing their children" because they were "unfamiliar with 'the system' here" (9).

The researchers found that "although the overall educational levels of parents were indeed low, most of the parents could read books with limited text and several were able to read quite well" (8). Despite the doubts teachers had about the parents' ability to help their children, story books and other literacy materials were sent home with the children. Some teachers developed activities for parents to do with their children at home that would reinforce what was being done in the classroom. These activities were similar to the *tarea* (homework) that parents were familiar with from their native countries. Some of the activities were actually quite fragmented. However, the important finding from this study was that parents did get involved. They wanted to help their children at home, and they *could* help them. Teachers need to trust that parents will engage in talking, reading, and writing with their children. These activities all contribute to English language learners' school success.

Although it is not easy, teachers at schools that take an intercultural orientation try different approaches to involving the parents of emergent bilinguals. A good first step is to listen to the parents and encourage them to voice their concerns either during meetings at school or through home visits. In addition, entire schools can undertake projects such as the math story book, and individual teachers can encourage parents to participate as Claudia and Gayleen did.

Implementing Transformative Pedagogy

A third characteristic of schools that take an intercultural orientation is that they implement a transformative pedagogy. As Cummins (1996) explains:

> Transformative pedagogy uses collaborative critical inquiry to enable students to relate curriculum content to their individual and collective experience and to analyze broader social issues relevant to their lives. It also encourages students to discuss ways in which social realities might be transformed through various forms of democratic participation and social action. (157)

An example of transformative pedagogy comes from Shelly, who taught seventh- and eighth-grade social studies. Her students' first languages included Spanish, Hmong, and Khmer, the language spoken in Cambodia. Since the seventh-grade social studies curriculum at her school begins with a unit on how people research the past, Shelly decided to have her students research their own past and connect their past to the present. Under the broad theme of "Culture: A Pattern of Civilization," Shelly and her students explored the question, "What's my part in my family and my culture?"

To launch her unit, Shelly discussed with her students the job descriptions for an archaeologist and an anthropologist. Next, she told them that *they* would be archaeologists and anthropologists. She shared examples of fossils, artifacts, legends, pieces of art, folk beliefs, and old written documents to give students ideas about how scientists research the past. The students then brainstormed what aspects of their own cultural background they would explore during the unit. They chose the following seven items:

1. *Customs/Traditions*: Discuss five cultural traditions/customs.

2. *Religious Traditions* (if applicable): Discuss five religious traditions.

3. *Recipes/Food*: Share five favorite family recipes.

4. *Legends*: Record three legends.

5. *Music*: Share the lyrics of three songs or list names of musical compositions.

6. *Holidays*: Discuss five holidays.

7. *Values*: Discuss family values and important issues.

After each student had picked a topic from the list, they interviewed their families to find out about coming to the United States and California. This information was compiled for a class map so that students could compare their migrations with those of others in their class. In addition, students brought in "artifacts" from their homes and created a class museum of cultural pieces.

Another activity in this unit was a timeline. Rather than having students simply look at timelines in a text, Shelly asked them to construct a timeline of their own lives. When her students did not know dates, Shelly suggested that they ask their families. This family involvement was so successful that Shelly has decided to make it a regular part of the unit in the future. She also discovered that timelines served as a nonthreatening way for some students to share things about their past, including

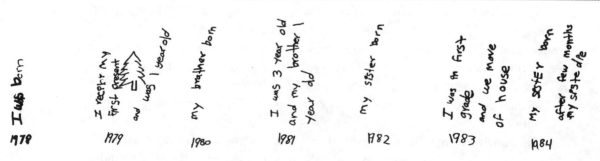

FIGURE 7–6. *Juan's timeline*

tragic deaths in the family. Juan, a Mexican student, recorded the birth and death of a sister, his separation from his parents when they came to the United States to work, and his arrival in this country (see Figure 7–6).

After the students had completed their timelines, they displayed them around the room and shared what they considered to be significant events. They also created a large whole-class timeline with dates of historical events they were studying. Students helped fill in that timeline and enjoyed adding to it each time they studied a new event. Shelly explained how the personal timelines helped scaffold her students' understanding of history better: "They have been able to compare their short lives with centuries of events, to put history in perspective, and to develop the concept that all things are connected through time."

During the unit, students worked in pairs or individually to complete projects based on the list they had brainstormed. For example, Patricia and Suiem coauthored a bilingual Spanish/English book on Mexican holidays. They included religious holidays such as Epiphany and described how it is celebrated in Mexico, where people eat a special bread, *rosca de reyes* (bread of the kings), that has a small baby Jesus doll hidden in it. The person who gets the piece of bread with baby Jesus has to throw a party for their family and friends. The two students also researched information about Mexican history. One page of their book contained their drawings of five important leaders of the Mexican Revolution.

Each student also completed an individual project. One of the most powerful examples of the positive results from this project came from Patricia's book, *My Culture of México*. In this project of over twenty neatly handwritten pages in Spanish, Patricia included the national hymn of Mexico, selected pieces of poetry, two legends, summaries of holidays, traditions, religious customs, and values and attitudes of the Mexican people. The section "Valores familiares en México" (Family Values in Mexico) demonstrates how a project such as this can help students understand and take pride in their culture (see Figure 7–7).

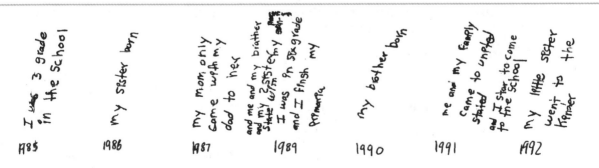

FIGURE 7–6. *Continued*

FIGURE 7–7. *Family values*

Shelly used transformative pedagogy and found creative ways to involve her students in a variety of activities as they studied culture. At the end of the inquiry unit, she wrote this reflection:

> The class really developed sophisticated concepts about culture. As we have continued to study other cultures it is obvious that they have a framework within which to work. By having them study their own culture first, they were able to personally define the meaning of custom, tradition, culture, religion, family, values, and perspective.

Taking an Advocacy Role in Assessment

A fourth characteristic of schools that take an intercultural orientation is that they design assessments that allow all their students, including their English language learners, to demonstrate what they have learned. Often, emergent bilinguals have learned much more than they can show on quizzes, tests, and essays written in English. However, these same students can show what they know when teachers use alternative forms of assessment, including assessment in their first language.

Both Denise and Shelly used a variety of methods to assess their students' learning. Denise read stories about immigrants and then discussed the stories with them. She could do an informal assessment of her students' comprehension during the class discussions and later as they filled in the Venn diagram showing differences and similarities between immigrants and refugees. She also evaluated their interviews as she listened to students share in their small groups and then read their interview notes. In addition, she was able to check the progress of their development of English proficiency as she read over their Pilgrim doll stories.

Shelly also used a variety of means to assess her students. She evaluated the students' learning by reading their timelines and by having them do projects with a partner and individually. For the projects, she gave students several choices, including making a home video; doing a mural or illustration of their family or culture; compiling a book or report on family myths, legends, traditions, or recipes; producing a family newsletter, including family events and articles written by family members; creating and performing a drama; or putting together a scrapbook or collection of articles, advertisements, or pictures that displayed aspects of their culture.

Shelly explained the value of assessing the final individual projects:

> The project was the culmination of the students' self-exploration of their own culture. Most of the students were very eager to do something with the information they had spent four weeks gathering. Since the class had developed particular guidelines that everyone used to explore his/her culture, I could have given them an essay exam based on these questions. In fact, the students were surprised that I did not give them a test. I think that this project worked much better.

> The students completed a variety of projects, utilized their talents, and practiced reading, writing, and verbal language skills. They were able to work in groups and share their knowledge. I believe that they learned so much more by sharing than if they had simply studied for a test. Many of them continued to record new information long after I had made my final check of their research notebooks.

It is important to note that Shelly allowed her students to use both English and their first languages. This not only validates their first language and culture, it makes it easier for students to show what they do know.

According to Cummins (1996), when schools adopt an intercultural orientation, the result is students who are academically and personally empowered. Students in

Shelly's class, like Patricia, developed academic skills and raised their self-esteem by completing their projects. Individual teachers like Shelly and Denise can help schools move toward an intercultural orientation. Teachers who adopt an intercultural orientation find ways to incorporate students' languages and cultures into the school program. They encourage parent involvement. They adopt transformative pedagogical approaches and use forms of assessment that allow all their students to demonstrate what they have learned.

KEY POINTS

➤ Ruíz describes three historical orientations toward the first language of ELLs: language as a handicap, language as a right, and language as a resource.

➤ Cummins proposes that schools can take one of two orientations: assimilationist or intercultural.

➤ Schools that take an intercultural orientation take an additive view of students' first languages and cultures, involve parents in the school, use transformative teaching methods, and take an advocacy approach to student assessment.

➤ Effective programs acknowledge parents' funds of knowledge and involve parents as partners in the education of their children.

➤ Teachers implement a transformative pedagogy by building on students' backgrounds and cultures.

➤ Teachers take an advocacy role in assessment.

APPLICATIONS

1. Discuss with classmates a unit and/or materials you have used that support an intercultural orientation.

2. List some ways that you or teachers you have observed have incorporated students' languages and cultures into the curriculum.

3. Visit one or two of your second language students' homes. What did you learn about the child and the family that you did not know before the visit? Share what you learned with classmates.

4. How have teachers at your school involved the parents of language minority students?

5. What are some ways other than testing have you used to assess your students that let them show what they know? List these and prepare to share them.

6. Does your school take an intercultural orientation or an assimilationist orientation? List specific facts that support your conclusion.

8

How Should We Teach Reading to Emergent Bilinguals?

Susanne, a third-grade teacher in a school where most of the students are Hispanics who speak English as their second language, was determined that in her classroom her students would become competent readers through engagement with books. At a state bilingual education conference she bought many books, and nearly all had a Latino theme, because she knew her classroom library had few books related to her students' backgrounds.

Though she expected her students to connect with the books, she had no idea how much culturally relevant bilingual books would excite them. She described what happened as she introduced the first book to her students:

> This afternoon I picked up *In My Family: En mi familia* by Carmen Lomas Garza. Time being limited, my purpose was simply to show the new books I had bought which were available in both English and Spanish and to encourage them to investigate and enjoy the Spanish text. The fever began as a slow burn as we discussed the wonderful cover illustration depicting an outdoor dance floor, people of all ages dancing, a musical ensemble, and simple lightbulbs strung from posts. I asked my students what they thought of the cover and where they thought the dance was taking place. A roar went up. "MEXICO!"

> I decided to read a bit to see what sort of connections my students would make with the first short vignette described in the book, "The Horned Toads: *Los chameleons.*" The room erupted in wild conversations during the reading. Students were unable to contain their excitement; they had stories to tell and, all decorum aside, they were going to tell them! They shared with their neighbors, friends, and, of course, me. They knew about horned toads, desert

environments, and fire ants that "really sting." By the next vignette, "Cleaning Nopalitos: *Limpiando nopalitos*," there was no way to calm the wonderfully noisy groundswell of storytelling and sharing. I was entering *their* culture, a culture and tradition they were passionate to share.

By using bilingual books that connected to her students' cultural background (Y. Freeman et al. 2003), Susanne found a way to engage her students in meaningful reading. Often, emergent bilinguals struggle with reading, especially when they are trying to learn to read in their second language. The first step in bringing ELLs to literacy is to find ways to engage them, and this is what Susanne was able to do by choosing books that connected with their culture.

Engagement in Reading

In his research with native English speakers, Guthrie (2004) has identified engagement as critical for literacy development. Guthrie and Davis (2003) define engaged readers as students who have integrated reading into their definition of who they are and willingly read to the exclusion of other activities, particularly when faced with choices. Meltzer and Hamann (2004) in their review of literacy for second language students, also identify engagement as a key for success. Students are more likely to become engaged readers when teachers choose books that connect to their students' lives, the way Susanne did.

Similarly, in their report on the results of the Program for International Student Assessment (PISA) in reading, Brozo, Shiel, and Topping (2007/2008) found that students who were engaged readers read at higher levels than students who were less engaged. They defined engaged readers as students who read a diversity of texts, read for pleasure frequently, and had a positive attitude toward reading. What makes the PISA findings significant is that younger engaged readers scored higher than older students who were less engaged, and students from low socioeconomic levels who were engaged readers scored higher than students from higher socioeconomic levels who were less engaged. Normally, socioeconomic status and age are factors that best predict success on tests of reading, but as the PISA studies show, engagement can have a stronger effect than either of those predictors.

Emergent bilinguals may receive initial literacy instruction in their first language, their second language, or both, depending on the program they are in. A synthesis of the research on literacy for second language learners by the National Literacy Panel (August and Shanahan 2006) confirms that students who receive primary language literacy instruction develop higher levels of reading proficiency than those taught completely through a second language. This follows logically from the research results on engagement. Students who are taught to read in a language they don't yet speak or understand well are much less likely to be engaged in reading than those who are taught in their native language, a language they do understand.

Effects of Reading First

Many emergent bilinguals who are taught to read in their second language with materials that are not engaging become *word callers*. That is, they learn to pronounce the words in the text, but they do not develop adequate levels of comprehension. Research reported by the National Literacy Panel confirms the observations of many teachers: "[T]here is little or no difference between the performance of language minority students and their native-speaking peers on measures of word reading accuracy" (August and Shanahan 2006, 61). ELLs do seem to pick up basic decoding skills at the same rate as native speakers. However, when it comes to comprehension, they lag behind. As the NLP report states:

> The few available studies that compared language minority students with their native-speaking peers . . . yielded highly-consistent results, indicating that the reading comprehension performance of language minority students falls well below that of their native-speaking peers. (62)

One reason that emergent bilinguals as well as native English speakers have become word callers is that many schools implemented reading programs based on Reading First grants. These programs emphasized beginning decoding skills—phonemic awareness, phonics, and fluency. The Reading First Impact Study: Final Report (Institute of Educational Sciences 2008) summarized the results of this intensive effort:

> The findings presented in this report are generally consistent with findings presented in the study's Interim Report, which found statistically significant impacts on instructional time spent on the five essential components of reading instruction promoted by the program (phonemic awareness, phonics, vocabulary, fluency, and comprehension) in grades one and two, and which found no statistically significant impact on reading comprehension as measured by the SAT 10. (xvii)

What the research shows, then, is that when initial literacy instruction focuses on developing basic decoding skills (phonemic awareness, phonics, and fluency), students do learn to decode, but they do not develop high levels of comprehension, and they do not become engaged in reading. If this is true of native English speakers, it is even more pronounced for emergent bilinguals.

One of the assumptions behind Reading First was that once students learned to read, they could read any text. Their skills would naturally evolve as they encountered more difficult and different types of texts. Basic skills would give them the foundation needed for any future reading. However, this is not the case. Unfortunately, when emergent bilinguals struggle with more complex texts, often the response from teachers is to give them additional basic skills practice. In fact, in many schools the extra practice in comprehension for ELLs consists almost entirely of short test practice texts based on the state reading test. These passages are designed to teach specific skills. What ELLs really need is engaging texts at a level they can read. Teachers can use more limited texts as scaffolds to help students develop more advanced reading skills.

Gradual Release of Responsibility Model of Reading

Whether reading is taught in a student's first or second language, finding appropriate texts is one way that teachers can move students progressively toward higher levels of reading proficiency. Effective teachers follow an approach to teaching reading that keeps the focus on comprehension, the gradual release of responsibility model (Pearson and Gallagher 1983). This model reflects Vygotsky's (1962) concept, the zone of proximal development. Vygotsky argued that we learn when we work collaboratively with an adult or a more knowledgeable peer. What we can do now with help we can do later independently.

The gradual release model illustrates how teachers can begin by providing a great deal of support for students learning to read. Then, gradually, they release the support. Beginning readers need the most support. Since they can't read, the teacher reads to them. Over time, the responsibility for reading shifts from the teacher to the student. The goal is for the student to read independently. Figure 8–1 illustrates this gradual release of responsibility model. Teachers who follow this model provide scaffolded support as students learn to read.

The first classroom activity in the gradual release model is reading aloud. At this stage, the teacher does all the work of reading. The teacher reads and students listen. As they listen, students acquire a sense of how texts work. They also begin to pick up new vocabulary and syntactic structures. Perhaps most important, they start to understand how exciting stories and informational texts can be. The second stage of the gradual release model is shared reading. During this time, the students begin to

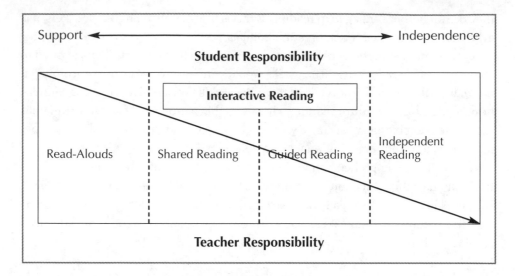

FIGURE 8–1. *Gradual release of responsibility (Pearson and Gallagher 1983)*

share the task. They follow along as the teacher reads an enlarged print text the whole class can see, or they look at their own copy of a story the teacher reads, chiming in on repeated phrases. During interactive reading, pairs or small groups of students read together supporing one another. The fourth stage is guided reading. The teacher works with small groups of students to teach specific skills that they practice. Here, the responsibility shifts more to the students. Although the teacher provides strong support, the students have the primary responsibility for reading. The final activity in the gradual release model is independent reading.

Read–Alouds

Effective teachers, like Susanne, read aloud to their students every day. They do this whether they are kindergarten teachers or high school teachers. Most often, the teacher reads to the whole class. However, at times, the teacher may read to just a small group. With older students, the teacher may read aloud from a chapter book while the students simply listen. However, many picture books are appropriate for older students as well. In addition to reading more complex books to older readers, teachers generally read for longer periods of time. Another difference between reading aloud to younger and older readers is that teachers often reread favorite books several times for younger readers. Since books for older readers are longer, the teacher reads a part each day, often a chapter, but does not reread the book.

There are several benefits of reading aloud to students. First, the teacher models fluent reading. It is important for students to hear a fluent reader, especially when the book is in their second language. This gives them a feel for the rhythm of the language as well as the pronunciation of words. Students also begin to understand elements of plot, character, and setting and the concepts of beginning, middle, and end. In addition, a teacher can choose informational books to read aloud that help build background knowledge for a theme the class is studying. Hearing a good book can also pique students' interest in the topic and in reading. Further, reading aloud provides support for struggling readers and students still developing proficiency in a second language. Above all, when teachers read aloud, students enjoy the experience. Read-alouds help students come to value reading.

Shared Reading

To shift the responsibility for reading gradually from the teacher to the student, teachers move from reading aloud to shared reading. Shared reading is often a regular feature in lower-grade classrooms. Typically, teachers read and reread a big book, a book with enlarged type and pictures that all the children can see easily. This is important for younger students who are just beginning to develop concepts of print and need to learn to match the words in the text with the teacher's oral language. Usually, the teacher moves a pointer under the words as she reads.

Shared reading sessions can be conducted with the whole class. However, they can be done in small-group settings as well. In smaller groups, teachers can better monitor how students are responding to the reading. The teacher can also encourage all the students to chime in on repeated portions of the text. This is especially important for ELLs.

Although shared reading is used most commonly with younger students, it also is essential for many older students, especially those who still struggle to read grade-appropriate texts (Allen 2002). Since most big books are written for younger children, the content and pictures are usually not appropriate for older students. Teachers of older students more often read aloud from a class text as students follow along in their individual copies. Teachers may put a reading selection on a transparency and project it so that all the students can read it, or the teacher may scan in some pages and project them in a PowerPoint presentation. The teacher stops periodically to ask questions about the reading or to have students make predictions. Teachers can also model how proficient readers make sense of text by using a think-aloud.

Interactive Reading: A Bridge to Guided Reading

Interactive reading is an intermediate stage between shared reading and guided reading. Students are given more responsibility because they now read to and with other students. Students can be paired in such a way that each pair has a stronger reader to support a less proficient reader. The less proficient reader can begin to chime in and pick up the intonation pattern of the language as the two read together.

In bilingual and dual language classes, students often work in bilingual pairs. Depending on the language of instruction, the native speaker becomes the more proficient reader. When instruction switches to the other language, the student who was less proficient now becomes the more proficient reader. This provides a good balance so that each student has a chance to take the lead.

Another way to bridge the step between shared and guided reading is through the use of listening centers. Students can listen to books and follow along as they hear fluent readers read texts. They can also read along interacting with the taped text. Both these options can help struggling readers begin to read more fluently and expressively.

Guided Reading

The next stage of the gradual release model is guided reading. Here, the responsibility shifts much more to the students. During guided reading, students do more reading on their own under the guidance of their teacher and with her support. Guided reading allows students to apply the skills they have developed during shared reading. Typically, the teacher works with a small group of students who have similar instructional needs. The teacher uses short books during the guided reading lesson or a passage from a longer text. Often, the teacher uses leveled books. These are small books that are organized by various criteria, such as the number of words, the syntactic complexity, and the text-picture match. The students may reread a familiar book first. Then the teacher introduces a new book and guides the students as they read it with her. As she reads with the students, the teacher teaches specific skills, such as using context clues or checking to see if the sentence makes sense. Afterward, students read the book on their own applying the specific skills the teacher has taught. They may also do writing related to the book. Throughout the lesson, the teacher uses the text to teach certain reading strategies in context.

There are several differences between shared and guided reading. Shared reading is most often done as a whole-class activity. Guided reading involves small groups of students. In shared reading the teacher often uses a text all the students can see, although teachers of older students may read a normal-sized book while the students follow along in their books. For guided reading, each student has a copy of the book. The key difference between shared and guided reading is that in shared reading the teacher does most of the reading and the students chime in, while in guided reading the students do most of the reading with support from the teacher. Both shared and guided reading provide opportunities for implicit and explicit teaching of skills.

Independent Reading

In many schools students are given some time for independent reading on a regular basis. In some schools everyone reads at the same time each day, and in other schools individual teachers schedule the time for independent reading. The time period varies. Generally, older and more proficient readers are given more time to read on their own. Often, the reading period is referred to as D.E.A.R. time (drop everything and read), or SSR (sustained silent reading). *Silent* is a relative term. Especially in lower grades, students may read aloud to themselves or with a partner. In many dual-language schools, teachers organize bilingual pairs, and the two students support one another when reading in either language. Pilgreen (2000) provides many different ideas for teachers about managing SSR time and includes examples for ELLs.

During independent reading students select and read books or magazines for enjoyment or information. One key for successful independent reading sessions is for students to make good choices of texts to read. For that reason, teachers usually spend time teaching students to choose appropriate books, and teachers monitor student choices so that students won't be bored by easy books or frustrated by hard ones. Teachers may also organize the books in the room to make choosing the right book easier. In addition to helping students make good choices of books to read during independent reading, teachers can also confer with their students about their independent reading. This practice can provide teachers with insights into how well students are managing their independent work, and it can help teachers decide on what skills individual students should be helped to develop.

Krashen (2004a) has summarized the research on what he terms free voluntary reading. Almost without fail, studies have shown that students make gains in reading comprehension when they are given time to read. The few studies that do not show gains were usually very short-term studies. It takes time to establish a routine for independent reading. When teachers give students time to read on a regular basis over at least a semester, the students show clear gains in their reading comprehension.

Using Culturally Relevant Bilingual Books

A key to successful independent reading is for teachers to find engaging books as Susanne did when she introduced her students to culturally relevant bilingual books. Her students showed a kind of enthusiasm she had never seen before. This is a crucial first step. Then, following the gradual release of responsibility model, she read these books aloud, conducted shared and guided reading sessions, and provided time for students to read independently. In this process, Susanne helped her students build a solid base for future reading development.

Some teachers have been reluctant to use bilingual books in their classes. In the following sections, we review three misconceptions that have kept teachers from using bilingual books, we discuss the different types of bilingual books, and we explain how teachers can choose and use bilingual books. Figure 8–2 is a bibliography of the books we discuss.

Three Commonly Held Misconceptions

"If I'm going to teach these kids English, why would I use books that have Spanish in them? They should only be using books in English."

"I can't use bilingual books with my students because they have both English and Spanish in the same book. That's like concurrent translation."

"There are so many wonderful bilingual books, but how can I use them with my students if I'm supposed to keep the two languages separate?"

Over the years, we have had questions like these posed to us by teachers working with English language learners when we have promoted culturally relevant bilingual books in our talks and in our writing (Freeman, Freeman, and Freeman 2003). While we agree with teachers that concurrent translation, moving back and forth between languages, is ineffective because students only pay attention to their stronger language, we are also convinced that bilingual books have a place in classrooms. This is especially true now that so many high-quality, culturally relevant Spanish/English bilingual books are available. Comments like the ones above arise from three misconceptions many teachers hold. We discussed these misconceptions in Chapter 6. We review them briefly here and then suggest bilingual books that relate to each one.

One commonly held misconception is that all instruction should be given in the target language. In this approach, referred to as the direct method, all instruction for a student learning English would be in English with no use of the first language. Bilingual books include both languages, so students could look at the first language version of the book for primary language support, and this goes against the basic assumptions behind the direct method. This direct method holds that more teaching in English produces higher levels of English proficiency. However, research shows clearly that students who develop their first language fully make greater gains in

Ada, Alma Flor. *I Love Saturdays and domingos*. New York: Atheneum Books, 2002.

————. *Me encantan los Saturdays y los domingos*. Miami: Santillana, 2004.

————. *Me llamo María Isabel*. New York: Libros Colibri, 1993.

————. *My Name Is María Isabel*. New York: Atheneum Books, 1993.

Altman, Linda Jacobs. *Amelia's Road*. New York: Lee & Low Books, 1993.

————. *El camino de Amelia*. Translated by Daniel Santacruz. New York: Lee & Low Books, 1993.

Argueta, Jorge. *A Movie in My Pillow: Una película en mi almohada*. San Francisco: Children's Book Press, 2001.

————. *La fiesta de las tortillas: The Fiesta of the Tortillas*. Miami: Santillana, 2006.

————. *Xochitl and the Flowers: Xóchitl, la niña de las flores*. San Francisco: Children's Book Press, 2003.

Bradman, Tony. *No hay nadie como yo*. Translated by R. Aguirre. Boston: Houghton Mifflin, 1999.

————. *There's Nobody Quite Like Me*. Boston: Houghton Mifflin, 1999.

Byrd, Lee. *The Treasure on Gold Street: El tesoro en la Calle Oro*. El Paso, TX: Cinco Puntos Press, 2003.

Carden, Mary, and Mary Cappellini. *I Am of Two Places*. Crystal Lake, IL: Rigby, 1997.

————. *Soy de dos lugares*. Crystal Lake, IL: Rigby, 1997.

Cohn, Diana. *¡Sí se puede! Yes, We Can!: Janitor Strike in L.A.* El Paso, TX: Cinco Puntos Press, 2002.

Colato Laínez, René. *Playing Lotería Mexicana: El juego de la lotería Mexicana*. Lanham, MD: Luna Rising, 2005.

————. *René Has Two Last Names: René tiene dos apellidos*. Houston, TX: Piñata Books, 2009.

————. *Waiting for Papá: Esperando a Papá*. Houston: Arte Público Press, 2004.

Dole, Mayra. *Birthday in the Barrio: Cumpleaños en el barrio*. San Francisco: Children's Book Press, 2004.

Dumas-Lachtman, Ofelia. *Pepita Talks Twice: Pepita habla dos veces*. Houston: Piñata Books, 1995.

Garza, Carmen Lomas. *Family Pictures: Cuadros de familia*. San Francisco: Children's Book Press, 1990.

————. *In My Family: En mi familia*. San Francisco: Children's Book Press, 1996.

Garza, Xavier. *Charro Claus and the Tejas Kid*. El Paso, TX: Cinco Puntos Press, 2008.

————. *Lucha libre: The Man in the Silver Mask*. El Paso, TX: Cinco Puntos Press, 2005.

Hayes, Joe. *A Spoon for Every Bite: Una cuchara para cada bocado*. El Paso, TX: Cinco Puntos Press, 2005.

————. *¡El cucuy! A Bogeyman Cuento in English and Spanish*. El Paso, TX: Cinco Puntos Press, 2001.

————. *La llorona: The Weeping Woman*. El Paso, TX: Cinco Puntos Press, 2006.

————. *Pájaro verde: The Green Bird*. El Paso, TX: Cinco Puntos Press, 2002.

Herrera, Juan Felipe. *Calling the Doves: El canto de las palomas*. Emeryville, CA: Children's Book Press, 1995.

————. *Super Cilantro Girl: La superniña del cilantro*. San Francisco: Children's Book Press, 2003.

————. *The Upside Down Boy: El niño de cabeza*. San Francisco: Children's Book Press, 2006.

Jiménez, Francisco. *La mariposa*. Boston: Houghton Mifflin, 1998.

————. *The Circuit: Stories from the Life of a Migrant Child*. Albuquerque: University of New Mexico Press, 1997.

————. *Cajas de cartón*. Boston: Houghton Mifflin, 2000.

Kurusa. *La calle es libre*. Caracas, Venezuela: Ediciones Ekaré-Banco del Libro, 1983.

————. *The Streets Are Free*. Scarborough, Ontario: Firefly Books, 1985.

Medina, Jane. *My Name Is Jorge on Both Sides of the River*. Honesdale, PA: Boyds Mills Press, 1999.

Mora, Pat. *The Bakery Lady/La señora de la panadería*. Houston: Piñata Books, 2001.

————. *Yum! ¡MmMm! ¡Qué rico!: Americas' Sproutings: Haiku by Pat Mora*. New York: Lee & Low, 2007.

Palacios, Argentina. *A Christmas Surprise for Chabelita*. New York: Andrews McMeel, 1994.

————. *Sorpresa de Navidad para Chabelita*. Mexico: Bridge Water Books, 1994.

Pérez, Amada Irma. *My Diary from Here to There: Mi diario de aquí hasta allá*. San Francisco: Children's Book Press, 2002.

————. *My Very Own Room: Mi propio cuartito*. San Francisco: Children's Book Press, 2000.

Rodríguez, Gina Macaluso. *Green Corn Tamales/Tamales de elote*. Tucson, AZ: Hispanic Books Distributors, 1994.

Sáenz, Benjamin Alire. *A Perfect Season for Dreaming: Un tiempo perfecto para soñar*. El Paso, TX: Cinco Puntos Press, 2008.

Salinas, Bobbi. *Cinderella Latina: La cenicienta latina*. Oakland, CA: Piñata Publications, 2003.

Torres, Leyla. *El sancocho del sábado*. New York: Farrar Straus Giroux, 1995.

————. *Saturday Sancocho*. New York: Farrar Straus Giroux, 1995.

Vela, Guadalupe Espinoza. *Cuando regresa mi papá*. Salem, MA: Pedestal Publishing, 2008.

————. *When My Dad Comes Home*. Salem, MA: Pedestal Publishing, 2008.

Womersley, Judith. *Carlos*. Boston: Houghton Mifflin, 1999.

FIGURE 8–2. *Bilingual books*

English proficiency than those taught only in English (Lindholm-Leary 2001; Rolstad, Mahoney, and Glass 2005; August and Shanahan 2006).

In Alma Flor Ada's *Me llamo María Isabel* (1993) / *My Name Is María Isabel* (1993) María's teacher insists on using only English in her classroom. She even changes María's name from María Isabel to Mary López, a name that María doesn't recognize when the teacher calls on her. Using the first language with students like María has both affective and cognitive benefits.

A second misconception that many teachers of bilingual students hold is that they should avoid translation (Cummins 2007). While translation is discouraged in classrooms, there have been many studies showing that bilingual children are quite highly skilled translators who serve as language brokers for their parents and other adults (Orellana et al. 2003).

The bilingual book *Pepita habla dos veces* / *Pepita Talks Twice* (Dumas-Lachtman 1995) brings out both the skills and the difficulty young bilinguals have when they are called upon to be translators. Pepita is asked so often by family and neighbors to translate that she decides it is too hard so she is only going to speak English. However, she discovers that using her bilingual abilities is very important as she saves her dog from being hit by a car. When the dog doesn't respond to English commands, Pepita calls to him in Spanish.

While students like Pepita have developed sophisticated translation skills, often helping adults with important business transactions, schools seldom draw on these skills or even acknowledge them (Jiménez 2000, 2005). Cummins (2007) suggests that using translation in the classroom promotes the acquisition of English as teachers and students translate important messages. Translation promotes biliteracy development when students write and translate their own books. In addition, when bilinguals show their abilities, they are more valued by monolingual English-speaking peers, and they develop their self-esteem.

A final, and perhaps more controversial, misconception is what Cummins (2007) has called the two solitudes assumption. This assumption holds that as students are learning in two languages, the two languages should be kept separate at all times. While Cummins acknowledges that it is important to keep largely separate spaces as students learn in the two languages, there are also times that the two languages should be brought together. For example, Cummins points out the importance of allowing students to use both languages by drawing on cognates, producing bilingual books and multimedia projects, and engaging in sister class exchanges.

An example of a project in which students produced a bilingual book is *Soy de dos lugares* and its English translation, *I Am of Two Places* (Carden and Cappellini 1997). Bilingual elementary school children wrote and illustrated their own bilingual poems about how it feels to be bilingual. A good example is the poem, "*Corazón Partido*" / "Divided Heart," written by Lorena Lozada. The young author writes about her divided heart with the lines, *Quiero estar allá pero me gusta más aquí. / Siento que me corazón está partido* (I want to be there but I like it more here. / I feel as if my heart is divided) (24).

These three misconceptions have kept some teachers from using bilingual books. However, current research shows that first language development supports the acquisition of English, that bilinguals use their two languages to translate in daily transactions, and that there are times when students benefit by using both their languages. The misconceptions all come from taking what García (2009) calls a monoglossic view of bilingualism, seeing the bilingual person as two monolinguals. Using bilingual books, on the other hand, is consistent with a heteroglossic view. From this perspective, the teacher recognizes that the two languages are constantly in dynamic interaction. (See Chapter 6.)

Types of Bilingual Books

There are three types of bilingual books. In some cases, there are separate versions of a book—one in English and one in Spanish. The two books are exactly alike, including the cover and the illustrations, except for being written in different languages. For instance, *Saturday Sanchocho* and *El sancocho del sábado* (Torres 1995) tell of a young girl and her grandparents living in a small town in Colombia. The grandmother wants to make the typical Saturday *sancocho*, or stew, but only has a dozen eggs in the house. She and her granddaughter go to a marketplace in the center of town and through much bargaining with different vendors, they are able to exchange what they have to get all the ingredients they need for a delicious chicken *sancocho*.

The flip book, another type of bilingual book, is organized differently. A reader can read the book in one language or flip the book over to read it in the other language. *Yum! ¡MmMm! ¡Qué rico! Brotes de las Américas / Yum! ¡MmMm! ¡Qué rico! Americas' Sproutings* (Mora 2007) is a flip book of haiku poetry about crops of both North and South America, which includes informative narratives about them as well. As with separate books, the illustrations, pagination, and covers of these flip books are the same in both languages.

The third type and most common format for bilingual books is a single book with both Spanish and English text on the same page or on facing pages. The storyteller Joe Hayes has provided many books formatted like this including *A Spoon for Every Bite / Una cuchara para cada bocado* (Hayes 2005), the tale of a conceited rich man who spends his fortune buying spoons when his poor neighbors tell him about someone who uses a different spoon for every bite. The story's twist is that the spoons the poor neighbor refers to are tortillas used for scooping up food.

Caveats When Choosing Bilingual Books

There are some considerations that teachers should take into account as they choose bilingual books. Teachers should be aware of certain formatting issues when two languages are in the same book. Often, the English title of the book on the cover and title page is much larger than the Spanish and in a font that is clearer to read. Within the books, when both languages are on a page, the English is usually printed above the Spanish. Sometimes the Spanish is in a font that is more difficult to read or in another color. As Nathenson-Mejía and Escamilla have pointed out,

> [t]hese differences, though they may appear to be insignificant, hinder the reading experiences of the child reading in Spanish. The placement of the Spanish below the English . . . reinforces the lower status that Spanish occupies in the dominant U.S. culture. (Nathenson-Mejía and Escamilla 2003)

An even more important consideration than formatting when looking at bilingual books is that one language is a translation. Whether the book was originally written in Spanish or in English, the translation into the other language must be a good one (Schon and Berkin 1996). In some cases, such as the books by Alma Flor Ada, the author is a proficient bilingual who wrote both versions. Too often, however, translations are literal and do not represent natural language. It is essential that translations be of the highest possible quality. Teachers who are not proficient readers of both languages should check the quality of the translation with a native speaker. While it may not always be possible to find the perfect bilingual books to use, teachers should carefully consider issues such as text placement and quality of translation when choosing books.

Characteristics of Texts That Support Reading in Bilingual Books

No matter which format the bilingual book is published in, when choosing books teachers should carefully consider whether or not the text has characteristics that support readers (Freeman and Freeman 2006, 2009). Figure 8–3 lists characteristics of texts that support readers. Books with these characteristics can help teachers scaffold instruction for emergent bilinguals. In the following sections, we discuss each question on the checklist.

The first question on the checklist is, "Is the language of the text natural?" Often, the first books students are given have very limited text. Even those books, however,

> **Checklist: Characteristics of Texts That Support Reading**
>
> 1. Is the language of the text natural?
>   When there are only a few words on a page, do these limited-text books sound like real language, something people really say?
>
> 2. Are the materials authentic?
>   Authentic materials are written to inform or entertain, not to teach a grammar point, a letter-sound correspondence, or a series of related syllables.
>
> 3. Is the text predictable?
>   Text is more predictable when readers have background knowledge of the concepts.
>   *For emergent readers*: Books are more predictable when they follow certain patterns (repetitive, cumulative) or include certain devices (rhyme, rhythm, alliteration)
>   *For developing readers*: Books are more predictable when students are familiar with text structures (e.g., beginning, middle, end; problem-solution; main idea, details, examples, and so on)
>
> 4. Are the materials interesting and/or imaginative?
>   Interesting, imaginative texts engage students.
>
> 5. For picture books, is there a good text-picture match?
>   Is the placement of the pictures predictable?
>   A good match provides nonlinguistic visual cues.
>
> 6. Is the text culturally relevant?
>   Do the situations and characters in the book represent the experiences and backgrounds of the students?

FIGURE 8–3. *Characteristics of texts checklist*

should sound natural. The words in the texts should be something the children recognize as language people use. *Carlos* (Womersley 1999), a limited-text counting book, has an English and Spanish version. The delightfully illustrated text in both languages is natural. The main character, Carlos, explains he has five fingers, four friends, three freckles, two grandmothers, and one baby sister with no teeth.

A second, related question asks, "Is the text authentic?" Authentic books are written to inform or entertain, not to teach a particular sound-letter correspondence, grammar point, or, as is often the case with Spanish, the sounds of related syllables. A good example of an authentic limited-text book is *No hay nadie como yo* (Bradman 1999) with the English version *There's Nobody Quite Like Me* (Bradman 1999). These two pattern books tell how a little girl is like her friends and even like her twin sister in many ways, but "There's nobody quite like me," or in Spanish, *No hay nadie como yo* (13). Books such as these connect to young readers because they validate who they are and talk about actual experiences the readers have.

The third checklist question asks, "Is the text predictable?" For emergent readers, bilingual books are predictable if they are like other books children have read. In *Green Corn Tamales: Tamales de elote* (Rodríguez 1994), the nana (grandma) asks for help from the family to make tortillas. This book follows the same pattern as the Little Red Hen tale. The children respond to nana's request by saying they will not help. Of course, once the tamales are all made, they eagerly volunteer to help eat them.

This book also contains a predictable pattern of question and response. In addition, it contains code switching:

> "Not I," said my brother Jaime.
> "*Yo no*," said cousin Larry.
> "Not I," said *tio* José.

Since many bilingual students naturally move between languages in this way with other bilinguals around them (Gutiérrez et al. 1999), the responses in the book that include code switching are predictable.

Older developing readers find texts more predictable when they follow familiar patterns such as a clear beginning, middle, and end or when they contain an easily identifiable problem and solution. A classic story from Venezuela, *La calle es libre* (Kurusa 1983), also available in English as *The Streets Are Free* (Kurusa 1985), presents a problem. Children living in the slums on the hills outside of Caracas want a place to play because, although the streets are free, they are also dangerous. The children work together to find a solution, and eventually locate an area for a park that the community helps to build. The problem-solution pattern the book follows makes it more predictable for readers.

The next question is, "Is the text interesting and/or imaginative?" Readers are more engaged when the texts they are given to read are interesting and imaginative, and, as Guthrie (2004) has shown, engagement leads to higher levels of reading proficiency. *Pájaro verde: The Green Bird* (Hayes 2002) is a very imaginative book. In this beautifully illustrated New Mexico folktale, an enchanted prince who has been transformed into a green bird falls in love with one of nine sisters. Each of the sisters has a different number of eyes beginning with the youngest, who has only one eye. The green bird marries the two-eyed sister, turns back into a prince, and takes her to live in a beautiful castle. However, the rest of the tale revolves around the jealous sisters' plot to destroy their sister and her good fortune and the prince's secret, enchanted transformations to a bird.

Another example of an interesting, imaginative book is *Charro Claus and the Tejas Kid* (Garza 2008), a Santa Claus tale that takes place along the Texas-Mexican border. Santa Claus enlists the help of his *compadre*, a former *charro* (Mexican cowboy), to help deliver Christmas presents on Christmas Eve to the children living all along the Rio Grande.

An important question to consider for picture books is: "Is there a good text-picture match?" As Rog and Burton (2001/2002) point out, one of the factors influencing the difficulty of texts for readers is "the degree of support offered by illustrations" (348). Many of the bilingual books already mentioned include illustrations that provide support for the text. Another book with a clear text-to-picture match is *Sorpresa de Navidad para Chabelita* (Palacios 1994) / *A Christmas Surprise for Chabelita* (Palacios 1994). In this story, Chabelita's mother must go to live and work in a city far from home, so Chabelita lives with her grandparents. She goes everywhere with them, including the marketplace where her grandfather talks to his friends and her grandmother buys all her fruits and vegetables. The pages describing both of these events are especially well illustrated.

Culturally Relevant Texts

The last question on the checklist asks, "Is the text culturally relevant?" Culturally responsive teaching is one of six factors the Center for Research on Education, Diversity and Excellence identified as important for Latino student success (Padrón, Waxman, and Rivera 2002). One way to engage in culturally responsive teaching is by using culturally relevant books. When readers can connect what they read to their own lives, they are more engaged and have more success in reading. Freire (Freire and Macedo 1987) makes this point powerfully by explaining that "[r]eading does not consist merely of decoding the written word or language; rather, it is preceded by and intertwined with knowledge of the world" (29).

The books discussed above have different characteristics that support readers. However, all the books included in this chapter have this final characteristic. For Spanish-speaking ELLs and many other second language students, they are all culturally relevant. That is, the books connect to the students' backgrounds, ethnicity, and cultural experiences. By using culturally relevant bilingual texts, teachers help emergent bilinguals reclaim both their culture and their language. Jiménez (1997) found that struggling Latino students were better able to read and understand texts that were culturally familiar.

Not only do students choose culturally relevant books more often than other books, they comprehend these books better as well. Y. Goodman (1982) conducted research using miscue analysis and retellings with speakers of Navajo, Hawaiian Pidgin, Samoan, and Spanish. She reported that those young readers understood better when they read books connected to their own experiences. As Goodman notes:

> [T]he more familiar the language of the text, the actions of the characters, the description of the setting, the sequence of the events—the closer the readers' predictions will match the author's expression and the easier the text will be for the reader to comprehend. (302)

Drawing on this research and her own miscue analysis studies with Spanish-speaking students in both rural and urban settings, Ebe (2010; Paulson and Freeman 2003) developed a rubric that teachers can use to help them determine the cultural relevance of texts. The rubric (see Figure 8–4) consists of a series of questions, each of which highlights certain features of cultural relevance for readers.

The first item asks readers if the characters in the story are like those of their families. This question gets at students' ethnicity and the connections they can make with the books and their own ethnic background. In *René Has Two Last Names / René tiene dos apellidos* (Colato Laínez 2009), a newcomer from El Salvador is confused when his second last name is missing from the label on his desk. When the class project is to make a family tree, René shows his classmates and his teacher how important his mother's side of the family is. He validates the Hispanic custom of using both the mother's and father's last names.

Me encantan los Saturdays y domingos (Ada 2004), or the English version, *I Love Saturdays and domingos* (Ada 2002), is an ideal book for children from bicultural families. The little girl in the story goes to her Anglo, English-speaking grandparents' house on Saturdays and to her Latino, Spanish-speaking grandparents' home on Sundays. The activities she does with each set of grandparents are representative of their different worlds. Many emergent bilinguals come from backgrounds like this girl's.

The second consideration for choosing culturally relevant books is, "How often have you had experiences like the ones described in the story?" In *My Diary from Here to There: Mi diario de aquí hasta allá* (Pérez 2002), the author writes about herself as a young girl leaving Mexico and about keeping a diary of memories, fears, and new experiences as she travels to her new home. Many emergent bilinguals or their parents have had experiences like this.

In *The Bakery Lady: La señora de la panadería* (Mora 2001) and *La fiesta de las tortillas: The Fiesta of the Tortillas* (Argueta 2006), readers connect to familiar foods as well as to the adventures of the characters in the story. In *The Bakery Lady: La señora de la panadería*, the main character, Monica, spends many hours in her grandparents' Mexican bakery and wants to become a baker herself. In *La fiesta de las tortillas: The Fiesta of the Tortillas*, a mysterious spirit of the corn invades the family's Salvadoran restaurant business and brings the family closer together. As readers engage with texts like these, they are able to connect the experiences and the themes to their own lives.

The next question on the rubric, "Have you ever lived in or visited places like this?," asks about the setting. In *My Very Own Room: Mi propio cuartito* (Pérez 2000), Pérez tells how a young girl living in a large city who no longer wants to share her bedroom with her several brothers is able create a room of her own in their small family home. Many emergent bilinguals live in settings like this.

In contrast to the city setting, Herrera describes a rural setting in *Calling the Doves: El canto de las palomas* (Herrera 1995) as he recalls his childhood memories as a

Cultural Relevance Rubric

1. Are the characters in the story like you and your family?

   Just like us .... Not at all

   | 4 | 3 | 2 | 1 |

2. Have you ever had an experience like one described in this story?

   Yes .... No

   | 4 | 3 | 2 | 1 |

3. Have you lived in or visited places like those in the story?

   Yes .... No

   | 4 | 3 | 2 | 1 |

4. Could this story take place this year?

   Yes .... No

   | 4 | 3 | 2 | 1 |

5. How close do you think the main characters are to you in age?

   Very close.., Not close at all

   | 4 | 3 | 2 | 1 |

6. Are there main characters in the story who are: boys (for boys) or girls (for girls)?

   Yes .... No

   | 4 | 3 | 2 | 1 |

7. Do the characters talk like you and your family?

   Yes .... No

   | 4 | 3 | 2 | 1 |

8. How often do you read stories like these?

   Often .... Never

   | 4 | 3 | 2 | 1 |

FIGURE 8–4. *Cultural relevance rubric*

migrant child. *Amelia's Road* (Altman 1993) and the Spanish version, *El camino de Amelia* (Altman 1993), tell the story of a migrant girl who hates roads because she is constantly moving and has to keep changing where she lives. Children who have lived in settings like those described in these stories can picture the places in the stories and are, thus, better able to understand what they are reading.

The fourth question is "Could the story take place this year?" Sometimes teachers have used folktales and historical readings from students' home countries. However, students are usually more interested in reading about the present. As Gray (2009) points out in her study, students "wanted books that were connected to their lives today" (476). For example, *The Treasure on Gold Street: El tesoro en la Calle Oro* (Byrd 2003) is the true story of a street in El Paso where the neighborhood has adopted a mentally challenged adult who is loved by all, especially the children. Another book, *¡Sí, se puede! Yes, We Can!* (Cohn 2002), is a fictional story based on the real-life janitor strike that took place in 2000 in Los Angeles. With the help of his teacher, the young boy in the story finds a way to support his mother, one of the key strike organizers. Both of these stories could be experienced by children today.

The next question on the rubric asks, "How close do you think the main characters are to you in age?" Readers are usually more interested in reading a book if the characters are close to them in age. For example, in *Waiting for Papá: Esperando a Papá* (Colato Laínez 2004) Beto remembers escaping from El Salvador with his mother when he was five. His father promises to follow but, in the story, his father has still not been able to come to the country when Beto celebrates his eighth birthday. This book would be good for younger students.

Birthday in the Barrio: Cumpleaños en el barrio (Dole 2004) is a birthday book that would appeal to older students. In this story, Chavi unites her Cuban American community in Miami to arrange a traditional *quinciñera* birthday celebration for a friend of her sister whose family cannot afford to do it for her.

Girls often want to read about other girls, and boys want to read about other boys. The next question on the rubric relates to gender: "Does the story have boy characters (for boy readers) and girl characters (for girl readers)?" *Xochitl and the Flowers: Xóchitl, la niña de las flores* (Argueta 2003) is the story of a Salvadoran family who moves to live in San Francisco. The family begins a flower business like the one they had in El Salvador by selling flowers in the streets, but Xochitl, a young girl, learns she needs the help of her neighbors for her family to establish a nursery and a more stable business.

In *Playing Lotería: Jugando lotería* (Colato Laínez 2005) a young boy's parents send him to Mexico to spend a summer with his grandmother despite his worries that he does not speak Spanish and she does not speak English. He soon helps his grandmother in her job as a caller for the game of *lotería*, picking up Spanish in the process.

The next question is "Do the characters talk like you and your family?" Medina's *My Name Is Jorge on Both Sides of the River* (1999) is a book of poems in both Spanish and English that powerfully depict experiences of Latino children and families in schools. In one of the poems Jorge, the main character, applies the often used slang label for Anglos to his teacher, saying, "Crazy *gabacha*. Who understands her?" (41). Latino children reading this poem all recognize this slang term. Similarly, Salinas uses slang in *Cinderella Latina: La cenicienta latina* (2003). For example, the father goes to *la pulga* (the flea market), where the sign says *Compramos chatarra y vendemos antigüedades* (We buy junk and sell antiques).

The following question asks about genres: "How often do you read books like these?" Books are more relevant when students have read other books of the same genre. Some bilingual books are extremely imaginative autobiographies. For example, in *A Movie in My Pillow: Un película en mi almohada* (Argueta 2001) the author recalls the volcanoes of his homeland, El Salvador, the delicious cornmeal *pupusas* (stuffed tortillas), and his grandmother's stories. He combines these memories with his adventures as a young boy in San Francisco. His memories make a kind of movie in his pillow. In *The Upside Down Boy: El niño de cabeza* (Herrera 2006), Herrera remembers his first months in the big city of his new country. In the city, everything seems upside down. Chickens come in plastic bags, the school schedule is confusing, and his tongue feels like a rock when he tries to speak English.

Several bilingual books are folktales, a genre that many Latino students are familiar with because they have heard them from their parents and grandparents. Both *¡El cucuy! A Bogeyman Cuento* in English and Spanish (Hayes 2001) and *La llorona: The Weeping Woman* (Hayes 2006) are familiar to children from Mexico. They delight in hearing the stories read and modifying them with versions they have heard from relatives. As students read additional autobiographies, folktales, or other genres, the books become easier to comprehend because the students become more familiar with the way each genre is structured.

When teachers choose bilingual books that have the characteristics of texts that support readers and are culturally relevant, they can engage emergent bilinguals in reading. The books we have described are all Spanish/English bilingual books. Spanish speakers make up nearly 80 percent of all the emergent bilinguals in the United States. However, increasingly, bilingual books in other languages are becoming available as the second language population of the United States changes and grows.

Uses of Bilingual Books

Bilingual books can be used in a variety of ways:

1. They can provide students a preview in the first language of the text to be read in the second language.

2. They can serve as a resource when comprehension starts to break down.

3. They can provide opportunities for linguistic investigations and cognate activities.

In this section, we provide examples of bilingual books that can be used in each of these three ways.

Vela's *Cuando regresa mi papá* (Vela 2008) is an excellent limited-text patterned book for young readers that could be read and discussed with native Spanish speakers first in Spanish as a preview for the English version, *When My Dad Comes Home* (Vela 2008). This is the story of a young boy whose father is away in the Middle East in the military. The boy keeps imagining what he will do with his father when he returns. Once Spanish-speaking students have read and discussed the book in their first language, they will better understand the English version. The first language preview makes the second language version more comprehensible.

La mariposa (Jiménez 1998), available in both Spanish and English, is taken from Jimenez's chapter book, *The Circuit* (Jiménez 1997). In *La mariposa* the author recounts his own difficult experience entering first grade as a monolingual Spanish speaker. This book is one that many Spanish-speaking children connect with. Previewing and discussing it first in Spanish would give Spanish-speaking children the opportunity to share their own experiences and feelings in their first language before they read the story in English. Because this story is so powerful, the preview would help students more fully engage in the English version and extend their understanding of both languages. In fact, the entire book, *The Circuit*, is often read in secondary schools with students because it connects so well to the Mexican American migrant experience. For native Spanish-speaking students, reading this novel *Cajas de cartón* (Jiménez 2000) in Spanish provides important background for reading the novel in English. In dual language classes, teachers could read the English version first to provide a preview for English speakers of the Spanish version.

Secondly, bilingual books can serve as a resource for understanding the second language. When students struggle with an important idea in a book, they can look at the first language text to be sure they are on the right track. Then they can return to reading in the second language. A bilingual book that could serve as such a resource is *Lucha libre: The Man in the Silver Mask* (Garza 2005). Boys would be motivated to try to read this book about Mexican wrestling matches in their second language, and they could check difficult passages by looking at the text in their first language. For girls, an engaging story is *Super Cilantro Girl / La superniña del cilantro* (Herrera 2003). In this story, a girl worries because her mother goes across the border into Mexico and does not return. The heroine, Esmeralda, picks cilantro leaves and wishes that she could go across the mountains and bring her mother back. She grows bigger, turns green, and flies to save her mother. She awakes the next day and her mother is home. Readers wonder if this really happened or was just a dream. Students could read the story in their second language and then check their understanding by reviewing the text in their first language.

A third use for bilingual books is linguistic investigation. When students are learning a second language, it is interesting for them to compare and contrast their native language with the language they are learning. For example, they could compare sentences in the two languages to identify differences in word order. Even in the title of *A Perfect Season for Dreaming / Un tiempo perfecto para soñar* (Sáenz 2008), the adjective *perfect* precedes the noun in English but *perfecto* follows the noun in Spanish. This beautifully illustrated tale is about a grandfather who dreams about traveling armadillos, a mariachi band of dogs, flying pigs, and piñatas. He only shares his strange imaginings with his granddaughter. She, of all the people around him, understands. Students could compare and contrast the Spanish and English versions to note differences in the order of words in parallel sentences in the two languages.

Students can also use bilingual books to investigate cognates, words related in origin that have the same or similar meanings in different languages. So, for example, *family* in English is *familia* in Spanish. Finding cognates is facilitated when the texts of both languages are on the same page as in Carmen Lomas Garza's books about the life experiences of Mexican Americans living in the United States, *In My Family: En mi familia* (Garza 1996) and *Family Pictures: Cuadros de familia* (Garza 1990).

Conclusion

Research shows that many emergent bilinguals develop adequate word identification skills. They can decode most grade-level texts once they reach a certain level of English and literacy proficiency. As a result of Reading First grants, reading instruction in most parts of the United States has focused on beginning literacy skills, such as phonemic awareness, phonics, and fluency. Both native English speakers and second language students acquire these skills at about the same rate.

When it comes to comprehension, emergent bilinguals lag behind native English speakers. Since they don't understand much of what they read, many second language students become disengaged from reading. While other students continue to develop their reading proficiency, emergent bilinguals fall progressively farther behind each year.

When teachers follow the gradual release of responsibility model and use culturally relevant bilingual books with the characteristics of texts that support reading, they offer their students more opportunities to become both bilingual and biliterate. Students become engaged in reading these books and build vocabulary and comprehension skills as they read them. Teachers can also use bilingual books to provide a first language preview or as a source of data for linguistic investigations.

Bilinguals naturally use both of their languages as they communicate in different settings. While there are times that languages should be kept separate for instruction, there are also times when the two languages should be brought together. Bilingual books bring the two languages together in ways that teachers can use to help emergent bilinguals develop biliteracy.

KEY POINTS

→ Engagement is a key to reading success for English language learners.

→ ELLs who receive primary-language literacy instruction achieve higher levels of reading proficiency than students taught to read in a second language.

→ ELLs taught to read in their second language with a focus on basic skills needed for decoding (phonemic awareness, phonics, fluency) learn to decode, but they do not comprehend texts as well as native-English-speaking peers.

→ Effective literacy instruction follows a gradual release of responsibility model that includes read-alouds, shared reading, interactive reading, guided reading, and independent reading.

→ Three misconceptions have kept some teachers from using bilingual books, but emergent bilinguals benefit from reading culturally relevant bilingual books.

→ Teachers should use books that have the characteristics of texts that support reading.

→ Teachers can use the culturally relevant rubric when choosing books for ELLs to read.

→ Bilingual books can be used in a variety of ways, even when the teacher is not bilingual.

APPLICATIONS

1. Engagement is key to reading success, especially for emergent bilinguals. Bring to class two books that you have found to engage your students. Explain how you used the books and why you think the books were engaging for your students.

2. Many English language learners have become good "word callers." The Reading First report explains that ELLs were comparable to native speakers in their decoding ability, but they scored much lower on tests of comprehension. This suggests that students were spending too much time on decoding and other skills activities and too little time reading engaging texts. What has been your experience with the ELLs you have worked with? Are they "word callers"? What seems to be a way to engage them in reading?

3. We described the different stages of the gradual release of responsibility approach to teaching reading, including read-alouds, shared reading, interactive reading, guided reading, and independent reading. Consider a group of students you are working with. Choose a text that would be appropriate for each of these gradual release activities. Bring the books to class and explain why you chose those books for each stage. If possible, use the books with your students and explain how it went.

4. In this chapter, we discussed three commonly held misconceptions about using bilingual books in the classroom. List the three misconceptions. Which of these have you heard teachers or others say? How do you respond to these objections now that you have read the chapter? Give your response to each of the misconceptions.

5. What are some ways you can use bilingual books in your classroom? This week choose one of the ways and use a bilingual book in your teaching. Bring the book to class and be prepared to explain how it went.

6. Find at least two of the bilingual books listed in this chapter that you have not used before. Read it with some of your students this week. Bring the books to class and be prepared to describe your experience.

9

*How Can Teachers Help ELLs
Develop Academic Language?*

Emergent bilinguals most often acquire oral English first. Then, as teachers read to and with them using culturally relevant, engaging stories, students begin to learn to read and write English as well. While the language in stories is somewhat similar to oral language, emergent bilinguals also need to learn to read informational texts, discuss them, and write descriptions, explanations, reports, and analyses. These tasks require a different kind of language than the language of conversations and story books.

The language registers used in schools to read, write, and discuss academic subjects are referred to as *academic language*. As Goldenberg and Coleman (2010) observe:

> the challenge for teachers is to use strategies, approaches, and techniques that promote grade-level content learning (e.g. social studies, science) *and* English language development, both of which are needed for students to enter the educational mainstream. (89)

Even though it seems clear that teachers of ELLs need to use strategies and techniques to promote both content learning and language development, Goldenberg and Coleman caution that "we lack a research base demonstrating how or even whether this can be accomplished in an all-English instructional context" (90).

For this reason, as we explained in Chapter 6, well-implemented, long-term bilingual programs are most effective in promoting academic achievement for emergent bilinguals. The key in these programs is for teachers to teach subject matter content and academic language in both the students' languages. As we discussed in Chapter 7, teachers can teach both language and content by using transformative pedagogy as part of an intercultural orientation. In this chapter, we consider what constitutes academic language, the instructional techniques teachers can use to promote academic language, and ways to assess academic language proficiency.

Academic Discourse

In Chapter 4 we discussed Gee's (2008) idea that learning takes place when people join social groups. At early stages, they are like apprentices who are learning how to talk, think, believe, and even dress like others in the group, or what Gee refers to as a Discourse. Gee explains that there is a difference between a primary Discourse and a secondary Discourse. Humans develop a primary Discourse in the process of growing up in a social group. They learn the rules for communication and interaction from people in their families and their community. Emergent bilinguals need to develop a secondary Discourse when they begin to interact with English speakers. Native English speakers use a different language to communicate than ELLs do, and they interact in different ways. In schools, all children need to learn an additional secondary Discourse, the general school Discourse. That is, they need to learn how to behave in certain ways, discuss topics in class, and read and write in response to teachers' requirements.

In addition, students need to refine these general skills to fit the expectations of teachers in the different subject areas. Writing a good book report is different from writing a good science report. Reading a math text is different from reading a novel. In other words, students need to learn to use the language suitable for each content area, especially as they reach middle school and high school. The basic reading and writing skills and the general vocabulary that emergent bilinguals acquire in the early grades need to be further developed to meet the academic demands of the upper grades.

Disciplinary Literacy

Shanahan and Shanahan (2008) conducted research showing that students need to develop new reading skills to comprehend content texts at the middle and upper grades. These researchers identify three skill levels: basic, intermediate, and disciplinary. Figure 9–1 lists the skills needed at each of these levels.

At the basic level, students need decoding skills, knowledge of high-frequency words, and basic levels of fluency. These skills, which generalize across texts, underlie reading at the intermediate and disciplinary levels. Books this basic are often stories, and the language of the books is similar to everyday conversational language.

Reading Level	Skills	Typical Texts
Basic grades 1–3	Decoding skills, knowledge of high-frequency words, basic fluency	Stories with language similar to oral discourse
Intermediate grades 4–8	Increased vocabulary and fluency, comprehension strategies	Fiction texts and some content or expository texts
Disciplinary grades 9–12	Specialized vocabulary and syntax, advanced comprehension strategies	Advanced texts in social studies, math, and science as well as language arts

FIGURE 9–1. *Reading levels and skills (based on Shanahan and Shanahan 2008)*

At the intermediate level, students increase their reading vocabulary and fluency. They also develop comprehension strategies, such as making predictions and monitoring their reading to see if it makes sense. These skills are often taught in upper elementary and middle school grades. Students at the intermediate level can usually read most fiction texts, and they can also read more basic informational texts.

The third level is the disciplinary level. Students need to develop the specialized vocabulary and syntax of the different content area texts they are required to read in middle school and high school. They also have to understand that as they read in different disciplines, they must attend to different aspects of the text.

For example, when reading history, proficient readers learn to check and question sources. They also pay attention to patterns of time or cause and effect. In contrast, as they read science, students check diagrams and charts carefully. They assume the information is accurate and read to see if they understand the steps of an experiment and the significance of the results. In mathematics, students should read more slowly. They need to check figures and equations carefully. They also need to understand that many everyday words, like *table*, have specialized meanings that may be different in history, science, and math. All these challenges make reading disciplinary texts more difficult. Basic and intermediate reading skills do not enable second language students to succeed with texts like these.

Shanahan and Shanahan (2008) observe that most students, not just ELLs, struggle to develop disciplinary literacy. To a great extent, their struggles come because teachers assume that once a child can read, that child can read anything. This view is often expressed in the saying, "First you learn to read. Then you read to learn." Teachers in upper grades are not usually trained in how to teach the literacy skills needed for their subject areas. They may believe that this is the job of the English teacher. However, unless math, science, and social studies teachers also teach their students how to read and write in their disciplines, students will not develop the academic language and literacy they need to succeed in school.

Cummins' Distinction Between Conversational and Academic Language

In the same way that we can distinguish between basic or intermediate literacy and disciplinary literacy, we can also differentiate between two kinds of language proficiency that emergent bilinguals develop: conversational language and academic language. One of the first researchers to draw this distinction was Cummins (1981). Cummins observed that English language learners were overrepresented in the special education population of schools in Canada. As he investigated reasons for the high number of ELLs who were placed in special education classes, he discovered that although these students appeared to have developed the ability to use English for daily communication, they had difficulty understanding lectures in school, reading textbooks, and writing school papers. In other words, these students spoke and comprehended everyday conversational English quite well, but they lacked the academic English needed to complete school tasks.

Cummins' observations were consistent with studies of Finnish children in Sweden conducted by Skutnabb-Kangas and Toukomaa (1976). These researchers reported that the Finnish immigrants in Sweden appeared to be quite fluent in Swedish. However, when they were given tests in Swedish that involved complex cognitive operations, the Finnish children were not able to score at expected grade-level standards.

Cummins' own research in Canada supported Skutnabb-Kangas and Toukomaa's research. Cummins analyzed the teacher referral forms and psychological assessments of over four hundred English language learners. He found a consistent pattern of results. The students were perceived as having good oral English fluency, but they scored low on academic tests. For example, one referral read, "Arrived from Portugal at age 10 and was placed in a second grade class; three years later in fifth grade, her teacher commented that 'her oral answering and comprehension is so much better than her written work that we feel a severe learning problem is involved, not just her non-English background'" (4–5). Another referral stated, "Referred for reading and arithmetic difficulties in second grade, teacher commented that 'since PS attended grade one in Italy, I think his main problem is language although he understands and speaks English quite well'" (4).

Since students appeared to speak English well, teachers and administrators assumed that their low scores on academic tasks reflected limited cognitive ability. Cummins' distinction between conversational and academic language was intended to show that there are two types of language proficiency. Most students, like those described on the referral forms, develop oral fluency in a language much more quickly than they acquire academic language proficiency. Estimates are that it takes about two years to develop conversational fluency in a new language and four to nine years to develop academic language.

Cummins originally referred to conversational language as Basic Interpersonal Communicative Skills (BICS) and academic language as Cognitive Academic Language Proficiency (CALP). These terms were critiqued in part because some interpreted them to mean that certain ELLs lacked basic cognitive abilities or CALP. Cummins (2008) has responded to these concerns. To avoid any misunderstanding and to more clearly indicate the difference between the two kinds of language ELLs need, he now uses the terms *conversational fluency* and *academic language proficiency*. He defines academic language proficiency as "the extent to which an individual has access to and command of the oral and written academic registers of schooling" (Cummins 2000, 67).

Cummins' Quadrants

Cummins created a model to represent the difference between the two types of language proficiency. This model is shown in Figure 9–2.

The model consists of a horizontal and a vertical line that cross to form four quadrants. Each of these lines represents a developmental continuum of language competence. The horizontal line extends from context-embedded communication to

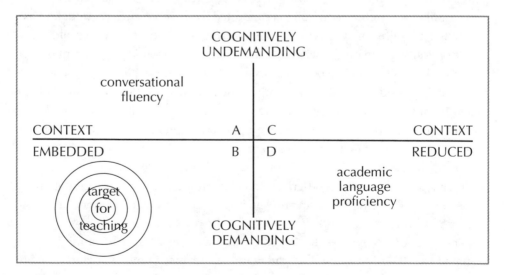

FIGURE 9–2. *Cummins' quadrants (based on Cummins 1981)*

context-reduced communication, and the vertical line goes from cognitively undemanding to cognitively demanding tasks.

Cummins (1981) explains that the extremes of the horizontal continuum:

> are distinguished by the fact that in context-embedded communication the participants can actively negotiate meaning (e.g. by providing feedback that the message has not been understood) and the language is supported by a wide range of meaningful paralinguistic (gesture, intonation, etc.) and situational cues; context-reduced communication, on the other hand, relies primarily (or at the extreme of the continuum, exclusively) on linguistic cues to meaning. (11)

All language occurs in some context. However, the amount of nonlinguistic support can vary greatly. For example, in talking with someone face to face, we pick up much of the message from tone of voice, facial expression, gestures, and so on. If the conversation is about something we know well, our background knowledge supplies extra context. In addition, if we can see what we are discussing or if we have pictures or other visual cues, it is easier to follow the conversation, even if we lack full language proficiency. A good example of context-embedded language would be discussion about the weather with a friend as we stand in the rain under our umbrellas waiting for a ride to school. Even if some of the words or sentences are not clear, we can follow the thread of the conversation quite well and also contribute to it.

At the other end of the horizontal axis is language that is context reduced. Here, we have to depend much more on the words than on any other cues. An example might be reading a test question on a standardized test. Often test questions are not related to one another, so other sections of the test do not provide extra clues. In addition, there are no visual cues. The test taker has to rely on knowledge of the language. Context-reduced language is not limited to written language. Many ELLs have trouble following lectures in school if the teacher simply talks. On the other hand, the teacher can make the lecture more context embedded by using a PowerPoint, a graphic organizer, or a video clip. While these supports are helpful for all students, they are especially beneficial for ELLs because the visuals reduce the students' dependency on linguistic cues for making sense of the lecture.

The vertical scale on Cummins' diagram goes from cognitively undemanding to cognitively demanding. In describing this continuum, Cummins (1981) comments, "Cognitive involvement can be conceptualized in terms of the amount of information that must be processed simultaneously or in close succession by the individual in order to carry out the activity" (12–13).

Cognitive demand does not depend so much on the subject as on a person's background knowledge. The conversation about the weather is cognitively undemanding for most people because they know a great deal about weather. They don't need to expend a great deal of mental energy to decide whether it is raining or not. On the other hand, learning a new math concept could be very demanding. A young child learning how to multiply two numbers would have to devote a great deal of attention and memory to the task. Of course, most older students would find multiplication quite easy and not very demanding cognitively. This continuum, then, represents a developmental sequence. As students become more familiar with a procedure or task, the cognitive demand is reduced.

The two continuums form four quadrants. Quadrant A contains language that is context embedded and cognitively undemanding. The example of the weather would fall into this quadrant. The teachers and administrators who referred children for special education assessed students' English proficiency by using evidence from Quadrant A. They assumed that if students demonstrated conversational fluency, they were fully proficient in English.

However, an emergent bilingual who has developed conversational fluency may still lack academic language proficiency. The same student who does well in settings where English is context embedded and cognitively undemanding (Quadrant A) may struggle listening to a lecture or taking a test, because in those settings the language is context reduced and cognitively demanding (Quadrant D). Although many tests and school tasks fall into Quadrant D, teaching should not be targeted to Quadrant D. When school administrators ask teachers to prepare students for standardized tests by giving them practice tests frequently or by reading passages similar to those on the test and answering questions, the teaching falls into Quadrant D. These tasks are cognitively demanding and context reduced.

What ELLs need is instruction that is cognitively demanding but also context embedded. They need scaffolded instruction to make difficult academic concepts comprehensible. When teachers use graphic organizers, have students work in cooperative groups, and engage them in hands-on activities to teach important concepts, they are teaching in Quadrant B. They are providing contextual support while still maintaining high cognitive demand. When the target for teaching is in Quadrant B, students develop the academic language they need to perform well on Quadrant D types of tasks that are cognitively demanding and context reduced.

This distinction between conversational and academic language is important. Previously, large numbers of ELLs were placed in special education classes because many of the tests used to measure English language proficiency only tapped their conversational fluency. The results of the tests and teachers' daily interactions with the students led teachers to believe that many ELLs had developed the English they needed for school. However, since the students did poorly on written tests that measured academic knowledge and problem solving ability, it was assumed that their low scores reflected a cognitive deficit, and they were placed in special education classes. What Cummins was able to show was that the low scores on tests of academic knowledge reflected a lack of academic English proficiency, not a learning difficulty. There are now tests for ELLs that are better designed to determine their academic language proficiency so that fewer emergent bilinguals are mislabeled and placed in special education classes.

The Threshold Hypothesis

A second important theoretical construct that Cummins (1979) developed is the Threshold Hypothesis. This hypothesis is related to the Interdependence Hypothesis we discussed in Chapter 6. The Interdependence Hypothesis holds that there is a common underlying proficiency (CUP) across languages, and, as a result, emergent bilinguals can draw on knowledge and skills they developed in one language as they listen, speak, read, and write in a second language. In other words, because of the common underlying proficiency, knowledge and skills transfer, and this provides bilinguals with a cognitive advantage.

The Threshold Hypothesis helps to explain the conditions under which transfer takes place and provides cognitive benefits for emergent bilinguals. In order to enter a home or any building, it is necessary to cross a threshold—that raised board below a door. When we cross the threshold, we have entered a home or other building. In the Threshold Hypothesis, Cummins presents an image of students crossing different thresholds as they develop increased academic proficiency in their two or more languages. Cummins describe three threshold levels (see Figure 9–3).

Emergent bilinguals at the lowest level have not developed age- or grade-level academic language proficiency in either their first or second languages. These students do have conversational fluency but a lack of academic language proficiency may lead to negative cognitive effects. What Cummins refers to in the Threshold Hypothesis is academic language proficiency, not conversational fluency. Many of the students described in the referral forms Cummins reviewed fell into this category.

Students who have developed grade-level academic proficiency in one of their languages fit the second level of Figure 9–3. For example, older students who arrive from Mexico with grade-level literacy and academic content knowledge in their first language would be at this level. Cummins says that these students experience neither positive nor negative cognitive effects of bilingualism. Of course, if the student from Mexico with a good academic background is tested in English, she will not appear to have any academic language proficiency. This is why it is important to assess the academic proficiency of bilingual students in both their first and second languages.

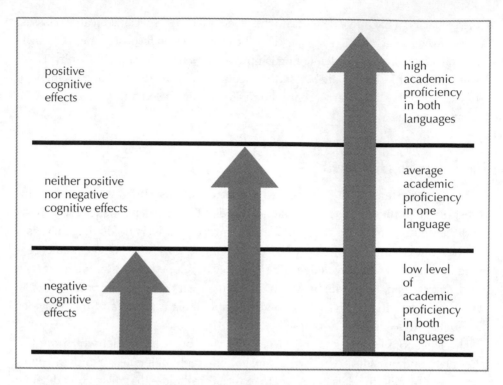

FIGURE 9–3. *Threshold Hypothesis (adapted from Cummins 1979)*

The goal for designing instructional programs for emergent bilinguals should be to help them reach the top level of Figure 9–3, proficient bilingualism. When students develop literacy and learn content in both their first and second languages they experience the positive cognitive effects of bilingualism because concepts learned in either language transfer to the other language. Effective, long-term bilingual programs help students develop full academic language proficiency in two languages.

Time to Develop Academic Language

Researchers estimate that the amount of time needed to acquire academic language proficiency ranges from four to nine years (Cummins 2008; Collier 1989; Hakuta, Butler, and Whitt 2000). Factors that influence the time it takes to develop academic proficiency are age on arrival and previous schooling as well as the kind of curriculum the school offers for emergent bilinguals. In addition, immigrants living in difficult situations and facing daily stresses outside school cannot be expected to succeed academically as quickly as students living in more favorable conditions.

Even though estimates of the time it takes to develop academic language proficiency vary, all researchers agree that an ELL will take several years to compete academically with native-English-speaking peers. This should not be surprising. If you were to move to Lithuania to live, it would take you about two years to develop the conversational language needed to carry out daily living tasks using the new language. You would be able to go to stores, ask for basic necessities, exchange common greetings, use the bus system, and engage in conversations on topics you already know about. You would not, however, be ready to attend college classes, or take notes or tests, or write essays in Lithuanian at that point. That would take considerably longer.

Bridging from Conversational to Academic Language

The challenge facing teachers of emergent bilinguals is to find ways to scaffold instruction and help students move from conversational to academic language. Gibbons (2002, 2009) provides numerous examples showing how teachers can support students' development of academic language through carefully sequenced lessons.

For example, Gibbons (2002) describes how a fourth-grade teacher provided multiple scaffolds during a lesson on magnetism. First, she involved students in a hands-on science activity with magnets. Each group was given a different experiment to carry out. They also were told that they would be reporting the results of their experiment to the class. As Gibbons notes, the group work was an authentic context for communication. Students needed to talk with group members as they completed the experiment.

Next, the teacher briefly introduced two key vocabulary words, *attract* and *repel*. She built her explanation on the language the children had been using. For example, she explained that another way to say *push away* is *repel* and that this is a more scientific word. As she explained the words, she demonstrated their meaning using magnets.

Once she had introduced the key vocabulary, the teacher guided students as each group reported on the results of their experiments. Here she used verbal scaffolds, such as questions. She helped clarify what students were saying. She also helped them begin to use the words *attract* and *repel* as they gave their reports. As Gibbons (2002) comments, "The overall aim of the teacher-guided reporting was to extend children's linguistic resources and focus on aspects of the specific discourse of science" (45). This extended portion of the lesson was designed to help students begin to talk and think like scientists, or in Gee's (2008) terms, to be part of the science Discourse.

Following the oral reports, students wrote about their experiments in their science journals. This writing was scaffolded by the earlier activity with the magnets, the teacher's explanation of key words, and the oral reports. The journal entries, in turn, later became a source of information for more formal science reports on magnets. At each stage of this lesson, the teacher provided the scaffolds the students needed to engage successfully in the activities of the classroom. In the process, they learned both academic English and academic content knowledge.

Gibbons (2002) explains that this example shows how a teacher can move her ELLs along a mode continuum from conversational to academic language. The term *mode* is used by systemic functional linguists to refer to the manner of communication. For example, the mode could be spoken or written. Martin (1984) points out that some spoken language, such as the language used when someone reads an academic paper, has many features of written language. On the other hand, some written language, such as a text message, is very informal and has many features of spoken language. Often, emergent bilinguals write the way they speak. Their written language lacks many of the features of academic discourse even though it is in written form. For that reason, Martin refers to language as more spoken-like or more written-like. Academic language, whether oral or written, has the features of formal written language.

During the lesson on magnets, the teacher moved her students along the mode continuum from conversational to academic English. Gibbons analyzes the language the students produced at each stage. As they talked together during the science experiment, the students used phrases like "Look, it's making them move." Here, the speaker does not have to specify what *it* or *them* refers to since all the children can see the objects. Later, as they reported back to the class, the children had to be more specific and name the objects—the pins and the magnets. They also began to use the words *attract* and *repel,* guided by the teacher. Later, as they wrote in their journals, they used complete sentences and paragraphs as well as specific terms. In writing a formal report, the students would need to reshape the language once more to fit the requirements of the science report genre.

Figure 9–4 illustrates the movement along the mode continuum from language that is more like spoken language to language that is more like written academic language. As this example shows, an important role for the teacher is to provide scaffolded instruction that helps ELLs build the academic language they need for school success.

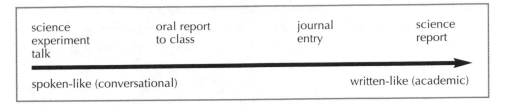

FIGURE 9–4. *Mode continuum*

Characteristics of Academic Language

Cummins' theoretical framework, the quadrants model, shows that academic language is context reduced and cognitively demanding. But what exactly are the characteristics of the context-reduced cognitively demanding language used in science, social studies, math, and literature? When students use the academic registers of school to discuss, read, and write about these subjects, just what kind of language do they need to use?

Differences in Vocabulary

One difference between conversational and academic language is the vocabulary. Corson (1997) examined two different large collections of words. One was the Birmingham corpus, which lists words that ESL students, children and adults, need for daily communication. He found that only two of the 150 most frequent words, *very* and *because*, have Latin or Greek roots. The rest are drawn from Anglo-Saxon vocabulary.

The vocabulary of everyday English comes primarily from Anglo-Saxon. These are short words like *bread* and *house*. This is the vocabulary that makes up most of the conversational language that ELLs acquire. In contrast, academic texts contain a high number of words with Greek and Latin roots, such as *transportation* and *sympathy*. Corson also examined the 150 most frequent words in the University Word List. This list, which includes words ESL students need to read academic texts, includes two words with Germanic roots and four others that entered English from French. The rest have Greek and Latin origins.

Corson's study shows that English vocabulary can be divided into two types of words, those with Anglo-Saxon origins used in everyday conversation and those from Latin and Greek sources that occur frequently in academic texts. Academic vocabulary contains both general academic terms that occur in different content areas and content-specific technical terms, such as *rectangle* in math or *mitosis* in science. ELLs first acquire the vocabulary needed for everyday communication, and this is what gives them conversational fluency. One way that emergent bilinguals can develop academic vocabulary is through extensive reading. Corson found that "popular magazines had three times as many rare words as television and informal conversation" (1997, 764).

Teaching Academic Vocabulary

One of the keys for successful vocabulary-building programs is that students are given only a few words each week (Marzano 2004), and these words are thoroughly learned. It is much better for students to gain a deep understanding of a few key words each week than to be exposed to a long list of words that they quickly forget. It is important to keep in mind that one of the best ways to build background is to engage students in reading accessible texts. In some classes, teachers try to preteach almost every word they think will be unfamiliar to students. The problem in trying to teach too many words is that time given to teaching vocabulary is time taken away from reading.

The words students learn should represent the most important concepts they are studying. For example, in her lesson on magnets, the teacher chose to focus on two essential words, *attract* and *repel*. She demonstrated the meaning of the words using magnets so that even ELLs at beginning levels could associate the words with the concepts they represented. She then guided students as they gave oral reports using the words. Subsequently, students included these terms as they wrote in their science journals.

Graves (2006) argues that any effective vocabulary program includes four components: it (1) provides rich and varied language experiences; (2) teaches individual words; (3) teaches word learning strategies; and (4) fosters word consciousness. In classes where teachers implement these four components, emergent bilinguals build academic vocabulary.

PROVIDE RICH AND VARIED LANGUAGE EXPERIENCES
In his review of research on ELLs, Graves (2006) concluded that "students need to develop their oral language skills in both their native language and in English" (34). The teacher in the lesson on magnets had her students work in small groups where they could use their first language or English as they discussed an academic subject. Small-group work benefits emergent bilinguals because they have more opportunities to talk than in whole-class settings. The teacher also had each group report on their experiment. As students reported, she scaffolded their oral language.

In addition to opportunities to develop oral language skills, ELLs need extended time for silent reading. Krashen (2004a) has summarized a great deal of the research on free voluntary reading. He concludes that programs in which students read for extended periods of time on a regular basis improve all aspects of their language proficiency.

For example, research by Anderson and Nagy (1992) showed that students who read extensively make impressive gains in their vocabulary. They conclude that, "for children who do a fair amount of independent reading, then natural learning could easily lead to the acquisition of five to ten thousand words per year" (46). As they read, students pick up content knowledge as well as vocabulary.

TEACH INDIVIDUAL WORDS

A number of writers have provided specific strategies for teaching individual words (Fisher and Frey 2008; Marzano and Pickering 2005; Graves 2006; Whitaker 2008; Frey and Fisher 2009; Allen 2007). All of these writers emphasize the need to choose only a few words to teach each week. The words should be selected from the unit of inquiry or theme being studied. This allows teachers to ensure that the instruction is contextualized.

Instruction should also be explicit. For example, Whitaker explains one strategy that involves filling in a graphic organizer. She describes how a teacher helped students learn a content-specific word, *force*.

The students were given a graphic organizer originally developed by Frayer. As Whitaker explains, "This graphic organizer is divided into four main sections to include the definition, characteristics, examples, and non-examples of words being studied. Revolutionary for its time, this model requires students to both analyze words and apply word knowledge" (2008, 153).

For the word *force*, students worked in groups to fill in the four squares of the Frayer model. For their definition, they put "a push or pull." They listed several characteristics, such as "measured in Newtons." Then they wrote examples like catching or throwing a ball and nonexamples like *mass* and *weight*. As they worked together to fill in the four boxes, the students discussed what *force* meant and, in the process, refined their understanding of this key term. This simple graphic organizer scaffolds instruction for ELLs and struggling readers. The students are also supported in their learning by working in small groups. They have opportunities to discuss the meanings of words and clarify their understandings.

TEACH WORD LEARNING STRATEGIES

According to Graves (2006), a third research-based component of an effective program for building vocabulary is teaching word learning strategies. These strategies include using context clues, using word parts, and using the dictionary and other resources.

Graves states, "Using context clues to infer the meanings of unknown words is the first word-learning-strategy I consider because it is the most important one" (2006, 94). All readers use context clues as they read. However, skilled readers make better use of context clues than struggling readers. ELLs who read well in their first language can transfer their skills, including using context clues, to a second language. However, many older ELLs do not read well in their first language or in English. For both struggling readers and ELLs, some explicit instruction in how to use context can be useful. Teachers can demonstrate how to use context clues by thinking aloud as they read a passage. Teachers can show different ways they use surrounding words to figure out unfamiliar vocabulary.

The second word learning strategy that Graves lists is using word-part clues to infer meanings of words. Words that make up the academic vocabulary of English often have Latin or Greek roots as well as prefixes and suffixes. Students can use these word parts to infer the meaning of words in context.

Kieffer and Lesaux (2010) report on a study they conducted in which teachers taught the use of suffixes to middle school students. The teachers chose one or two suffixes for each theme studied during the year. Then they went through a series of steps to teach suffixes that occurred frequently. They taught words that had a recognizable base, such as *invention* and *celebration*.

First, the teachers made sure that students understood the meaning of the base word. Students had to know the meaning of a word like *strategy* before learning derived forms, such as *strategic* or *strategize*. Teachers also divided the suffixes into different levels of difficulty. For example, a word formed by adding *er* to a verb to create a noun (*teach* → *teacher*) is easy to decompose, while a word formed by adding *-ity* to an adjective to form a noun (*durable* → *durability*) is more difficult to recognize or break into its parts.

Teachers introduced each suffix using carefully chosen examples. They involved students in different activities to recognize suffixes and use them to infer word meanings. For example, they showed students how a suffix like *tion* changes an action into a person, place, or thing (*contribute* → *contribution*). They also kept a cumulative chart and came back to the different suffixes repeatedly during the year. This method of teaching word parts explicitly in meaningful contexts helped increase students' vocabularies.

TEACH STUDENTS TO DRAW ON COGNATES

For English language learners with well-developed vocabularies in their first language, a very effective word learning strategy is to draw on cognates (Freeman and Freeman 2004). Of course, some students speak languages that are not related to English, and there are few, if any, cognates. However, many ELLs do speak languages related to English. The largest number of ELLs, nearly 80 percent, are Spanish speakers. Graves (2006) refers to studies that estimate that 20 percent to more than 30 percent of English words have Spanish cognates.

Academic English words with Latin and Greek roots are often cognates with Spanish words. For example, *hypothesis* has the Spanish equivalent *hipótesis*. Many everyday terms in Spanish are part of the academic language register in English. However, as Spanish-speaking students read or interact in classrooms, they often fail to draw on this knowledge base. Goldenberg (2008) notes, "Teachers cannot assume that transfer is automatic. Students sometimes do not realize that what they know in their first language (e.g., cognates such as *elefante* and *elephant*, or *ejemplo* and *example*; or spelling and comprehension skills) can be applied in their second" (16).

Teachers can help students access cognates by engaging them in activities that increase their awareness of similar words across languages. Williams (2001) lists several strategies teachers can use. For example, a teacher might begin by putting book pages on an overhead transparency and having students find cognates as a group. Then students can work in pairs to identify cognates. The teacher can also put a chart up in the classroom, and students can list the cognates they find on the chart. This activity can extend throughout a unit of study, and students can list as many cognates as possible related to the topic. They can find both general academic words, such as *análisis* and *analysis*, and content-specific words, such as *triángulo* and *triangle*. The students can also develop a classroom cognate dictionary using the words from the cognate chart.

USING REFERENCE TOOLS

The third word learning strategy that Graves (2006) recommends is to teach students how to use the dictionary and related reference tools. To teach students about dictionaries, a teacher needs to find dictionaries at the right level. For beginning ELLs, for example, a picture dictionary is a useful resource. For more advanced ELLs, student dictionaries are appropriate. Many dictionaries and other reference tools are available online, and students need to learn how to access and use those. For example, many students can find information about a topic on Wikipedia. This resource can help them clarify words that are labels for the complex concepts they study in different academic fields.

Graves offers several tips for helping students use dictionaries effectively and efficiently. He suggests giving students guidelines like these:

▶ When reading a definition, be sure to read all of it, not just part of it.

▶ Remember that many words have more than one meaning.

- Be sure to check all the definitions a dictionary gives for a word, not just one of them.

- Decide which definition makes sense in the passage in which you found the word.

- Often the dictionary works best when you already have some idea of a word's meaning. This makes the dictionary particularly useful for checking on a word you want to use in your writing. (112)

These are good guidelines, since students often read only the first entry in a dictionary without considering whether that definition fits the word in the context of their reading. Teachers could display Graves' suggestions in the classroom.

FOSTERING WORD CONSCIOUSNESS

Each of the components for vocabulary development that Graves lists is crucial. Students need to engage in class discussions and to read and write extensively to build their vocabulary. Teachers should teach some content-specific words directly. They can also provide students with strategies for learning words independently. In addition, teachers should plan activities to help students develop word consciousness. According to Graves:

> The term *word consciousness* refers to an awareness of and interest in words and their meanings. As defined by Nagy and Anderson (1992), word consciousness involves both a cognitive and an affective stance toward words. Word consciousness integrates metacognition about words, motivation to learn words, and deep and lasting interest in words. (7)

Teachers can foster word consciousness by pointing out similarities and differences across languages. For example, English has *crocodile* and in Spanish, the word is *cocodrilo*. The class could discuss how letters sometimes get transposed as they move across languages. Since ELLs speak a language other than English, discussion of cognates and false cognates, such as *assist* (help) and *asistir* (to attend), can also spark interest in language.

Teachers can also make a point of using new words as they lecture or lead class discussions. If the teacher has come across a new word in her reading, she can ask if anyone in the class has heard the word, and she can ask them what they think it might mean. The teacher can also read the section where the word appears and think aloud about how the context gives clues to the word's meaning. It is important that students know that teachers also learn new words as they read.

Teachers who show an active interest in words help their students develop word consciousness. They provide a model, showing students that words are important. When students see that their teachers are interested in words and that teachers continue to learn words, they also become more conscious of all the words they encounter each day. The goal for any program of vocabulary development should be to foster word consciousness. When ELLs and struggling readers become interested in words and become aware of the power of words, they build the academic vocabulary they need to succeed in school.

Differences in Style

Vocabulary is not the only difference between conversational and academic language. Biber (1986) analyzed the differences between two large samples of language. The first was a collection of five hundred written text samples of about two thousand words each. These included fiction, such as detective stories, as well as press reports and academic papers. Biber also added text from professional letters. The oral language sample consisted of recorded conversations, broadcasts, and public speeches. This spoken-language database contained eighty-seven texts of about five thousand words each.

Biber found three differences between the style of the language used in the two text samples. First, the spoken texts were more interactive and showed more personal involvement. The written texts showed less personal involvement. They were more detached in style. For example, when students do a biology experiment, talk about it as they work, and report back orally, the language they use is more interactive, less formal, and less precise than the language these same students use when they write up the experiment. Biber refers to this difference between spoken and written language as interactive versus edited text.

A second stylistic difference between the two types of texts was that the written texts were more abstract while the spoken texts were more concrete. Written texts achieve abstraction by the use of a number of features, such as nominalizations and passives. Nominalization is a process of turning a verb into a noun. For example, the verb *destroy* can be changed to the noun, *destruction*. Nominalization allows writers to pack more information into each sentence. At the same time, the sentences become more abstract because the person or thing doing the action is removed. In "The beetles destroyed the redwood trees" the actor—the beetles—is named. In "The destruction of the redwood trees is of great concern" no actor is named, so the idea is conveyed in an abstract manner. In the same way, passives remove the actor. An active sentence, "The beetles destroyed the redwood trees," becomes more abstract when it is made passive: "The redwood trees were destroyed." The result is an abstract and more formal style.

Spoken language, in contrast, is more concrete and situated. Speakers name the agents who carry out actions. They also indicate the time and place more specifically. Spoken language, as a result, is more situated in particular contexts. The language is also more informal. For example, when students discuss a field trip they took, they can use informal language to talk about specific events that occurred in particular places at certain times. Their language is situated and informal. If, however, they write about the field trip, they use a more abstract, formal style to report what happened and to make generalizations about what they learned.

A third difference in style that Biber (1986) found was that the oral texts were more immediate, and the written texts were delivered in a reported style. A reported style is characterized by language that tells about events that occurred in the past and in a different place. Writers usually use past tense and write about places that are not near a reader. In contrast, the immediate style of oral language uses present tense more often. Speakers talk about current events or events that have recently occurred, and they often talk about local events.

When teachers read books to their students and students respond either in groups or in the whole class, their language is less formal as they talk about their immediate response. On the other hand, when students write a report about that book, discussing plot, character, theme, and setting or comparing the book with something else they have read, this reported style is more structured and much more distant.

The three differences in style that Biber identified through his analysis of the two types of texts were not differences in vocabulary, but differences in syntactic and semantic features. The spoken texts were more interactive, situated, and immediate. The written texts were more edited, abstract, and reported. These features give written academic texts an authoritative tone. Emergent bilinguals often have difficulty reading and writing academic texts because they expect that these texts will contain the same kind of language that is used in everyday conversations. However, as the study by Biber reveals, there are qualitative differences between conversational language and academic language.

Differences in Lexical Density

Text analyses by systemic functional linguists, such as Halliday (1989) and Schleppegrell (2004), found that academic language has greater lexical density than conversational language. Earlier, we mentioned that academic language contains many nominalized forms. Nominalization is the process of turning verbs or adjectives into nouns. For example, through the process of nominalization the verb *produce* or the adjective *productive* can be changed to the noun *productivity*.

Now consider the following pairs of sentences:

(i) The workers *produce* parts for automobiles at a high rate, and this has increased the company's profits.

(ii) The automobile parts factory workers' high *productivity* resulted in increased profits for the company.

(i) The workers at the plant were very *productive*, and this increased the company's profits.

(ii) The workers' high *productivity* increased the company's profits.

The first sentence in each pair contains a concrete subject (the workers) that is doing the work. In contrast, the subjects of the second sentences are more abstract (productivity). Nominalization is one way that writers of academic texts create an abstract style. At the same time, the second sentences contain more information in each clause. In linguistic terms, these sentences have greater lexical density (Halliday 1989). Lexical density is greater when each clause in a sentence contains more lexical words.

Linguists distinguish between two kinds of words: lexical and grammatical. Lexical words are nouns, verbs, and some adjectives and adverbs, such as *green* or *fortunately*. These are the words that carry the main meaning of a message because they refer to people, places, things, or qualities we can picture. On the other hand, grammatical words include articles, prepositions, conjunctions, pronouns, and other words that connect the content words and show the relationships among them.

In each pair of sentences above, the first sentence has two clauses, and the second sentence has only one. Since the first and second sentences in each pair express the same idea, we can see that the information expressed in two clauses in the first sentences is compressed into one clause in the second sentence of each pair through the use of nominalization. If we count the number of lexical words in each clause in the first sentences of each pair, we find that the percentage of lexical words is 48 percent. In the second set of sentences, in contrast, 78 percent of the words are content words. These results are typical of the findings of linguists who analyze extensive samples of spoken and written language. Written language often has double the lexical density of spoken language. The higher rate of lexical words increases the cognitive demand on the reader.

Writing Sentences in an Academic Style

Teachers can help students write in an academic style by improving their sentences and paragraphs. Often ELLs write either short, simple sentences or very long sentences that consist of a series of short sentences joined by common conjunctions, such as *and* or *because*. Their sentences also have low lexical density.

One way to help students move past this early stage is to build their vocabulary by introducing other, more precise, words to show the relationships between ideas. These transition words are often referred to as signal words because they signal to the reader how two ideas are related. Signal words may connect ideas within a sentence or across sentences. Fisher, Rothenberg, and Frey (2007) explain how a team of ninth-grade teachers worked to help their students write more complex sentences.

The teachers examined student writing and found that their ELLs often left transitions out. The teachers introduced a word list that grouped signal words by function. The functions included addition, example, comparison, contrast, cause and effect, concession, and conclusion. For each function, several words were listed. For example, for addition, the list included *also, and, besides, furthermore, in addition, indeed, in fact, moreover, so,* and *too*.

The teachers posted this list in their rooms as a word wall. They took time on a regular basis to review the words with their students. As they read aloud to their students, they made a point of emphasizing words in the texts that were on the list. According to Fisher and his colleagues, "Over time, students started to notice the terms in their reading and began incorporating them into their writing" (51). The process the teachers used enabled emergent bilinguals in their ninth-grade classes to write more complex sentences.

Another way to help ELLs write sentences in an academic style is through sentence combining activities. Research has shown that these activities improve student writing (Kilgallon and Kilgallon 2007). The teacher can write a series of short sentences and then have students work in groups to rewrite the sentences using signal words to connect them. Each group could put their results up on butcher paper or on an overhead transparency and explain how they combined the sentences.

Teachers can use sentence combining to introduce various ways to combine sentences. For example, the teacher could show students how to use relative clauses to combine two sentences, such as "Scientists follow a set of procedures" and "These procedures help ensure that their experiments are carried out properly," to produce "Scientists follow a set of procedures that help ensure that their experiments are carried out properly." Then students could practice combining sentences by making one sentence a relative clause.

Since academic writing contains many sentences with complex nominal phrases, teachers could work with advanced ELLs to further refine their writing and create an academic style. First, the teacher would show students how verbs and adjectives such as *replace* or *creative* can be turned into nouns like *replacement* or *creativity*. Then, working together, the teacher and a small group of advanced ELLs could identify sentences in one of their content texts that contained nominalized forms.

Once students understand the process of nominalization, they could try rewriting to produce sentences that contain nominalized forms. For example, using the example from our discussion of lexical density, the teacher could give students a sentence such as "The workers *produce* parts for automobiles at a high rate, and this has increased the company's profits," and guide them to rewrite using nominalizations to produce a sentence like "The automobile parts factory workers' high *productivity* resulted in increased profits for the company." With proper scaffolding, teachers could instruct their advanced ELLs to write sentences such as this that reflect the academic style found in many school textbooks.

Writing Paragraphs in an Academic Style

The main challenge for students in writing paragraphs in an academic style is to write cohesive paragraphs. Often ELLs and other struggling students produce paragraphs that consist of a series of unrelated sentences. Academic writing demands that sentences be linked clearly to develop one idea in each paragraph.

One way teachers can help students write cohesive paragraphs is to show them how to use signal words to connect sentences. Students who can use signal words to connect clauses within a sentence can extend this skill to connect sentences in a text. Teachers can use the same strategies described earlier to introduce a series of words for each function and provide meaningful, contextualized activities for using signal words.

Teachers can also show students how to create cohesive paragraphs by following certain patterns to connect the sentences. First, the teacher would explain that sentences in English can be divided into two parts, the topic and the comment. The subject is the topic, and the rest of the sentence serves to say something about the subject. For example, in a sentence like "The boy passed the test," the topic, what we are talking about, is "the boy," and the rest of the sentence—"passed the test"—is a comment about the boy. It tells us what he did.

Once students understand that sentences are made up of a topic and a comment, the teacher can show that in cohesive paragraphs each sentence has the same topic, each sentence has a topic that is a subcategory or example of the topic in the first sentence, or that the comment of one sentence is the same as the topic of the following sentence. Most paragraphs have a combination of these patterns, but they should be introduced and practiced one at a time. Brown (2009) refers to these three patterns as constant topic, derived topic, and chaining.

> Nine **planets** make up the solar system. **They** can be grouped into the inner planets and the outer planets. All the **planets** move in orbits around the sun. As **they** move, the planets rotate. **Each one** is surrounded by an atmosphere that consists of a layer of gases. The **planets** range in temperature from very hot to very cold. **They** are fascinating to study.

FIGURE 9–5. *Constant topic*

Figure 9–5 illustrates a constant topic. In this paragraph, the topic of each sentence refers to planets. The author used pronouns (*they, each one*) to vary his writing. The sentences are all clearly connected by the constant topic.

> The nine **planets** that comprise the solar system differ in various ways. **Mercury** is one of the inner planets. **Jupiter** is an outer planet. **Mars** is made up of rock. **Neptune** consists of gases. **Earth** takes 365 days to orbit the sun. **Uranus** takes 84 years. **Venus** is the hottest planet, and **Pluto** is the coldest.

FIGURE 9–6. *Derived topic*

The next organizational pattern, a derived topic, is shown in Figure 9–6. In this paragraph, the first sentence has *planets* as the topic. Then, each of the following sentences has one of the planets as the topic. Having topics that represent subcategories of a topic is a common way to connect the sentences in a paragraph.

> The **solar system** is made up of nine **planets**. These **planets** all orbit around the **sun**. The **sun** is a **star**. **Stars** vary in **temperature** and **color**. The **hottest** stars are **bluish-white** and the **coolest** stars are **red**. **Red** stars are still very hot, more than 5,500 degrees Fahrenheit.

FIGURE 9–7. *Chained topic*

The most common pattern in academic writing is shown in Figure 9–7. In this pattern the comment, or last part, of one sentence connects to the topic of the following sentence. For example, in Figure 9–7, the first sentence ends with *planets*, and then *planets* is the topic of the following sentence. This chaining pattern allows the writer to link a series of related topics.

Teachers can teach each of these patterns by providing clear examples and then having students practice writing paragraphs using each one. Paragraph cohesion should be taught in the context of content-area studies. Students reading about the Civil War in the United States could write paragraphs about the war. Students can also analyze key passages from their textbooks to identify the patterns the authors used. Often, writers include a combination of constant, derived, and chained topics in the same paragraph.

Writing in Academic Genres

The different types of texts within an academic discipline are referred to as *genres*. The term *genre* is most often used to describe types of text used in art and literature. For example, we might view an impressionist or a cubist painting or read a novel, a play, or a poem. Each of these is structured differently, and each represents a different genre.

Systemic functional linguists have extended the term *genre* to include other kinds of texts, including the text types that are commonly used in schools. Each subject area has different text types. For instance, science has procedures, and history has historical explanations. When students understand how these different text types or genres are organized and which features are associated with them, they can make better predictions as they read them, and they can produce writing that follows the pattern of the text type that is appropriate to an assignment. For example, if a teacher asks the students to write a science report, they should organize their writing and include features in ways expected of science reports and not in ways typical of a book report.

Schleppegrell (2004) describes three types of genres used in schools: personal, factual, and analytical. Personal genres report on personal experiences. For example, a student might write about what she did on a field trip. Factual genres, in contrast, present facts. When students write a report on a historical character, their writing is in the form of a factual genre, and it should not include personal opinion. Analytical genres analyze events and often argue for a particular interpretation. A paper on the best solution to a math problem would be an example of an analytical genre.

Each genre has specific language features. Procedures are usually written as numbered lists with verbs in the imperative form (1. *Fill* the beaker with water). A procedural recount of the steps taken in conducting an experiment would be written in past tense and would include signal words showing sequence. This procedural recount might be accompanied by a diagram to illustrate the steps.

Genres are best taught by content-area teachers. Language arts teachers often teach the form and features of different types of poetry, for example. In the same way, teachers of math, science, and social studies should specifically teach the structures and features of the different kinds of writing in their discipline. This requires content teachers to examine the kinds of writing their students read and are expected to produce and then carefully scaffold instruction so that students can read and write academic genres successfully. One way to be sure to include the teaching of academic language and academic writing style in content areas is to develop both content and language objectives when teaching.

Language and Content Objectives

Teachers are accustomed to basing their instruction on content objectives. Content objectives are based on state or national standards. Objectives have been developed for each content area at the different grade levels. For example, a math objective for middle school might be "Students will be able to solve simple algebraic equations and explain the operations they used to solve the problems using proofs."

Teachers with English language learners in their classes also need to develop language objectives based on the state English language proficiency standards. Language objectives should be related to content objectives to contextualize teaching for ELLs. The teachers that Kieffer and Lesaux worked with, for example, chose the suffixes they taught to expand students' academic vocabulary from the unit themes.

Language objectives can target different levels—vocabulary, sentence, paragraph, or text (genre). Following the state English language proficiency standards, teachers of ELLs should develop a comprehensive plan for language skills to be taught and then write language objectives that relate to their content objectives.

For example, if the big question for an inquiry unit is "What are the cycles we find in our lives, our environment, and our history?" and the students are studying the water cycle, a content objective might be for students to demonstrate their understanding of the water cycle by drawing a diagram, labeling the phases, and writing a short paragraph explaining what happens during each phase of the cycle. A text-level language objective could be for students to refer to a diagram and write a science report about the water cycle. At the paragraph level, students could use signal words showing sequence, such as *first*, *next*, and *then*. At the sentence level, students could focus on subject-verb agreement (water evaporates). And at the word level, students could study words with a *tion* suffix (*evaporation, precipitation, condensation*).

Teachers would not want to assign language objectives from the different levels at the same time, but through various assignments, they could teach and assess ELLs' developing language proficiency. Teachers can also vary language objectives depending on the proficiency level of the ELLs in a class. In addition, they can draw on the different language domains—speaking, listening, reading, and writing. For example, in writing, a beginning-level ELL might label the steps in a science experiment while an intermediate ELL might list the steps in a science procedure, and an advanced student could write a recount of an experiment using past-tense verbs and connecting sentences with signal words that show sequence.

Assessing Academic Language

English language learners are assessed more often than native English speakers since they are assessed both for their language proficiency and for their content area knowledge. While ELLs can be assessed on content knowledge in their native language, most often, they are assessed in English. In fact, pressures from standardized testing in English resulting from the No Child Left Behind legislation has led to less content teaching in students' first languages and a decline in bilingual education programs (Crawford 2007).

Gottlieb (2006) outlines the steps required for assessing ELLs. Assessment starts with a home language survey. As Gottlieb explains, the survey "serves to differentiate monolingual English-speaking students from those who interact in another language and culture on a daily basis" (6). Students who are identified as coming from a home where another language is used are further tested. In some schools they are given a literacy survey. This survey provides valuable information on students' first language literacy and helps in proper placement. In addition, all identified students are given a standards-based, reliable, and valid test of English language proficiency, such as the Language Assessment Scales (LAS) or the Idea Proficiency Test (IPT). Older students are also given tests designed to measure academic achievement in their native language and in English. All these measures help determine the level of support students need.

Gottlieb (2006) lists additional assessments for ELLs that serve a variety of purposes. Schools are required to monitor ELLs' English language proficiency and their academic achievement through classroom assessments (created by teachers), and/or standardized portfolios, as well as district- or school-level measures.

ELLs are also assessed to meet accountability requirements in both language proficiency and academic achievement through state content and language assessments and district-level assessments. These measures along with teacher recommendations are often the basis for student reclassification from Limited English Proficiency status to Full English Proficiency. Finally, ELL assessment is also used for program evaluation at the school or district levels.

In accordance with the No Child Left Behind law, states are required to establish English language proficiency standards aligned to state academic content standards and to assess and report the English language proficiency of all ELLs on an annual basis. There are three measures, referred to as Annual Measurable Achievement Objectives (AMAOs). The first AMAO measures the annual increases in the number or percentage of students making progress in learning English. The second AMAO reports the annual increases in the number or percentage of students attaining English language proficiency by the end of each school year. And the third AMAO shows adequate yearly progress for the ELL subgroup in meeting grade-level academic achievement standards in English language arts and mathematics.

Gottlieb and Nguyen (2007) describe in detail how a large district that offers dual-language programs, transitional bilingual programs, and ESL programs has developed a comprehensive assessment system. The heart of the model is a pivotal portfolio. The assessment and accountability system implemented in this district can serve as a model for other districts around the country and can help districts design assessments needed for their AMAO reports.

Modifications of Standardized Tests

ELLs as well as native English speakers are required to take standardized tests in English designed to measure their content-area proficiency in language arts, mathematics and science. As Abedi and Lord (2001) note:

> English language learner (ELL) students score lower than students who are proficient in English on standardized tests of mathematics achievement in elementary school as well as on the Scholastic Aptitude Test and the quantitative and analytical sections of the Graduate Record Examination. Although there is no evidence to suggest that the basic abilities of ELL students are different from non-ELL students, the achievement differences between ELL and non-ELL students are pronounced. (220)

Abedi and Lord conclude that the difference in scores of ELL and native-English-speaking students can best be explained by recognizing the effects of English language proficiency on academic content test scores. As a result, attempts have been made to modify the tests or the testing situation to close this achievement gap.

In some cases, the tests have been translated into the students' first languages. However, testing experts argue that it is nearly impossible to produce equivalent tests in two languages since languages differ in a number of ways. Simply translating an English test into Spanish, for example, does not produce an equivalent test, even when the translation is a good one. ELLs may not benefit from a test in their native language if most or all of their content-area instruction has been in English, and they have not developed grade-level academic proficiency in their first language.

Other modifications include allowing students to use a bilingual dictionary, having someone read the test questions to them, and giving the students more time. These efforts for the most part have not been successful in creating assessments that remove the language factor for ELLs. However, Abedi and Lord (2001) report that linguistic modification of test items has resulted in increased test scores in math for ELLs.

The researchers modified items in one or more of several ways. For example, they replaced unfamiliar or infrequent vocabulary, they changed passive forms to active, they shortened long nominal (noun) groups, they replaced sentences with conditional clauses with simple sentences, they removed relative clauses, they simplified questions, and they made questions more concrete.

As an example of the kind of math problem ELLs face, consider the following question from a state's grade 6 exam:

> Students in Mr. Jacob's English class were giving speeches. Each student's speech was 7–10 minutes long. Which of the following is the best estimate for the total number of student speeches that could be given in a 2-hour class?
> A. 4   B. 8   C. 13   D. 19

The last sentence is particularly difficult. It has a long nominal group with a passive and a relative clause. The phrase "which of the following" may be confusing to students because they may have trouble deciding what "which" refers to. Linguistically modifying this sentence would produce an exam question that ELLs would be more likely to comprehend:

> Students in Mr. Jacob's English class were giving speeches. Each student's speech was 7–10 minutes long. About how many students could give speeches during a 120-minute class?
> A. 4   B. 8   C. 13   D. 19

Abedi and Lord (2001) found that when ELLs were given linguistically modified questions that assessed the same math concepts and functions, the students preferred the modified questions, and they scored significantly higher on a test with modified questions. This large-scale study suggests that linguistic modifications are the most effective way to ensure fair tests for ELLs. However, modifying tests linguistically is time-consuming and requires considerable expertise. Furthermore, even when tests are modified, ELLs score lower than native English speakers. Their lack of English proficiency makes learning content more difficult, and this results in lower test scores.

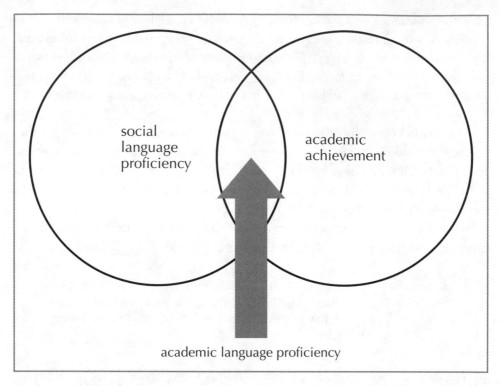

FIGURE 9–8. *Academic language proficiency (adapted from Gottlieb 2006)*

English Language Proficiency Standards

The English language proficiency standards developed by many states are based on the language arts standards that were written for native English speakers. Tests of state English language proficiency standards seldom measure ELLs' academic language proficiency. However, the TESOL (Teachers of English to Speakers of Other Languages) organization has developed English language proficiency standards (Gottlieb et al. 2006). These standards form the basis for performance indicators designed to serve as samples for measuring academic language proficiency.

Academic language proficiency can be conceptualized as the overlap between social language and academic achievement. Figure 9–8 illustrates the relationship between social language, academic achievement, and academic language proficiency.

There are five TESOL English language proficiency standards. The first is that English language learners communicate for social, intercultural, and instructional purposes within the school setting. This standard focuses on the language ELLs need in order to function effectively in a classroom and includes their ability to use language to communicate with peers and the teacher and to understand and participate in instructional activities.

The remaining four standards are similar. Each one corresponds to one of the primary content areas. Standard two is that English language learners communicate information, ideas, and concepts necessary for academic success in the area of language arts. Standards three through five address mathematics, science, and social studies. These TESOL standards describe the linguistic, cognitive, and sociocultural skills ELLs at different levels of proficiency need to succeed academically in English.

TESOL has developed sample performance indicators for each standard. These sample indicators are organized around five different proficiency levels, five grade-level clusters, and four language domains of speaking, listening, reading, and writing. Each sample performance indicator consists of three parts: a language function, the academic content, and the support or strategy. For example, in the area of science and the topic of Earth's materials for students at level four (next to the highest) in grades four and five, a sample performance indicator is "Discuss and give examples of uses of natural phenomena from collections or pictures" (Gottlieb et al. 2006, 43). Here the content is "natural phenomena," the language function is "give examples," and the support is "from collections or pictures."

The performance indicators can be modified to fit students at different proficiency levels by changing the language function or the support. For example, for grades 1 to 3 in science with the topic of plants and animals, the performance indicators for writing for each of the five levels of proficiency are shown in Figure 9–9.

As Figure 9–9 (taken from the TESOL PreK–12 English Language Proficiency Standards, page 65) shows, the content for each indicator is the same. However, the supports and language functions are different. Beginning students are asked to draw and label, intermediate students compare using graphic support, and advanced students maintain journals or learning logs. More advanced students receive less support and are asked to complete more demanding tasks to demonstrate their understanding of the content.

Level 1	Level 2	Level 3	Level 4	Level 5
Draw and label local plant or animal species from real-life observations, experiences, or pictures.	Draw and describe physical attributes of local plant or animal species from real-life observations, experiences, or pictures.	Compare physical attributes of local plant or animal species from real-life observations, experiences, or pictures, using graphic support.	Rewrite notes on or comparisons of local plant and animal species from real-life observations or experiences to produce sentences and paragraphs.	Maintain journals or learning logs describing local plant or animal species and environments based on real-life observations or experiences.

FIGURE 9–9. *Sample performance indicators (from TESOL Pre-K–12 English Language Proficiency Standards 2006)*

How Can Teachers Help ELLs Develop Academic Language?

These sample performance indicators have been used as models by states that have developed their own English language proficiency standards and exams. They are only samples because each state has its own content standards, although all content standards are based on national standards developed by professional organizations. The TESOL standards are excellent guides for the difficult task of assessing academic language.

Conclusion

English language learners need to develop academic language to succeed in school. Academic language may be defined as the registers of language used in schools. Students with academic English can read, write, and discuss academic subjects. Academic language differs from conversational language in both vocabulary and style. Teachers can help students develop academic language by developing both content and language objectives. Language objectives should account for different linguistic levels—words, sentences, paragraphs, and whole texts.

To teach academic language effectively requires that teachers develop language objectives that fit with their content objectives. For each content objective, teachers can ask themselves, "What language forms and functions will my ELLs need to read, write, and discuss this content?" Assessing academic content for ELLs is a challenge since, even with modifications, tests often measure students' English proficiency rather than their content knowledge. Valid and reliable assessments can be developed by basing assessments on performance indicators that combine linguistic, cognitive, and sociocultural factors. The TESOL sample performance indicators serve as a model for states as they develop their English language proficiency exams.

KEY POINTS

→ The language register used in schools to read, write, and discuss academic subjects is referred to as *academic language*.

→ Many ELLs develop basic and intermediate levels of reading proficiency but fail to develop disciplinary literacy.

KEY POINTS

➤ Cummins distinguishes between two kinds of language proficiency: conversational fluency and academic language proficiency.

➤ Cummins' quadrants model illustrates that conversational fluency is context embedded and cognitively undemanding while academic language is context reduced and cognitively demanding. Teachers should provide instruction in Quadrant B that is both context embedded and cognitively demanding.

➤ Cummins holds that bilinguals must reach a certain threshold of proficiency in two languages to receive the cognitive benefits of bilingualism.

➤ It takes about two years to develop conversational fluency, but it takes from four to nine years to develop academic language proficiency in a second language.

➤ Teachers can scaffold instruction to bridge from conversational to academic language.

➤ Teachers should teach the different levels of academic language: word, sentence, paragraph, and text.

➤ Teachers should write both content and language objectives as they teach academic language and subject matter content to ELLs.

➤ ELLs are assessed more than native English speakers because they are assessed for both language proficiency and academic content.

➤ Even when ELLs are tested for academic content, the tests are often measures of English proficiency.

➤ Some linguistic modifications help ELLs demonstrate their knowledge of academic content.

➤ TESOL has developed standards for assessing academic language proficiency.

APPLICATIONS

1. Interview five teachers. Ask them to explain the difference between social language and academic language. Bring your results to class or your study group for discussion.

2. Look back at Cummins' quadrant (Figure 9–2). List several activities you have done with your students or that you have observed that fit in Quadrant B (cognitively demanding and context embedded).

3. This chapter suggests several ways to teach academic vocabulary. Try one or more of these and write up what you did and how it worked.

4. The chapter also suggests ways to help students write cohesive paragraphs. Try teaching a lesson or a series of lessons on the organizational patterns listed in the chapter. Write up what you did and the results.

5. What genres have you taught? Make a chart with the genres and the language features associated with each genre. Use the example below as a model for your chart:

Genre	Language Features
Science procedure	Numbered steps Imperative verbs
History report	Adverbs of time Chronological organization

6. Choose a unit of inquiry that you teach. List two or three content objectives. Then, for each, list at least one language objective. Finally, write performance indicators that you could use to assess this objective for beginning, intermediate, and advanced ELLs. Use Figure 9–9 as a guide.

References

Abedi, J., and C. Lord. 2001. "The Language Factor in Mathematics Tests." *Applied Measurement in Education* 14 (3): 219–34.

Ada, A. F. 1990. *Una Semilla Nada Más*. Carmel, CA: Hampton-Brown.

Aguila, V. 2010. "Schooling English Learners: Contexts and Challenges." *Improving Education for English Learners: Research-Based Approaches*, ed. F. Ong, 1–20. Sacramento: California Department of Education.

Allen, J. 2002. *On the Same Page*. Portland, ME: Stenhouse.

———. 2007. *Inside Words: Tools for Teaching Academic Vocabulary Grades 4–12*. Portland, ME: Stenhouse.

Anderson, R., and W. Nagy. 1992. "The Vocabulary Conundrum." *American Educator* 16 (4): 14–18, 44–47.

August, D., and T. Shanahan, eds. 2006. *Developing Literacy in Second-Language Learners: Report of the National Literacy Panel on Language Minority Children and Youth*. Mahwah, NJ: Lawrence Erlbaum.

Baker, C. 2006. *Foundations of Bilingual Education and Bilingualism, 4th Edition*. Clevedon, UK: Multilingual Matters.

Batalova, J., and M. McHugh. 2010a. *Number and Growth of Students in U.S. Schools in Need of English Instruction*. Washington, DC: Migration Policy Institute.

———. 2010b. *States and Districts with the Highest Number and Share of English Language Learners*. Washington, DC: Migration Policy Institute.

Beebe, L. 1987. "Introduction." *Issues in Second Language Acquisition: Multiple Perspectives*, ed. L. Beebe, 1–14. New York: Newbury House.

Biber, D. 1986. "Spoken and Written Textual Dimensions in English: Resolving the Contradictory Findings." *Language* 62 (2): 384–414.

Bliatout, B., B. Downing, J. Lewis, and D. Yang. 1988. *Handbook for Teaching Hmong-Speaking Students*. Folsom, CA: Folsom Cordova Unified School District.

Bourdieu, P., and J. Passeron. 1977. *Reproduction in Education, Society and Culture*. London: Sage.

Brown, D. 2009. *In Other Words: Grammar Lessons for Code-Switching, Composition, and Language Study*. Portsmouth, NH: Heinemann.

Brown, H. 1980. *Principles of Language Learning and Teaching*. Englewood Cliffs, NJ: Prentice-Hall.

Brown, J., A. Collins, and P. Duguid. 1989. "Situated Cognition and the Culture of Learning." *Educational Researcher* 18 (1): 32–42.

Brown, R. 1973. *A First Language: The Early Stages*. Cambridge, MA: MIT Press.

Brozo, W., G. Shiel, and K. Topping. 2007/2008. "Engagement in Reading: Lessons Learned from Three Pisa Countries." *Journal of Adolescent & Adult Literacy* 51 (4): 304–17.

Bruner, J. 1985. "Models of the Learner." *Educational Researcher* 14 (6): 5–8.

Bunting, E. 1988. *How Many Days to America?* Boston: Clarion.

Canale, M., and M. Swain. 1980. "Theoretical Bases of Communicative Approaches to Second Language Teaching and Testing." *Applied Linguistics* 1: 1–47.

Cazden, C. 1992. *Whole Language Plus: Essays on Literacy in the United States and New Zealand*. New York: Teachers College Press.

Chomsky, N. 1975. *Reflections on Language*. New York: Pantheon.

Cloud, N., F. Genessee, and E. Hamayan. 2000. *Dual Language Instruction: A Handbook for Enriched Education*. Boston: Heinle & Heinle.

Cohen, A., and E. Olshtain. 1993. "The Production of Speech Acts by ESL Learners." *TESOL Quarterly* 27 (1): 33–56.

Cohen, B. 1983. *Molly's Pilgrim*. New York: Lothrop, Lee & Shepard.

Collier, V. 1989. "How Long? A Synthesis of Research on Academic Achievement in a Second Language." *TESOL Quarterly* 23 (3): 509–32.

Collier, V., and W. Thomas. 2004. "The Astounding Effectiveness of Dual Language Education for All." *NABE Journal of Research and Practice* 2 (1): 1–19.

———. 2009. *Educating English Learners for a Transformed World*. Albuquerque, NM: Dual Language Education of New Mexico/Fuente Press.

Corcoran, A. November 2009. "How Did We Get So Many Somali Refugees—The Numbers Are Telling." Refugee Resettlement Watch. Available at http://refugeeresettlement watch.wordpress.com/.

Corson, D. 1997. "The Learning and Use of Academic English Words." *Language Learning* 47: 671–718.

Cortés, C. 1986. "The Education of Language Minority Students: A Contextual Interaction Model." *Beyond Language: Social and Cultural Factors in Schooling Language Minority Students*, ed. D. Holt, 3–33. Los Angeles: Evaluation, Dissemination and Assessment Center, California State University, Los Angeles.

CNN. 2010. "Arizona Schools Chief Says Ethnic Studies Law Takes Focus off Race." Available at http://articles.cnn.com/2010-05-12/politics/arizona.ethnic.studies_1_new-immigration-law-tucson-unified-school-district-ethnic-studies?_s=PM:POLITICS.

Crawford, J. 2007. "The Decline of Bilingual Education: How to Reverse a Troubling Trend?" Available at www.elladvocates.org/.

Crystal, D. 2000. *Language Death*. Cambridge, UK: Cambridge University Press.

Cummins, J. 1979. "Linguistic Interdependence and the Educational Development of Bilingual Children." *Review of Educational Research* 49 (2): 222–51.

———. 1981. "The Role of Primary Language Development in Promoting Educational Success for Language Minority Students." *Schooling and Language Minority Students: A Theoretical Framework*, 3–49. Los Angeles: Evaluation, Dissemination and Assessment Center, California State University, Los Angeles.

———. 1989. *Empowering Minority Students*. Sacramento: California Association of Bilingual Education.

———. 1996. *Negotiating Identities: Education for Empowerment in a Diverse Society*. Ontario, CA: California Association of Bilingual Education.

———. 2000. *Language, Power and Pedagogy: Bilingual Children in the Crossfire*. Tonawanda, NY: Multilingual Matters.

———. 2001. *Negotiating Identities: Education for Empowerment in a Diverse Society*. 2d ed. Ontario, CA: California Association of Bilingual Education.

———. 2007. "Rethinking Monolingual Instructional Strategies in Multilingual Classrooms." *Canadian Journal of Applied Linguistics* 10 (2): 221–40.

———. 2008. "BICS and CALP: Empirical and Theoretical Status of the Distinction." *Encyclopedia of Language and Education*, ed. N. Hornberger, 71–84. New York: Springer Science and Business.

Derewianka, B. 2007. "Changing Approaches to the Conceptualization and Teaching of Grammar." *International Handbook of English Language Teaching*, ed. J. Cummins and C. Davison, 843–58. New York: Springer Science+Business Media.

Díaz, S., L. Moll, and H. Mehan. 1986. "Sociocultural Resources in Instruction: A Context-Specific Approach." *Beyond Language: Social and Cultural Factors in Schooling Language Minority Students*, 187–230. Los Angeles: Evaluation, Dissemination and Assessment Center, California State University, Los Angeles.

Dolson, D., and J. Mayer. 1992. "Longitudinal Study of Three Program Models for Language Minority Students: A Critical Examination of Reported Findings." *Bilingual Research Journal* 16 (1–2): 105–57.

Dulay, H., and M. Burt. 1974. "Natural Sequences in Child Second Language Acquisition." *Language Learning* 24: 37–53.

Ebe, Ann. 2010. "Culturally Relevant Texts and Reading Assessment for English Language Learners." *Reading Horizons* 50 (3): 193–210.

Ellis, R. 1990. *Instructed Second Language Acquisition*. Oxford, UK: Blackwell.

———. 1998. "Teaching and Research: Options in Grammar Teaching." *TESOL Quarterly* 32 (1): 39–60.

Faltis, C., and S. Hudelson. 1998. *Bilingual Education in Elementary and Secondary School Communities*. Boston: Allyn and Bacon.

Fisher, D., and N. Frey. 2008. *Word Wise and Content Rich, Grades 7–12: Five Essential Steps for Teaching Academic Vocabulary*. Portsmouth, NH: Heinemann.

———. 2009. *Background Knowledge: The Missing Piece of the Comprehension Puzzle*. Portsmouth, NH: Heinemann.

Fisher, D., C. Rothenberg, and N. Frey. 2007. *Language Learners in the English Classroom*. Urbana, IL: National Council of Teachers of English.

Fix, M., and R. Capps. 2005. "Immigrant Children, Urban Schools, and the No Child Left Behind Act." Migrational Policy Institute. Available at www.migrationalinformation.org/feature/display.cfm?ID=347.

Flint, D. 1998. *Where Does Breakfast Come From?* Crystal Lake, IL: Rigby.

Freeman, D., and Y. Freeman. 2000. *Teaching Reading in Multilingual Classrooms*. Portsmouth, NH: Heinemann.

———. 2004. *Essential Linguistics: What You Need to Know to Teach Reading, ESL, Spelling, Phonics, and Grammar*. Portsmouth, NH: Heinemann.

———. 2009. *Academic Language for English Language Learners and Struggling Readers: How to Help Students Succeed Across Content Areas*. Portsmouth, NH: Heinemann.

Freeman, Y., and D. Freeman. 1990. "New Attitudes for New Students." *Holistic Education Review* 3 (2): 25–30.

———. 1998. *ESL/EFL Teaching: Principles for Success*. Portsmouth, NH: Heinemann.

———. 2002. *Closing the Achievement Gap: How to Reach Limited Formal Schooling and Long-Term English Learners*. Portsmouth, NH: Heinemann.

———. 2006. *Teaching Reading and Writing in Spanish and English in Bilingual and Dual Language Classrooms*. Portsmouth, NH: Heinemann.

————. 2009. *La enseñanza de la lectura y la escritura en español y en inglés en clases bilingües y de doble inmersión*, segunda edición revisada. Portsmouth, NH: Heinemann.

Freeman, Y., A. Freeman, and D. Freeman. 2003. "Home Run Books: Connecting Students to Culturally Relevant Texts." *NABE News* 26 (3): 5–8, 11–12.

Freeman, Y., D. Freeman, and S. Mercuri. 2005. *Dual Language Essentials for Teachers and Administrators*. Portsmouth, NH: Heinemann.

Freire, P., and D. Macedo. 1987. *Literacy: Reading the Word and the World*. South Hadley, MA: Bergin and Garvey.

Frey, N., and D. Fisher. 2009. *Learning Words Inside and Out: Vocabulary Instruction That Boosts Achievement in All Subject Areas*. Portsmouth, NH: Heinemann.

Gándara, P., and F. Contreras. 2009. *The Latino Education Crisis: The Consequences of Failed School Policies*. Cambridge, MA: Harvard University Press.

García, E. 1999. *Student Cultural Diversity: Understanding and Meeting the Challenge*. 2d ed. Boston: Houghton Mifflin.

García, O. 2009. *Bilingual Education in the 21st Century: A Global Perspective*. Malden, MA: Wiley-Blackwell.

————. 2010. "Misconstructions of Bilingualism in U.S. Education." *NYSABE News* 1 (1): 2–7.

García, O., J. A. Kleifgen, and L. Flachi. 2008. *From English Language Learners to Emergent Bilinguals*. New York: Teachers College Press.

Gee, J. 1988. "Count Dracula, the Vampire Lestat, and TESOL." *TESOL Quarterly* 22 (2): 201–25.

————. 1992. *The Social Mind: Language, Ideology, and Social Practice*. New York: Bergin and Garvey.

————. 2008. *Social Linguistics and Literacies: Ideology in Discourses*. 3d ed. New York: Routledge.

Genesee, F. 1984. "Historical and Theoretical Foundations of Immersion Education." *Studies on Immersion Education*, ed. D. Dolson. Sacramento: California State Department of Education.

Gibbons, P. 2002. *Scaffolding Language: Scaffolding Learning*. Portsmouth, NH: Heinemann.

————. 2009. *English Learners, Academic Literacy, and Thinking: Learning in the Challenge Zone*. Portsmouth, NH: Heinemann.

Goldenberg, C. 2008. "Teaching English Language Learners: What the Research Does—and Does Not—Say." *American Educator*: 8–44.

Goldenberg, C., and R. Coleman. 2010. *Promoting Academic Achievement Among English Learners: A Guide to the Research*. Thousand Oaks, CA: Corwin.

Goldenberg, C., and R. Gallimore. 1991. "Local Knowledge, Research Knowledge, and Educational Change: A Case Study of Early Spanish Reading Improvement." *Educational Researcher* 20 (8): 2–14.

Gómez, L., D. Freeman, and Y. Freeman. 2005. "Dual Language Education: A Successful 50/50 Model." *Bilingual Research Journal* 29 (1): 145–64.

González, N., L. Moll, M. Floyd-Tenery, A. Rivera, P. Rendón, R. González, and C. Amanti. 1993. "Teacher Research on Funds of Knowledge: Learning from Households." *NCR-CDSLL Educational Practice Report.* Santa Cruz, CA: University of California.

Goodman, K., and D. Freeman. 1993. "What's Simple in Simplified Language?" In *Simplification: Theory and Application,* ed. M. L. Tickoo, 69–81. Singapore: SEAMEO Regional Language Center.

Goodman, Y. 1982. "Retellings of Literature and the Comprehension Process." *Theory into Practice: Children's Literature* 21 (4): 301–307.

Goodman, Y., and K. Goodman. 1990. "Vygotsky in a Whole Language Perspective." *Vygotsky and Education: Instructional Implications and Applications of Sociohistorical Psychology,* ed. L. Moll, 223–50. Cambridge, UK: Cambridge University Press.

Gottlieb, M. 2006. *Assessing English Language Learners: Bridges from Language Proficiency to Academic Achievement.* Thousand Oaks, CA: Corwin Press.

Gottlieb, M., L. Carnuccio, G. Ernst-Slavit, and A. Katz. 2006. *PreK–12 English Language Proficiency Standards.* Alexandria, VA: Teachers of English to Speakers of Other Languages (TESOL).

Gottlieb, M., and D. Nguyen. 2007. *Assessment and Accountability in Language Education Programs.* Philadelphia: Caslon.

Graves, M. 2006. *The Vocabulary Book: Learning and Instruction.* New York: Teachers College Press.

Gray, E. 2009. "The Importance of Visibility: Students' and Teachers' Criteria for Selecting African American Literature." *The Reading Teacher* 62 (6): 472–81.

Greene, J. 1998. *A Meta-Analysis of the Effectiveness of Bilingual Education.* Claremont, CA: Tomas Rivera Policy Institute.

Grosjean, François. 2010. *Bilingual: Life and Reality.* Cambridge, MA: Harvard University Press.

Guthrie, J. 2004. "Teaching for Literacy Engagement." *Journal of Literacy Research* 36 (1): 1–29.

Guthrie, J., and M. Davis. 2003. "Motivating Struggling Readers in Middle School Through an Engagement Model of Classroom Practice." *Reading & Writing Quarterly* 19: 59–85.

Gutiérrez, K., P. Baquedano-Lopez, H. Alvarez, and M. Chiu. 1999. "Building a Culture of Collaboration Through Hybrid Language Practices." *Theory into Practice* 38: 67–93.

Hakuta, K., Y. Butler, and D. Whitt. 2000. *How Long Does It Take English Learners to Attain*

Proficiency? Santa Barbara: University of California: Linguistic Minority Research Institute.

Halliday, M. 1989. *Spoken and Written Language.* Oxford, UK: Oxford University Press.

Halliday, M., and R. Hassan. 1989. *Language, Context, and Text: Aspects of Language in a Socialsemiotic Perspective.* 2d ed. Oxford, UK: Oxford University Press.

Harrison, K. 2010. "The Tragedy of Dying Languages." *BBC News.* Available at www .google.com/search?client=safari&rls=en&q=the+tragedy+of+dying+languages &ie=UTF-8&oe=UTF-8.

Hatch, E. 1983. *Psycholinguistics: A Second Language Perspective.* Rowley, MA: Newbury House.

Heath, S. 1983. *Ways with Words: Language, Life, and Work in Communities and Classrooms.* Cambridge, UK: Cambridge University Press.

———. 1986. "Sociocultural Contexts of Language Development." *Beyond Language: Social and Cultural Factors in Schooling Language Minority Students,* ed. D. Holt, 143–86. Los Angeles: Evaluation, Dissemination and Assessment Center, California State University, Los Angeles.

Hernández-Chávez, E. 1984. "The Inadequacy of English Immersion Education as an Educational Approach for Language Minority Students in the United States." *Studies on Immersion Education,* ed. D. Dolson, 144–83. Sacramento: California State Department of Education.

Horwitz, A., G. Uro, R. Price-Baugh, C. Simon, R. Uzzell, S. Lewis, and M. Casserly. 2009. *Succeeding with English Language Learners: Lessons Learned from the Great City Schools.* Washington, DC: Council of the Great City Schools.

Hymes, D. 1970. "On Communicative Competence." *Directions in Sociolinguistics,* ed. J. Gumperz and D. Hymes, 35–71. New York: Holt, Rinehart and Winston.

Institute of Educational Sciences (IES). 2008. *Reading First Impact Study: Final Report.* Washington, DC: U.S. Department of Education.

Jiménez, R. 1997. "The Strategic Reading Abilities and Potential of Five Low-Literacy Latina/O Readers in Middle School." *Reading Research Quarterly* 32 (2): 224–43.

———. 2000. "Literacy and the Identity Development of Latina/o Students." *American Educational Research Journal* 37 (4): 971–1000.

———. 2005. *Moving Beyond the Obvious: Examining Our Thinking About Linguistically Diverse Students.* Naperville, IL: North Central Regional Educational Laboratory (NCREL).

Johnson, K. 1995. *Understanding Communication in Second Language Classrooms,* ed. J. Richards. Cambridge Language Education. New York: Cambridge University Press.

Kieffer, M., and N. Lesaux. 2010. "Morphing into Adolescents: Active Word Learning for English Language Learners and Their Classmates in Middle School." *Journal of Adolescent & Adult Literacy* 54 (1): 47–56.

Killgallon, D., and J. Killgallon. 2007. *Grammar for High School: A Sentence-Composing Approach*. Portsmouth, NH: Heinemann.

Krashen, S. 1982. *Principles and Practice in Second Language Acquisition*. New York: Pergamon Press.

————. 1985. *Inquiries and Insights*. Haywood, CA: Alemany Press.

————. 1992. *Fundamentals of Language Education*. Torrance, CA: Laredo.

————. 1996. *Under Attack: The Case Against Bilingual Education*. Culver City, CA: Language Education Associates.

————. 1999. *Condemned Without a Trial: Bogus Arguments Against Bilingual Education*. Portsmouth, NH: Heinemann.

————. 2004a. *The Power of Reading: Insights from the Research*. 2d ed. Portsmouth, NH: Heinemann.

————. 2004b. "Skyrocketing Scores: An Urban Legend." *Educational Leadership* 62 (4): 37–39.

Larsen-Freeman, D., and M. Long. 1991. *An Introduction to Second Language Acquisition Research*. New York: Longman.

Lauer, P., M. Akiba, S. Wilkerson, H. Apthorp, D. Snow, and M. L. Martin-Glenn. 2006. "Out-of-School-Time Programs: A Meta-Analysis of Effects for At-Risk Students." *Review of Educational Research* 76 (2): 275–313.

Levinson, R. 1985. *Watch the Stars Come Out*. New York: E. P. Dutton.

Lindholm-Leary, K. J. 2001. *Dual Language Education*. Clevedon, UK: Multilingual Matters.

Long, E. 2004. *Mañana Iguana*. New York: Holliday House.

Long, M. 1983. "Does Second Language Instruction Make a Difference? A Review of the Research." *TESOL Quarterly* 14: 378–90.

————. 2001. "Focus on Form: A Design Feature in Language Teaching Methodology." *English Language Teaching in Its Social Context: A Reader*, ed. C. Candlin and N. Mercer, 180–90. London: Routledge.

Mahoney, K., J. MacSwain, and M. Thompson. 2005. *The Condition of English Language Learners*. Tempe: Arizona State University.

Martin, J. 1984. "Language, Register, and Genre." *Children Writing: Study Guide*, ed. Frances Christie. Geelong, Victoria, AU: Deakin University Press.

Marzano, R. 2004. *Building Background Knowledge for Academic Achievement: Research on What Works in Schools*. Alexandria, VA: Association for Supervision and Curriculum Development.

Marzano, R., and D. Pickering. 2005. *Building Academic Vocabulary: Teacher's Manual*. Alexandria, VA: Association for Supervision and Curriculum Development.

Matute-Bianchi, M. 1991. "Situational Ethnicity and Patterns of School Performance Among Immigrants and Non-Immigrant Mexican-Descent Students." *Minority Status and Schooling: A Comparative Study of Immigrant and Involuntary Minorities*, ed. M. Gibson and J. Ogbu. New York: Garland.

McGlothlin, J. 1997. *The Internet TESL Journal* 3 (10). Available at http://iteslj.org/Articles/McGlothlin-ChildLearn.htm.

McNeil, L., E. Coppola, and J. Radigan. 2008. "Avoidable Losses: High-Stakes Accountability and the Dropout Crisis." *Education Policy Analysis Archives* 16 (3): 1–45.

Medina, J. 1999. *My Name Is Jorge on Both Sides of the River*. Honesdale, PA: Boyds Mills Press.

Meltzer, J., and E. Hamann. 2004. "Meeting the Literacy Development Needs of Adolescent English Language Learners through Content Area Learning: Part 1: Focus on Motivation and Engagement." The Education Alliance at Brown University. Available at www.alliance.brown.edu.

Menken, K., and T. Kleyn. 2009. "The Difficult Road for Long-Term English Learners." *Educational Leadership* 66 (7). Available at www.ascd.org/publications/educational_leadership/apr09/vol66/num07/The_Difficult_Road_for_Long-Term_English_Learners.aspx

———. 2010. "The Long-Term Impact of Subtractive Schooling in the Educational Experiences of Secondary English Learners." *International Journal of Bilingual Education and Bilingualism* 13 (4): 1–19.

Menken, K., T. Kleyn, and N. Chae. 2007. *Meeting the Needs of Long-Term English Language Learners in High School*. New York: Research Institute for the Study of Language in an Urban Society.

———. Under review. "When Change Is the Only Consistency: The Case of Long-Term English Language Learners in Secondary Schools."

Miller, B. 2003. *Critical Hours: Afterschool Programs and Educational Success*. Quincy, MA: Nellie Mae Education Foundation.

Moll, L. 1994. "Literacy Research in Homes and Classrooms: A Sociocultural Approach." *Theoretical Models and Processes of Reading*, ed. R. Ruddell, M. Ruddell, and H. Singer. Newark, DE: International Reading Association.

Nathenson-Mejía, S., and K. Escamilla. 2003. "Bridging Cultural Gaps with Children's Literature." *Bilingual Research Journal* 27 (1): 101–16.

Numeroff, L., and F. Bond. 1985. *If You Give a Mouse a Cookie*. New York: HarperCollins.

Ogbu, J. 1991. "Immigrant and Involuntary Minorities in Comparative Perspective." *Minority Status and Schooling: A Comparative Study of Immigrant and Involuntary Minorities.*, ed. M. Gibson and J. Ogbu, 3–33. New York: Garland.

Ogbu, J., and M. Matute-Bianchi. 1986. "Understanding Sociocultural Factors: Knowledge,

Identity and School Adjustment." *Beyond Language: Social and Cultural Factors in Schooling Language Minority Students*, ed. D. Holt, 73–142. Los Angeles: Evaluation, Dissemination and Assessment Center, California State University, Los Angeles.

Olsen, L. 2010. *Reparable Harm: Fulfilling the Unkept Promise of Educational Opportunity for California's Long Term English Learners*. Long Beach: Californians Together.

Olsen, L., and A. Jaramillo. 1999. *Turning the Tides of Exclusion: A Guide for Educators and Advocates for Immigrant Students*. Oakland: California Tomorrow.

Olsen, L., and N. Mullen. 1990. *Embracing Diversity: Teachers' Voices from California Classrooms*. San Francisco: California Tomorrow.

Orellana, M., J. Reynolds, L. Dorner, and M. Meza. 2003. "In Other Words: Translating or 'Para-Phrasing' as a Family Literacy Practice in Immigrant Households." *Reading Research Quarterly* 38: 12–34.

Padrón, Y., H. Waxman, and H. Rivera. 2002. *Educating Hispanic Students: Obstacles and Avenues to Improved Academic Achievement*. Santa Cruz: Center for Research on Education, Diversity and Excellence.

Parrish, T., M. Pérez, and A. Merickel. 2006. *Effects of the Implementation of Proposition 227 on the Education of English Language Learners*. Sacramento, CA: American Institute for Research WestED.

Paulson, E., and A. Freeman. 2003. *Insight from the Eyes: The Science of Effective Reading Instruction*. Portsmouth, NH: Heinemann.

Pearson, P. D., and M. Gallagher. 1983. "The Instruction of Reading Comprehension." *Contemporary Educational Psychology* 8 (3): 317–44.

Petitto, L. 2000. "How Children Acquire Language: A New Answer." Available at www.dartmouth.edu/~lpetitto/langAc.html.

Piaget, J. 1955. *The Language and Thought of the Child*. New York: Meridian.

Pilgreen, J. 2000. *The SSR Handbook: How to Organize and Manage a Sustained Silent Reading Program*. Portsmouth, NH: Heinemann.

Pinker, S. 1994. *The Language Instinct: How the Mind Creates Language*. New York: William Morrow.

Power, B. 1999. *Parent Power: Energizing Home-School Communication*. Portsmouth, NH: Heinemann.

Prelutsky, J. 1996. *A Pizza the Size of the Sun*. New York: Greenwillow.

Preston, M. 2010. "The Texas Textbook Controversy and Failing American Consensus." True/Slant. Available at http://trueslant.com/michaelpreston/2010/03/16/the-texas-textbook-controversy-and-the-failing-american-consensus/.

Radford, A. 1981. *Transformational Syntax: A Student's Guide to Chomsky's Extended Standard Theory*. Cambridge, UK: Cambridge University Press.

Ramírez, J. 1991. *Final Report: Longitudinal Study of Structured English Immersion Strategy, Early-Exit and Late-Exit Bilingual Education Programs*. Washington, DC: U.S. Department of Education.

Rice, M. 2002. "Children's Language Acquisition." *Language Development: A Reader for Teachers*, ed. B. Power and R. Hubbard, 19–27. Upper Saddle River, NJ: Merrill Prentice-Hall.

Rog, L., and W. Burton. 2001/2002. "Matching Texts and Readers: Leveling Early Reading Materials for Assessment and Instruction." *Reading Teacher* 55 (4): 348–56.

Rolstad, K., K. Mahoney, and G. Glass. 2005. "A Meta-Analysis of Program Effectiveness Research on English Language Learners." *Educational Policy* 19 (4): 572–94.

Ruíz, R. 1984. "Orientations in Language Planning." *Journal of the National Association of Bilingual Education* 8: 15–34.

Scarcella, R. 1990. *Teaching Language Minority Students in the Multicultural Classroom*. Englewood Cliffs, NJ: Prentice Hall Regents.

Schleppegrell, M. 2004. *The Language of Schooling: A Functional Linguistics Perspective*. Mahwah, NJ: Lawrence Erlbaum.

Schleppegrell, M., and L. Oliveira. 2006. "An Integrated Language and Content Approach for History Teachers." *Journal of English for Academic Purposes* 5: 254–68.

Schon, I., and S. Berkin. 1996. *Introducción a la literatura infantil y juvenil*. Newark, DE: International Reading Association.

Schumann, J. 1978. *The Pidginization Process: A Model for Second Language Acquisition*. Rowley, MA: Newbury House.

Seliger, H. 1988. "Psycholinguistic Issues in Second Language Acquisition." *Issues in Second Language Acquisition: Multiple Perspectives*, ed. L. Beebe, 17–40. New York: Newbury House.

Selinker, Larry. 1972. "Interlanguage." *International Review of Applied Linguistics* 10: 201–31.

Shanahan, T., and C. Shanahan. 2008. "Teaching Disciplinary Literacy to Adolescents: Rethinking Content Area Literacy." *Harvard Educational Review* 78 (1): 40–59.

Short, D., and S. Fitzsimmons. 2007. *Double the Work: Challenges and Solutions to Acquiring Language and Academic Literacy for Adolescent English Language Learners—A Report to Carnegie Corporation of New York*. Washington, DC: Alliance for Excellent Education.

Skutnabb-Kangas, T. 1983. *Bilingualism or Not: The Education of Minorities*. Clevedon, UK: Multilingual Matters.

———. 2008. "Language, Education and (Violations) of Human Rights." Linguistic Human Rights Symposium, Geneva, Switzerland, October 13.

Skutnabb-Kangas, T., and P. Toukomaa. 1976. *Teaching Migrant Children's Mother Tongue and Learning the Language of the Host Country in the Context of the Socio-Cultural Situation of the Migrant Family*. Helsinki: The Finnish National Commission for UNESCO.

Slavin, R., and A. Cheung. 2003. "Effective Reading Programs for English Language Learners: A Best-Evidence Synthesis." Available at www.csos.jhu.edu/crespar/techReports/Report66.pdf.

Smith, F. 1983. *Essays into Literacy: Selected Papers and Some Afterthoughts*. Portsmouth, NH: Heinemann.

Soto, Gary. 1993. *Too Many Tamales*. Carmel, CA: Hampton-Brown.

Strauss, V. 2010a. "Heavily Accented Teachers Removed from Arizona Classrooms." *Washington Post*, 2 May. Available at http://voices.washingtonpost.com/answer-sheet/teachers/heavily-accented-teachers-remo.html.

———. 2010b. "Arizona Strikes Again: Now It's Ethnic Studies." *Washington Post*, 4 May. Available at http://voices.washingtonpost.com/answer-sheet/history/arizona-strikes-again-now-it-i.html.

Suárez-Orozco, C., M. Suárez-Orozco, and I. Todorova. 2008. *Learning a New Land: Immigrant Students in American Society*. Cambridge, MA: Harvard University Press.

Sue, S., and A. Padilla. 1986. "Ethnic Minority Issues in the United States: Challenges for the Educational System." *Beyond Language: Social and Cultural Factors in Schooling Language Minority Students*, 35–72. Los Angeles: Evaluation, Assessment and Dissemination Center, California State University.

Swain, M. 1985. "Communicative Competence: Some Roles of Comprehensible Output in Its Development." *Input in Second Language Acquisition*, ed. S. Gass and C. Madden, 235–53. Rowley, MA: Newbury House.

TESOL. 2006. *PreK–12 English Language Proficiency Standards*. Alexandria, VA: Teachers of English to Speakers of Other Languages.

Thomas, W., and V. Collier. 1997. *School Effectiveness for Language Minority Students*. Washington, DC: National Clearinghouse of Bilingual Education.

———. 2002. "A National Study of School Effectiveness for Language Minority Students' Long-Term Academic Achievement." CREDE. Available at www.crede.usc.edu/research/llaa/1.1_es.html.

Thompson, G. 1997. *The Apple Pie Family*. Austin, TX: Steck-Vaughn.

U.S. Census Bureau. 2006. "Results from the 2006 American Community Survey." Washington, DC: U.S. Census Bureau, Ethnicity and Ancestry Branch.

Valdés, G. 1996. *Con Respeto: Bridging the Distances Between Culturally Diverse Families and Schools*. New York: Teachers College Press.

———. 2001. *Learning and Not Learning English: Latino Students in American Schools*. New York: Teachers College Press.

Van Lier, L. 1988. *The Classroom and the Language Learner*. New York: Longman.

Vopat, J. 1994. *The Parent Project: A Workshop Approach to Parent Involvement.* York, ME: Stenhouse.

Vygotsky, L. 1962. *Thought and Language.* Trans. E. Vakar. Cambridge, MA: MIT Press.

———. 1978. *Mind in Society: The Development of Higher Psychological Processes.* Cambridge, MA: Harvard University Press.

Waters, K. 1989. *Sara Morton's Day: A Day in the Life of a Pilgrim.* New York: Scholastic.

Weaver, C. 2008. *Grammar to Enrich and Enhance Writing.* Portsmouth, NH: Heinemann.

Wells, G., and G. Chang-Wells. 1992. *Constructing Knowledge Together.* Portsmouth, NH: Heinemann.

Whitaker, S. 2008. *Word Play: Building Vocabulary Across Texts and Disciplines Grades 6–12.* Portsmouth, NH: Heinemann.

Williams, J. 2001. "Classroom Conversations: Opportunities to Learn for ESL Students in Mainstream Classrooms." *The Reading Teacher* 54 (8): 750–57.

Wink, Joan. 1993. "Labels Often Reflect Educators' Beliefs and Practices." *BEOutreach* 4 (2): 28–29.

Yang, L. 1992. "Why Hmong Came to America." *The Fresno Bee,* 27 December, B9.

Zanger, V., ed. 1996. *Math Story Book.* Boston: Joseph Hurley School.

Zentella, A. C. 2000. *Growing Up Bilingual.* Malden, MA: Blackwell.

Index